For Francis

ACKNOWLEDGEMENTS

The assistance of the Naval Historical Branch of the Ministry of Defence (Navy) in supplying correct dates and facts for the few warlike incidents described and the composition of the appendices is sincerely acknowledged. Commander Kenneth Clark, VRD* RNR Retd. very kindly loaned me his navigators work and note books for which I am very grateful. He also provided the original note scribbled on a signal pad during the attack on convoy "Faith" reproduced herein. The perceptive wit and skill of "Tugg" will, I hope, bring alive some of the incidents and I am indebted to him for his co-operation.

I would also like to thank Mr Peter Shepherd for his meticulous proof reading and Mrs Marilyn Todd for typing and retyping the manuscript.

Finally I wish to thank Vicki and Francis Scott for their encouragement which caused the pages to be written and Mr Charles Skilton and Mr Leonard Holdsworth who processed my scribblings into this book.

MORIN SCOTT

CONTENTS

APPENDICES

PROLOGUE

"YOU miserable little wart. You have a button undone *and* your lanyard isn't properly rigged. I shall guff you. What is your name and term?"

"Scott — St Vincent."

"Guff", or rather "fear of guff", made the world go round at the Royal Naval College, Dartmouth, and had done for at least fifty years and that — to a harassed thirteen year old — was for ever.

The glamour of being a prefect at Prep School and the admiration one had received from masters, parents, parents' friends and even other boys and girls on surviving the interview and then the examination to gain entrance had been crowned with the visits to Gieves to receive the complete outfit of uniform which marked one as an officer cadet in the Royal Navy.

Then came the awful reality of arrival in the train at Kingswear, crossing the ferry and being herded together by two God-like Cadet Captains and marched up that endless hill to the imposing college which surmounted it.

Even after arrival there seemed to be an endless succession of flights of stairs before one arrived at the barrack-like dormitory with its long row of beds and sea-chests each side.

For twenty-four hours one was bombarded with a stream of rules and requirements, interspersed with attempts to instil into one — along with fifty others — the rudiments of quick march, form fours, right turn, left turn, right dress, double march, quick march, salute, eyes right, eyes left, stand at ease, stand easy (ah, welcome relief) SAINT VINCENTS, SHUN.

After twenty-four hours the rest of the college arrived and term began properly before the new arrivals had even caught their breath.

Even getting up in the morning was a sort of frantic drill.

The bell rang. Up out of bed, grab a towel, feet in bath slippers and into the wash room. Into the salt water plunge bath (a salt water type of swimming bath with only two feet of ice cold water in it, in which one had to be totally immersed). Dry body and hair, clean teeth, wash face (replace all items in correct place and line), back to dormitory and dress in white flannel trousers, white flannel shirt, black socks, black boots (oh, those endless laces and hooks), tie, uniform jacket and cap, and run clear of the dormitory before the statutory eight minutes had elapsed.

Four years of that did at least teach me to dress quickly and be mightily impatient of others (especially women) who require much longer.

But "guff" was more than just rules and timetables. "Guff" was a constant sword of Damocles.

While there were College rules and requirements — for example, to be on time for schoolroom classes — there was the much more all-pervading aura of "Guff Rules".

Each batch of arriving cadets was grouped together as a term from their moment of arrival until their departure to the sea-going training cruiser after eleven terms. Each term was junior to those that had been in college longer and senior to those who arrived after, and one's seniority was clearly marked by the way one was required to wear the white lanyard (laundered weekly) with one's uniform reefer. New arrivals ("first termers") were almost strangled by it, "eleventh termers" wore theirs in a sweeping curve with the sliding turks head at the lowest position possible that still allowed the end to reach into the breast pocket where it held the keys to gunroom and dormitory sea-chest locker.

By the "Guff" system, any of the four hundred-odd cadets from terms senior to you could report you ("guff" you) for contravention of Guff Rules and punishment would follow.

The long list of Guff Rules defies memory after some fifty years, but a few examples will demonstrate the sort of discipline they instilled and in the best service tradition they contained one or two "catch-alls" to cover every and any circumstance.

Uniform buttons must never be undone.
All three blazer buttons must always be done up.
Hands must never remain in blazer side pockets.

(Hands could not remain in uniform side pockets or trouser pockets because there were none).

Caps must always be worn correctly.

Cap badges must be central.

Movement between classes must always be at the double.

Passing senior gunrooms must always be at the double.

It is not permitted to look into senior gunrooms.

Boot or shoe laces must never be undone while walking or doubling.

When in games clothes stockings must be properly gartered.

and so on, and so on.

By a "catch-all" rule one could not be "cheeky" to anyone a mere term above for fear of "guff".

Should you have a brother, a friend or someone from the same prep school in a term above you, it was not permitted to talk to him. If he chose, he could "take you out" between four-thirty and six p.m. on Wednesdays and Saturdays, when he could collect you from your gunroom and you could then walk around the quarter-deck gallery (nowhere else) together and chat away on any matter of mutual interest.

Everything was highly organised. the College Chaplain even remarked wryly one day that he believed there was an invisible notice outside the Chapel which said,

No Admittance Except When Marched

Matters improved with time and familiarity. Washing and dressing in eight minutes became habitual, avoidance of punishment became an art, and ways were found to beat the system.

By taking up fencing and rifle shooting the prescribed amount of afternoon exercise could be taken sheltered from the winter weather, and in the summer the river was a welcome escape from the boredom of cricket. During the third and fourth summers, the pleasure of sailing one's own boat could be enjoyed every afternoon with the additional joy (after qualifying suitably) of being able to sail up the river on a Sunday afternoon to consume a vast tea of scones with Devonshire cream and strawberry jam at Dittisham, where they had many years' experience of feeding hungry cadets.

At the beginning of the winter term in 1938 much classroom time was replaced by filling sandbags and building vast sandbag walls as air raid protection around the college. War with Germany was suddenly imminent and speculation was rife as to how many of the top terms would go straight to sea, as in 1914.

When Neville Chamberlain returned from München with his "piece of paper" and his wimpish cry of "Peace in our time", the mood in the College was one of disappointment and frustration. It was back to the classroom again.

Some weeks later, a hotly contested debate decided that the battleship had little to fear from air attack.

Chapter One

WAR CAME TO ME at the age of seventeen and three months and caught me at a somewhat inopportune moment. For the previous four years I had been an officer cadet at the Royal Naval College, Dartmouth, receiving a fairly normal education with the addition of a certain amount of time spent on navigation, on engineering and on what was referred to as "seamanship", which included, in the summer, the opportunity to go away in boats under oars, sail and motor on the River Dart. My hobby and main interest in life at that time was sailing, and life at the College was made more pleasant for the last two years by the fact that I was able to keep my own boat there (a twelve foot "National") and sail it almost every day instead of playing cricket.

However, dreams of becoming an Admiral in due course were shattered early on, when I was advised that my eyesight was not up to the standard for a deck officer and I had a choice of becoming an engineer, a paymaster or leaving the Navy. Having no interest in paperwork or engineering, and being somewhat aggravated by the Navy's refusal to allow me to stand on the bridge and look into the far horizon in the manner of the film stars of the period, I had elected to leave the Navy and had gone off to enjoy the summer holidays sailing in a twenty-five ton ketch up the West coast of Scotland for three weeks before commanding (for the third year running) the Royal Naval College entry in the Inter-Public Schools Sailing Races which were held in the Gareloch on the Clyde in Dragon class yachts. There seemed to be all the time in the world to make up one's mind what to do in life, and at that time the two most interesting possibilities were of sailing in an eight-hundred ton non-magnetic brigantine on a voyage of exploration and research in the Indian Ocean for two years or joining a yacht's crew for a round-the-world voyage in an ex-Bristol Channel pilot cutter, but between them, Neville Chamberlain and Adolf Hitler put the mockers on both those projects.

Following the Public Schools Races, I had accepted an invitation to sail as crew in an international six-metre, the property of a Glasgow shipowner, who also happened to be the Captain of the Royal Naval Volunteer Reserve on the Clyde. After the Saturday race, the crew was taking a drink aboard his one-hundred ton ketch and I paid little attention, as he listened closely, to the news broadcast at six o'clock, until he said when it was over,

"Well, we shall be at war within a week!"

This took me entirely by surprise, since I had not really read a newspaper or listened to a news broadcast for over a month, and I could not help remarking on my rather peculiar situation in that I had managed to retire from the Navy before even reaching the rank of midshipman. My host was amused and practical, and after a short pause said,

"Well, come and see me on Tuesday evening at the Clyde headquarters of the RNVR and I will get you into the RNVSR."

For those not acquainted with the division of the Naval Reserve in those days, I must explain that the Royal Naval Reserve (RNR) consisted of professional Merchant Navy officers and men, who were easily recognisable in Naval uniform for, instead of each single gold stripe on their arms, they wore a pair of intertwined half-sized stripes. The Royal Naval Volunteer Reserve (RNVR) consisted in the main of yachtsmen and other people interested in matters maritime as a hobby, who were granted commissions and wore a two-thirds width wavy gold stripe on their arm and were thus frequently referred to as the "Wavy Navy". Somewhat like the Territorial Army, they went to sea with the Navy for a fortnight each year and went along to the local division for one or two drill nights every week. Finally, My Lords Commissioners of the Admiralty had dreamed up the idea of forming the Royal Naval Volunteer Supplementary Reserve (RNVSR) which was officially described as "A list of gentlemen residing in the United Kingdom desirous of obtaining commissions in the Royal Naval Volunteer Reserve on the outbreak of hostilities". Until such time as they joined the RNVR proper, they wore no uniforms and did no drills, but in some parts of the country they formed themselves into "flotillas" and organised some training for themselves.

My host was as good as his word, and the following Tuesday I presented myself at the RNVR Headquarters in Glasgow and after a few words he put me into the RNVSR joining routine that was

2

taking place, which included the usual "cough please" medical inspection, with numbers of shivering, nude and self-conscious young men being examined by a somewhat harrassed RNVR doctor. While he was knocking his knuckles on my chest and feeling other parts of my body like a highly experienced slave-trader examining a possible purchase, I said to him quietly,

"Do you do eyesight examinations, Doc?"

He replied, "Yes, why?"

"Well, I only failed the Naval examination four weeks ago, so you're wasting your time."

"Do you want to get in?"

"Yes, that's why I'm here."

"Well, we'll see what we can do about it."

Eventually I stood on a brass strip nailed to the floor, squinted at the eye test chart and began to read off the letters with each eye until I got to the lower lines which were impossible to read.

"Is that the best you can do?"

"Yes, I'm afraid so."

"Well," said the doctor, looking round to see that nobody was observing what was going on, "That's no bloody good, you had better come closer."

Thus I was passed one hundred percent A1 fit and went home to Sussex to await a summons from My Lords Commissioners to go off to sea and help win the war, the kick-off of which was announced five days later by Neville Chamberlain.

So much for his "Peace in Our Time" promise of a bare ten months earlier.

Returning to the family home in Sussex and awaiting daily a request from My Lord Commissioners for my valuable services, I was afraid, like so many young men, that the war would be over before I got a chance to join in. Meanwhile, believing like most people that we were about to be bombed out of existence, I joined the local ARP organisation (Air Raid Precaution) as an ambulance driver. A new-fangled law had been introduced a few years earlier which required those wishing to drive a motor car on a public highway to take a driving test, and until that time to drive with an ignominious "L" plate on the front and back of the car and an experienced driver alonside them. For the previous twelve months I had been learning to drive a motor car on a private road which was not subject to the law, and had become reasonably proficient. With war declared, such formalities were swept aside, and I was issued with a delightful document which was entitled a "National Service Emergency Driving Licence", which enabled me to dispense with the "L" plates and the necessity of having an experienced driver alongside. This presented no great problem while driving a car, but I soon found out that I had to learn to drive all over again when confronted with an elderly Bean, which had in fact been put out of service as a laundry van and had only been pressed into service as an ambulance. Firstly, it was so ancient that it was not equipped with a self-starter, and secondly it was not equipped with synchromesh gears, and learning to drive what in those days was called a "crash gearbox" was quite an illuminating experience, and certainly very noisy and frightening to anybody else in the vehicle. Known as the "Has Been", we soon solved the self-starter problem by always parking the machine facing downhill outside the village hall which had become the ARP head-quarters. Fortunately it was a long hill.

On the receipt, by telephone, of "Air Raid Warning Yellow", the duty ambulance driver jumped into the "Has Been", selected a gear and depressed the clutch, then letting off the handbrake he allowed the machine to run down the hill until it had got up enough speed for him to take his foot off the clutch. The engine then started turning over, and with a bit of luck, spluttered into action before reaching the bottom of the hill, where it was turned round and driven back, steaming and hot, to be parked outside the village hall, pointing once more downhill, and ready for action in every way. Needless to say, this was normally followed by the "Air Raid Warning Green" (i.e. the All Clear), and the exciting action never came, except in one or two practice runs when the poor folks who were designated as casualties were considerably more frightened of a ride in "Has Been" than they were of the idea of being bombed by the Germans.

These civilian activities were cut short by a telephone call from the Captain RNVR on the Clyde who apologised for the errors, and informed me that the Admiralty had lost my papers for joining the RNVSR, but that he was able to arrange for me to go to sea almost immediately as a midshipman if I wished to do so. If the idea appealed, would I come up to Glasgow immediately. Needless to say, I caught the train that night and reported to him in St Enoch's Hotel the following morning after breakfast. There I was introduced to Captain Russell, Royal Navy, who seemed to me very austere and elderly, but it was explained to me that he had been appointed

4

HMS *Worcestershire*

Captain of the Bibby liner *Worcestershire*, which was to be commissioned shortly as an Armed Merchant Cruiser.

The conversion consisted of fitting six very ancient six-inch guns (dating from 1899 to 1902), and equipping her with a half Naval and half Merchant Navy crew to form part of the Northern patrol to prevent useful goods reaching Germany by sea. Her official complement was to include eight midshipmen, but the Admiralty only provided four of these, in fact three RNVR and one RNR, and the Captain was required to provide the others, and in this he was ably assisted by the Captain RNVR Clyde who had available the names and addresses of quite a number of people like myself who had joined the RNVSR and had their papers lost. Officially we all signed Articles, known as T124, which were Merchant Navy type Articles conducted by the shipping master and all that sort of nonsense, but which in fact constituted a sort of temporary joining up in the Royal Navy, whereby we all agreed to serve in a Naval vessel and to wear Naval uniform and to be awarded Naval ranks. It was only somewhat later that I found that one of the delights of this was that we were paid "Danger Money" of five pounds per month over and above our pay, and as such I was very much better paid than my

5

contemporaries in the Royal Navy or even in the RNR and RNVR, since a midshipman's salary was only seven pounds a month.

Elated beyond all imagination at being officially promoted to midshipman and instructed to join the staff in five days' time, I caught the train back to London to go home and pack all the necessary kit needed and have my uniform altered to show the RNR "patches" of a Royal Naval Reserve midshipman. Less than a week later I was travelling northward once more to Glasgow, and from there down the Clyde to the old derelict shipyard that had been Beardmore's, where I found the *Worcestershire* firmly gripped in the hands of the dockyard, and for the first time experienced the delights of trying to live on board the ship while work was being carried on both by day and night.

The ship had retained all of her Merchant Navy engineers and engine room crew, and all of her Purser's Department and cooks and stewards, together with other characters like shipwrights, bosun and one or two deck officers who had also signed the T124 agreement. These were then supplemented by an influx of RNR officers and a retired Lieutenant Commander Royal Navy as First Lieutenant, together with Chief Petty Officers, Petty Officers, Leading Seamen and Seamen, whose duties would be to man the elderly guns with which the ship had been fitted, and to provide the boarding parties and armed guards for the Merchant ships which we would stop and examine and send in to Scapa Flow for closer examination.

Orders had come from on high that as far as possible all combustible material was to be removed from the ship to reduce the risk of fire in action. By this time, most of the officers had joined the ship and over a few glasses of gin in the wardroom of an evening, the disappearance of creature comforts was much regretted. It was regretted even more when it was discovered that all these relatively valuable goods like carpets and comfortable chairs were being stored in an ancient warehouse without a roof, but it was not long before plans were laid and a raiding party was established which, after supper each evening, set out for the warehouse to retrieve as many articles as possible which could improve our comfort during the long months ahead on Northern Patrol.

I particularly remember being one of the legs of an enormous caterpillar which brought back the rolled-up wardroom carpet from the warehouse to the ship. It was probably something like fifty feet by fifty feet, and rolled into an enormous sausage which was only transported by some twenty-four officers being spaced along its length and weaving through the deserted dockyard and up the gangway like some fantastic prehistoric centipede. By similar methods a number of comfortable armchairs and sofas found their way back to the ship, together with minor items like cabin door curtains and carpets.

The standard armament for all the Armed Merchant Cruisers was to provide a broadside of four six-inch guns, and to this was added two three-inch anti-aircraft guns and two very ancient .303 machine guns for repelling aircraft. The six-inch guns had all been carefully preserved from the very large number of cruisers which were built around the turn of the century and fitted with numerous six-inch guns in upper and lower casemate mountings. *Worcestershire*, in fact, had one gun mounted on the forecastle on the centre line and one aft, and then two on either side to provide her four guns broadside, and I felt most honoured and most important to be appointed as Officer of Quarters to the gun on the forecastle. It was not until we had spent several weeks at sea on Northern Patrol and I had sampled the kind of weather and discomfort which is most noticeable when out on the exposed forecastle of the ship that I realised that the job had been given to me because nobody else wanted it. Nevertheless, at the age of seventeen, it was quite a thrill to be in charge of even a very ancient six-inch gun with a crew of nine men, and a very considerable destructive power.

Every Naval gun was accompanied throughout its life by a gun history sheet on which every shot fired, in practice or otherwise, has to be recorded. According to the engraving on the after end of the gun barrel, my gun had been manufactured in 1899, and according to the gun history sheet, had been constructed for a life of three hundred shots, and it was a matter of some amusement to me when I left the ship over a year later to note that the total of shots fired in my gun's life was two hundred and ninety-nine, so I was glad I was not going to be there to see the next one or two fired, in case the maker's estimate of life expectancy of the gun was too accurate!

For those with some interest in the technical details of the gun, it was a six-inch Mark VII breach-loading gun and fired a shell weighing one hundred and twelve pounds, which had to be inserted by hand into the breach and then rammed home with a wooden-handled rammer, rather resembling a household mop. The cartridge was not in a brass case, as is more common in these days, but merely

7

done up in a cloth bag, and this was likewise inserted by hand before the breech was closed, also by hand.

A few years previously my dear Mother had returned from an expedition of antique buying and displayed with great pride a tall cylindrical bucket with a leather handle painted green and with a Royal coat of arms upon it, which she proudly declared to be " one of Nelson's cartridge cases ", and thus obviously of interest to me as a budding Naval officer. We used it (and in fact I still use it today) as a wastepaper basket, but my pride in the family ownership of this valuable antique was somewhat diminished when I found that we carried dozens of identical units in *Worcestershire* (and in subsequent vessels) and that they were used for carrying the cartridges from the magazine to the breech-loading guns and were officially called Clarkson Cases. I regret I was not astute enough after the end of the war to purchase these for a few pounds per hundred and sell them to antique dealers all over the country as " genuine Nelson's cartridge cases ".

Eventually the great day of commissioning arrived. The Shipping Master came aboard and supervised the signing of the T124 Articles while the Naval draft arrived from Chatham barracks. Food stores were embarked that afternoon and well into the night, and early the following morning, with the aid of a pilot and several tugs, the ship was taken out of her berth at Beardmore's Yard and proceeded down the river to anchor off Greenock, where ammunition barges were soon alongside and the ship embarked a full stock of shells and cartridges for her six-inch guns and the appropriate ammunition for her two three-inch weapons.

The next day the ship sailed down from Greenock to the outer waters of the Firth of Clyde, where four shots were fired from each gun and the ship's magnetic compass was swung. On the completion of this, the ship was considered ready in all respects to proceed to sea and fight the Germans, and after spending one more night and the day at anchor off Greenock, the ship weighed anchor at dusk and proceeded down the Clyde to undertake her first stint at Northern Patrol between the Faroe Islands and Iceland. It can be seen that not a lot of time was made available for any forms of practice or drill on board — we were obviously expected to sort that lot out on our way to our first patrol line, and it was to be hoped that we did not encounter any enemy vessels during those few days.

We were, obviously, proceeding without navigation lights and with the ship entirely darkened, as were all other ships, and at that time of course no officers were really experienced in this form of night navigation, while modern devices like radar had not been invented. In fact, the ship did not even carry anything so sophisticated as an echo sounder. We were lucky that when we had a collision before leaving the Firth of Clyde it was merely a glancing blow from another ship of a similar size, the only damage inflicted on *Worcestershire* being to knock our starboard number three six-inch gun into the hospital, and naturally some wit observed that in view of its age, this was the best place for it. Looking back on the situation now, I realise how lucky we were to have only such minor damage with two unlit fifteen thousand ton ships actually managing to touch each other at night. In my ignorance and inexperience, it just appeared to me one of the sort of things that happened every few days in this exciting world at sea.

We took up our position on Northern Patrol a few days later. The object of Northern Patrol was to prevent merchant ships with valuable war materials reaching Germany, but since at this time Norway, Sweden, Finland, Denmark and Holland were all still neutral, many of their merchant ships were passing through our waters and a great number of fishing trawlers from all nations were also to be found. Every vessel sighted had to be stopped, and if the weather was sufficiently clement, boarded by a boarding party in one of our thirty-two foot cutters and examined. If there was any suspicion of anything untoward, an officer and a boarding party were left on board and the ship was directed to proceed to Scapa Flow where her cargo could be examined at leisure. When the weather was too bad for boarding, we would escort the ships to the Faroe Islands where we could rendezvous with armed trawlers who would take over the escort of the vessels and accompany them into Scapa Flow for examination as before.

It was an extremely wearing occupation, since we spent some eighteen to twenty-one days at sea with about fourteen days actually on patrol, and the remainder of the time going to and fro. While on patrol we would steam at a cruising speed of twelve knots, normally steering about West-South-West for twelve hours and then reversing course for the next twelve hours, and so on, until the fourteen day period was up. In theory there would be another ship thirty miles North of us and another one thirty miles South of us, and the theory was that we would intercept all ships while we were proceeding in a

Westerly direction during the day, and that our steaming in the opposite direction during the night would prevent any ships passing through unless they were going much faster than we were and out of sight to ourselves and our consorts.

Most of the patrol lines were occupied by Armed Merchant Cruisers similar to ourselves and certainly with similar armament, but there was a slight stiffening from time to time with the provision of a proper Royal Navy cruiser. Navigation was difficult, since none of the Armed Merchant Cruisers carried radar and modern gadgets like Decca and Satellite Navigators were still decades away, and in winter-time the weather was frequently so inclement that it was not possible to get a sight of the sun or stars for several days at a time, and this resulted in our actual position being extremely doubtful. The ship's company worked in three watches, known as the red, white and blue, which enabled us to keep one-third of our guns manned at all times and a skeleton staff in the gunnery control positions, while on the bridge we had a Navigating Officer of the Watch plus a midshipman, and on the gunnery control position above, a Gunnery Officer of the Watch also assisted by a midshipman.

In theory this should have given us all adequate sleep, but since it was necessary to go to action stations every time a ship was sighted and remain at action stations all the time the boarding boat was away (and this sometimes occurred up to five or six times a day) it was not uncommon for sleep to get into rather short supply. Except in particularly good weather, boarding was only possible by day, but we soon discovered that in the higher latitudes in the summertime, daylight was something that went on for almost twenty-four hours, and thus sleep became rather a valued commodity.

Our six-inch guns, now some forty years old, developed all sorts of problems and quite frequently the training mechanism (the gearing for swivelling the gun from left to right) failed, and this work had to be undertaken by attaching rope and tackles to the muzzle of the gun and employing spare ammunition numbers to train the barrel to left and right by orders from the Officer of Quarters, which gave us all the further feeling of being back in Nelson's day.

In winter, especially when operating North of Iceland, the temperature frequently fell very low indeed, and under these conditions the spray coming over the forecastle would freeze on deck and cover the whole of my gun and gun platform with a coating of ice, sometimes up to twelve inches thick in places. On these

10

occasions, it would sometimes take us up to thirty minutes to get the gun ready for action, chipping away at the ice on the canvas muzzle cover, and on one occasion even having to dig the rammer out of the deck. All the ready use shells which were stowed near the gun were completely frozen into their rack, and we could only consider using fresh shells brought up from the magazine. There was also a considerable danger in firing a shell from a gun which had any ice inside the barrel since this was reported to cause the gun barrel to open up like a tulip and kill all the gun's crew, and for this reason we were trained to fire a charge from the gun without a shell before loading any shells for subsequent firing. By the same token, while it was quite permissible to fire the gun with the canvas muzzle cover on if time was short, it was not advisable to do this when the canvas muzzle cover was covered with two or three inches of ice.

We all rather had the feeling that we had been thrown in at the deep end, but the spirit on board was very high, and everyone endeavoured to learn as fast as they could and to help train others, despite the difficulty of finding time for training in the relatively little spare time left after carrying out our ordinary duties.

One of the problems, of course, in night action was establishing one's identity as friend or foe, and endeavouring likewise to discover the identity of another vessel. This was achieved by having three groups of lights on the foremast, each group consisting of one red, one white and one green, and by an ingenious bit of electrical switching, these could be switched on by one switch on the bridge to give a certain pattern for challenging an enemy ship, and another position of the switch would give a reply to the challenge, and the particular combination of lights to give the right challenge and the right reply was changed at least once every twenty-four hours.

We had been on our first patrol only for a couple of days when at around two o'clock in the morning we suddenly found ourselves bathed in the light of half a dozen star shells on our port side and to starboard we could see the three challenging lights of recognition signal. Fortunately someone had made up the recognition signal correctly for our reply, and as soon as the switch was pressed, our lights shone out and declared ourselves to be friendly, while the very fact that we had received a challenge by the same method indicated to us that our "attacker" was friendly. It turned out to be one of the Town class cruisers which was filling one of the patrol berths, and there ensued a lengthy dissertation by shaded morse lamp to try and

11

decide whose navigation was in error, since we should have been separated by at least thirty miles.

Our high morale and enthusiasm for prosecuting the war was considerably dampened when we intercepted messages a few days later from *HMS Rawalpindi*, another Armed Merchant Cruiser (with similar guns to our own), stating that she was under attack by two battle cruisers. It transpired that these were the *Scharnhorst* and the *Gneisenau*, and so it was really no contest. Between them, these two ships were able to muster a broadside eighteen eleven-inch guns, twelve six-inch guns and fourteen 4.1 inch guns against the poor old *Rawalpindi*'s four six.inch guns of extremely ancient vintage and very limited range. *Rawalpindi*'s guns were of such short range that they were not able to fire even as far as the German 4.1 inch, so that she could very easily have been sunk without ever getting into range. In fact, the official reports say that the Germans opened fire at eight thousand yards, and it was even reported that the *Rawalpindi* scored a hit before she was finally destroyed. One officer and twenty-five ratings were picked up by the *Scharnhorst* and made prisoner, and a further ten survivors were picked up later by the *AMC Chitral*, which, considering the weather and the temperature of the water, was a fairly large number of survivors from a crew of some three hundred and fifty.

The incident certainly reinforced the belief among crews of the Armed Merchant Cruisers that the initials AMC actually stood for "Admiralty Made Coffins". Before the end of 1940, when I left *Worcestershire*, the *Jervis Bay* had been sunk by the *Admiral Sheer* and eight other AMCs had been torpedoed and lost, while the *Cheshire* had been torpedoed but managed to get into Belfast Lough and be beached. Two more AMCs were lost in the first six months of 1941 by torpedo, and one was sunk by a German armed raider which was fitted with much more modern guns than we were, and in fact *Worcestershire* herself was torpedoed (three months after I left her), but she received only one torpedo forward and managed to get back into the Irish Sea and subsequently was dry-docked in Liverpool and repaired.

Thirteen sunk and two damaged by torpedo in eighteen months was a depressing record.

The whole of 1940 was spent on Northern Patrol, a good deal of it on the Denmark Straits patch between Iceland and the ice pack, and the monotony of this was only relieved on two occasions — once when we were exchanged for a welcome fortnight in the warm weather of the Azores to do a stint on Western Patrol, and once when we were sent over to pick up a convoy from Halifax and escort it back across the Atlantic. This was just after the loss of the *Jervis Bay*, while she was performing similar duties, and we did not very much relish following in her footsteps. While we were going across to Halifax on a very bright moonlit night, we suddenly became aware that we were under fire from a vessel lying down-moon from us and having us in silhouette. She fired about twenty shells at us without managing to obtain a hit, and desisted quite rapidly when we fired a number of star shells in her direction to illuminate the scene. As soon as it was apparent what was happening, I was despatched to call the Captain and advise him of the situation. I stepped into his sea cabin at the back of the bridge and, without switching on the light, called out to him,

"Captain, sir! Captain, sir, we're under fire."

He took several seconds to wake up and I had to repeat my message before he finally said,

"What, what, what's happening?"

I said, "We're under shell fire, sir. There's another one coming over now," as I heard a shell screaming overhead.

At that he woke very quickly and came on to the bridge and took control, approving the order to fire star shells a few minutes later. Naturally the ship went to action stations and I made my way down to the forecastle and took command of my gun with shells continuing to pass over the ship until the star shells finally put a stop to the barrage.

The shells were coming from the starboard quarter and were finally assumed to be from a submarine on the surface which had mistaken us for a merchant ship. Presumably she was hoping for a hit or hoping that we would stop out of fear or that our speed was such that she would be able to catch up with us and polish us off in due course. We assumed the arrival of the star shell surprised and frightened her considerably and they probably dived immediately before our gunfire commenced. We remained at action stations for a further half hour and eventually reverted to normal cruising stations. When I arrived back on the bridge, the Captain sent for me and said,

"Snottie, the next time the enemy is firing at us and you are sent to wake me up, don't be so damned polite."

I only got one other piece of advice from this Captain, but I have treasured it all my life and passed it on to many others. On one occasion — I forget which — he asked me a question to which I did not know the answer, and I replied as smartly as I could, "I don't know, sir," at which he swung round on me and said,

"Snottie, always remember this, when a Senior Officer asks you a question to which you don't know the answer, never say 'I don't know, sir', always say 'I'll find out, sir' and then go and do it."

For anybody interested in the more serious doings of the Northern Patrol, I would heartily recommend the book entitled *The Blockaders* by A. Cecil Hampshire, which was published in 1980 by William Kimber & Co. It paints a comprehensive picture of the whole operation, while I can recount only one or two incidents which remain in my memory, most of which had very little effect on the war effort.

While I had never cared for cigarettes, I did occasionally smoke a pipe and had taken to smoking Burma Cheroots, which were extremely popular in a ship which still had some of the original officers who had been accustomed to sailing to Rangoon on regular runs before the war. Apart from being able to buy ordinary cigarettes at sixpence for twenty and pipe tobacco at a similar sort of price, we were also allowed a monthly ration of Naval pipe or cigarette tobacco, or if we desired it, tobacco in the natural leaf which was supplied at the remarkable price of one and six per pound. To prepare this leaf tobacco for smoking, it was necessary to find an old AB who knew how to make it up into what was technically known as a "prick", which was a torpedo-shaped wrapping of canvas and spun yarn. Traditionally you had to provide the AB with a tot of rum which he was supposed to use to soak the tobacco, but it was generally conceded that he drank this and spat on the tobacco instead. These pricks of tobacco were then laid bare by unwrapping the spun yarn and small amounts were cut off with a sharp knife, then rolled round before being inserted into a pipe or — more directly — into the mouth.

Chewing tobacco was something I had not tried, but I was persuaded to one night during the middle watch. Inserting the plug of tobacco into my mouth, I gave it one chew and that was enough for me. I rushed for the railing and spat it out, and thought I was going to follow with all my meals for the last three days. I managed to keep my meals, but I also kept the taste of the tobacco and could

14

not get rid of it for about six hours. Needless to say, I never tried it again.

Like most of the other AMCs, we were based on the Clyde and between our twenty-one day trips we used to lie at anchor for four or five days off Greenock, during which time we replenished fuel and other stores and allowed the ship's company to go ashore, transport being provided by drifters. Some kind soul had given the ship a gramophone of the old hand-operated, portable type, which was accomodated on the mess deck, but unfortunately only one record had been provided, which was a fairly raucous rendering of "I Will Pray". This became adopted by the lower deck as the ship's song, and it was always possible to tell when our liberty men were returning and approaching the ship because the strains of "I will pray every hour of the night and day" would come echoing across the water from the thirst-quenched lips of one hundred matelots in the drifter.

Many of our crew were retired Navy men, and some were older than others. One of the T124 stokers I recall wore, with pride, his Boer War medal ribbons, while a Naval Petty Officer who had completed his twenty.two years in the Service laid claim to the fact that he was struck in the chest with a Verey cartridge on November 11th, 1918, while keeping watch in harbour in the conning tower of a submarine. His name, I recall, was Stevens, and he was a caricature of a cockney and had that magnificent cockney turn of phrase and sense of humour. He had some marvellous reminiscences of a lifetime in the Navy, and some of these were passed across during night watches in the harbour when, respectively as Midshipman of the Watch and Petty Officer of the Watch, we stood at the gangway many an hour together. Two occasions particularly come to mind. Apropos of nothing in particular, he said on one occasion,

"Cor blimey, sir, aren't these hotels round here expensive?"

"Really." said I. "Which particular hotel are you referring to?"

"Why, that there Beresford in Glasgow, sir. Do you know, they charged me a quid for one room for one night?"

"Really, Stevens? What sort of room was it?"

"Oh well, sir, it was a nice enough little room, you know, sir. I mean, there was a little table with a lamp on it between the two beds."

15

"And I suppose that the other bed was not unoccupied?" said I, with a smile.

"Oh well, sir, we laid our clothes on the other bed."

On another occasion, Petty Officer Stevens and I were on gangway watch again and the Officer of the Watch, a T124 Lieutenant, who had been a second mate in one of the more infamous tramp companies between the wars, emerged on deck having over-indulged more than somewhat at the wardroom bar. In the manner of some drunks he picked on me for no real reason and upbraided me in a manner most unpleasant and obscene in front of Stevens and within hearing of the Quartermaster and Bosun's Mate. At the age of seventeen I was quite unable to cope with this situation and said nothing, while probably staring at him with my mouth open. I remember Stevens sucking his teeth and shifting his feet before he murmured quietly in my ear,

"I'll just be walking round the other side of the deck, sir, but I'll be back before 'e 'as time to hit you back."

* * * *

The patrols continued with relentless monotony. Three or four days on passage from the Clyde to our patrol line, twelve or fourteen days on patrol going to and fro like a sentry outside Buckingham Palace, and then three more days back to the Clyde where we lay for three to four days taking on fuel and other stores and granting the ship's company a little leave before going back again to our patrol line. Boredom was thus the main enemy, although what with watch-keeping, drills and exercises and boarding the numerous trawlers in the area, we did not have a lot of spare time during those long summer days of the higher latitude. When we boarded British trawlers, the boat usually came back full of fish, with the boarding of three or four trawlers providing more than enough for the whole ship's company for one meal.

During the Norwegian campaign, the destroyer HMS *Griffin* (in which I was later to serve) captured, by boarding, a German armed trawler and discovered that she was fitted with two torpedo tubes. As a result of this, we were instructed to board every trawler we sighted to make sure that she was not similarly fitted, and if our patrol line happened to cut across a profitable fishing area, this resulted in a vast number of boarding exercises. Eventually we were provided with a retired fishing skipper to assist us in identification,

16

and on one occasion at least he vouchsafed the bona fides of one trawler captain by recognising the photograph of the captain's wife in his cabin, since she had been a lady who had provided him with warmth and comfort on many a cold night in past years.

In the fashion of the times, we made up a concert party on board and endeavoured to give a performance every month or so. The midshipmen and Sub-Lieutenants were the mainstay of the concert party, but they were supported from time to time by some stalwarts amongst the crew, and on one occasion I recall the Commander and the Navigating Officer, very suitably dressed, bringing down the house with a passionate rendering of " If I could plant a tiny seed of love in the garden of your heart, would it grow to be a great big love one day or would it die and fade away? " — a popular music hall song of the previous war.

At times the bad weather provided some amusement, and I recall a happy afternoon spent trying to trap the grand piano which had run amok in the old passengers' smoke room. It was a fairly large room, about forty feet by sixty feet with a number of square tables, each provided with four chairs, all of which were chained down to plates on the deck. The piano had also been chained down, but broke its moorings when the ship heeled to some forty-five degrees and it then rampaged to and fro across the smoke room like a tank in a small forest, rapidly converting all the chairs and tables into matchwood. A " tiger catching party " was mustered and peered into the wreckage from one of the doorways, and each time the piano came temporarily to rest, they dashed in and tried to secure it, retreating rapidly when the piano broke loose again. By the time it was finally secured, it had lost all its legs and various wires were sticking out of the innards like angry antennae and few, if any, of the tables and chairs remained usable.

*   *   *   *

Of the many neutral ships stopped and boarded, the Finnish SS *Pori* of Mariehamn will always remain in my memory. At this time a winter war was going on between Russia and Finland, in which surprisingly the Finns seemed to be holding their own. Sympathy in Britain (and most of the world) lay with the Finns, who alone had offered serious resistance to the Russians. Estonia, Lithuania and Latvia had all been overrun and assimilated into the USSR some months beforehand.

Examination of her cargo manifest showed, among many other items, a number of aeroplane propellers, doubtless anxiously awaited in Finland. But, by our own rules, these were contraband of war and the ship had to be sent in to Kirkwall.

Such a small ship was not considered worthy of a regular prize crew, and since I was part of the examining boarding party and another larger ship had been sighted which also required boarding, I was left on board with Petty Officer Stevens and four seamen to ensure that the vessel duly arrived at Kirkwall, while the remainder of the boarding party returned to *Worcestershire*, which hoisted the cutter and steamed off in search of further prey.

Suddenly I seemed to be very alone, and the responsibility of command weighed heavily on my shoulders.

There was nothing to do but get on with it, and a course for Kirkwall was duly set and the Captain persuaded to ring down for "Full Speed Ahead", which produced from her wheezing and ancient engines a full five knots which occasionally rose to nearly six when the sea was smooth and the wind in our favour. I prayed that the weather would not turn against us.

Petty Officer Stevens was quite naturally a tower of strength as befitted his many years' experience. In no time at all he organised the seamen into two watches and found somewhere for them to eat and sleep, and likewise arranged some feeding arrangements for the two of us. How he conversed with the Finns, whose language bears no resemblance to anything even vaguely European, I never knew, but it seemed to present little problem to him.

I was convinced that the Finns were planning some desperate deed to avoid losing their propellers and also the nausea of delay at Kirkwall, and found it impossible to sleep peacefully, only dozing occasionally in a chair in the wheelhouse and continually waking up to check that we were still on course and that no devilment had been perpetrated while I slept.

It was a very long fifty-two hours before we were sighted by a Naval trawler from Kirkwall, which came to meet us and escort us to the examination anchorage.

The noise of the anchor going down was music in my ears and the relief was enormous when a few minutes later one of the examining officers of the Contraband Control Service came aboard and took charge of everything.

"You look a bit weary, Snottie," he said breezily. "You had

18

better get your party together and go ashore in my boat. They will fix you up with food and beds, which I expect you all need."

I needed no second bidding to relinquish my first command and bade farewell to the Finnish Captain, whose smiling face seemed suddenly different from his apparently villainous previous expression.

* * * *

After some six months of operation, we were ordered into Belfast to do a short refit in Harland & Wolff's shipyard there. This was mainly a thorough overhaul of the engine, which had been running fairly continuously since we commissioned, and the opportunity was taken to fill up all the cargo holds with empty forty gallon oil drums in the hope that this would keep the ship afloat after she had been torpedoed (and they were to prove their worth when the ship finally was hit by a torpedo nine months later).

In the 1980s we have become used to the sectarian problems and violence in Ireland, but it was a totally new experience to me in 1940 and was brought home when, on the first occasion that a few of us were in a dockside pub sampling a little Guinness, a burly dockyard matey approached us and said,

"I suppose you boys will be Protestants."

Frankly the religious convictions of my drinking partners were not something of which I was really aware, but since the remark was addressed to me, I looked round rather vaguely and said,

"Well, I don't know about the others, but I am, if it's of any interest."

Some of the others nodded in agreement, whereby our friendly dockyard matey, who stood about six feet four inches and was built like the proverbial brick outhouse, said in a stage whisper designed to be heard in every corner of the pub.

"Well, if there's any trouble at all, at all, me and the boys will be with you," and he nodded in the direction of half a dozen of his cronies. We subsequently discovered that this was the predominantly Catholic area, and even drinking Guinness was a comparatively dangerous occupation for Protestants, although in those days the unpleasantness was probably limited to a punch-up rather than a bit of bomb-throwing or machine-gunning.

While we had been plodding to and fro in the northern waters, the phoney war had finally ended with the invasion of Denmark and

19

Norway in May, our landings there and subsequent evacuation, and all this, as is well known now, was followed by the German sweep through Holland and Belgium, resulting in the mass evacuation at Dunkirk. Despite the general bleak appearance of the war, there was nothing very much that we could do about it except get on with our own job.

By chance we made friends with some officers who flew Fairey Battle Divebombers in 88 Squadron, which had recently pulled out of France and was now stationed at Belfast Airport. My particular drinking partner, a certain Pilot Officer Martin, was an air gunner (that is to say, a rear gunner in a Fairey Battle), who also held a Merchant Navy Second Mate's Certificate.

It transpired that at the beginning of the war he wished to join the Air Force and was refused permission because the Merchant Navy was considered a "Reserved Occupation". His rather unorthodox method of dealing with the situation was to register as a conscientious objector and obtain his discharge from the Merchant Navy, whereupon he walked straight along the road and into the RAF recruiting office, where he joined up as a rear gunner. The mortality rate of rear gunners was so high — even at the beginning of the war — that this was one category in which one had no difficulty in joining the forces, regardless of age or fitness. When a distant uncle of mine, who was a retired Colonel aged 62, desperately tried to join up to do his bit at the beginning of the war, this was the only type of active service for which he found he could be accepted, while apparently being too old for anything else.

It may seem odd to people used to flying to Spain or further for their holidays since an early age that, fifty years ago, flying was really quite an adventure and relatively rare.

True, there was a passenger service from Croydon to Paris, but very expensive and somewhat suspect from a safety point of view. Imperial Airways were running a flying boat service to various outposts of the Empire, and the Germans had a Zeppelin service to South America. Nevertheless, it was all somewhat experimental, not that far removed from today's space travel.

Although my main hobby was sailing, I was fascinated by aeroplanes, and keen to fly, so that when Sir Alan Cobham's Air Circus came to the small Sussex town where I lived and offered what were called "Joy Rides" lasting ten minutes and costing five shillings, I begged my parents for the necessary funds, which represented an enormous capital sum when compared with my sixpence a week pocket money.

"Certainly not," I was told. "What will you think of next?" Perhaps it was pure cussedness that made me join the Navy a few weeks later.

One July evening, for no particular reason, some of us attended a party at 88 Squadron Mess. Being not so good at carrying hard liquor as many years' practice have since made me, I was still not the first to pass out at around eleven p.m., but coming to at two a.m. I found the party in full swing and joined in again.

Folk music was all the fashion in those days, and the rafters rang to the choruses of such fine old traditional songs as "The Harlot of Jerusalem", "Caviar Comes from the Virgin Sturgeon", "She had to Go and Lose it at the Astor", "Barnacle Bill the Sailor", "The Good Ship Venus" and many other similar ballads. Most messes and ships seemed to have a particular favourite to which extra verses would be added by inventive and imaginative lyricists and, as I recall, 88 Squadron could manage some thirty-two verses of "Three Old Ladies Locked in the Lavatory".

In the friendly atmosphere of wine and song, I apparently allowed myself to volunteer to fly in Sailor Martin's place as rear gunner on a dawn patrol due to take off in a few hours' time. In a hazy spirit of Royal Navy/Royal Air Force co-operation and conviviality, permission for this changeover was readily obtained from 88 Squadron's C.O.

"Oh yes, bang on, what? Good for you chaps to get a bird's eye view of the sea and all that."

The First Lieutenant of *Worcestershire* was slightly less enthusiastic and not very much more coherent.

"Permission granted if that's what you want, Snottie, but remember that if God had meant us to fly, he would have given us bloody wings."

Encouraged madly by all this, I had two more drinks and passed out for the second time, and it seemed only a few minutes later that I was being awakened by a very respectful orderly who was thrusting a cup of tea at me.

"Good morning, sir. I understand you're flying the dawn patrol with Flight Lieutenant Stewart in Mr Martin's place. It's half past five now, and the Flight Sergeant will be along in ten minutes to take you to your plane."

21

It is an old adage in the Services that one should never volunteer for anything, and what appeared to be a pneumatic road drill attacking the back of my skull certainly made my particular contribution to the war effort seem highly unattractive at five-forty this July morning. The thought of lying down again and sleeping, or even dying, was much more attractive than standing up and doing anything at all, but at least there was one advantage. I had — as the saying goes — been dressed by the fairies and merely had to grasp my cap to be ready for the arrival of the Flight Sergeant.

He turned out to be an archetypal sergeant of the sort that has since appeared in many films. He looked as if sleep was something entirely beneath his dignity, and the general belief was that neither his parents nor grandparents had ever been married. He hauled off a salute that looked more like a double karate blow to his head and thigh, and blasted the morning with efficient information:

"Morning, sah! O five four O hours, sah. Understand as wot you is flying rear gunner in Mr Martin's plane, sah. Mr Stewart haims to take hoff in fifteen minutes, hand if you follow me, sah, I will get you your kit hand give you some hinstruction hin the Lewis Gun, sah."

At the risk of making the top of my skull fly away, I mustered up courage as quietly as I could, said "Very good, Sergeant," and put my cap on in the hope that it would keep my cranium in one piece.

I shuffled after the Flight Sergeant's parade ground marching steps and was helped into a flying suit, helmet and boots, and then walked what seemed miles across the airfield to an aeroplane in which dimmed lights showed. The noise of the Morse code came from inside, and as I started to climb aboard, "Sparky" reported to the Flight Sergeant,

"Radio gear all tested and in proper working order, Sarn't."

The Fairey Battle was a three-seater aircraft carrying a pilot who looked forward, a rear gunner who looked backwards and handled a single .303 machine gun, and a radio operator who, as far as I remember, was somewhere in the middle and could not see out at all. Like most peacetime designs, it did not really measure up to real war, but it was the only aircraft in the RAF that had any pretence to being a dive-bomber, and as such it was designated.

The Sergeant droned on,

"Well done, lad. Now listen 'ere, this is Mr Scott, a Naval

22

Officer, wot's come to be hintroduced to the mysteries of haviation. 'E'll be taking Mr Martin's place for this patrol."

We exchanged greetings as I climbed into the rear gunner's seat. Part of the canopy was open and the Flight Sergeant was standing in some toehold outside telling me all about the Lewis Gun in a drill book manner that did not sound very different to that prevalent in Whale Island, the Navy Gunnery School.

". . . this 'ere is the cocking lever wot you pulls back to cock the gun hinitially. Hafter the first round, the gasses from the hexplosion passing down this return tube. . ."

It was more than my skull could take, and I hastily interrupted with,

"That's all right, Sergeant, I'm well acquainted with the Lewis and all its stoppages. Just show me where I plug in the intercom and where the spare magazines are and I shall be OK."

In the gradually improving light from the imminent dawn, there emerged a group of people approaching the control tower. As they got closer, it was obvious that it was two people carrying a third, whose head lolled limply to one side in an unconscious manner and whose feet dragged like a rag doll's.

"Good gracious, Sergeant," I cried, "Has someone been injured?"

"Ho no, sah," replied the sergeant with some glee, "that's Flight Lieutenant Stewart, sah, your pilot, but hi assure you 'e'll be hall right as soon as 'e gets in the hair."

                *   *   *   *

One Sunday, a special concert was put on in one of the main theatres in Belfast, and since most of our officers and ship's company were on leave, I was able to occupy a seat in the centre of the front row. With the passage of time many of the stars are forgotten, but those that particularly come to mind are G. H. Elliott ("The Chocolate Coloured Coon"), who gave a magnificent performance of song and dance despite the fact that he was some sixty years of age, and there was also a delightful performance from Evelyn Laye. She sang "I'll See You Again" from "Bittersweet" and then asked for requests from the audience, at which I immediately requested "Dear Little Café" from the same show, and on the completion of this the tables were turned, because she invited me up on to the stage to join her in a duet of "Little Sir Echo". There were a number of the ship's company in the audience, and needless to say, my nickname for the rest of the time I was in the ship was "Little Sir Echo".

Some thirty years later I went to see a performance of "The Amorous Prawn" in which Evelyn Laye was playing, and during the interval sent round a card to her saying,.

"I am one of the hundreds of young officers who sang 'Little Sir Echo' with you during the war. May I pay a call upon you?"

This resulted in an invitation to have a drink in her dressing room after the show, when she stoically announced that she remembered me clearly, which was probably a brave and polite lie, but certainly her charm had by no means diminished. She was, and is, one of the truly great ladies of the theatre.

Our refit over, we returned once more to the monotonous duties, but by this time there were very many fewer German ships and very few neutral vessels passing through these waters, so that the number of ships on patrol was very much reduced and our main duty was covering the area between Iceland and the ice pack, where the real blockade runners were expected.

Life was made a little easier for us, since the ship had been fitted with a gyrocompass and an echo sounder, the former being particularly useful to the North of Iceland where there was a large area of magnetic anomaly. In these days, when such devices are commonplace, even in yachts, it is interesting to note that they were not part of the normal equipment of a fifteen thousand ton passenger ship. This was really the second step into the electronic era, since the first step had been taken some months before when the Kelvin Sounding Machine had been fitted with an electric motor. This really meant something to the midshipmen, because prior to the arrival of the electric motor, it was their duty to wind in the thousand odd feet of sounding machine wire and sounding lead when this machine was in use as we approached the Scottish coast. It was extremely hard work when the ship was proceeding at any sort of speed, and the arrival of the electric motor was really hailed as a benefit to humanity — or at least to midshipmen.

To my mind, it was really the dawn of modern technology.

In October or November we were required to take General the Viscount Gort, VC, and his staff from the Clyde to Iceland before doing a patrol in the Denmark Straits and then collect him and bring him back to Greenock when we returned. He had been made Inspector General of the Forces, and was required to inspect the defences of Iceland.

While he was on board during the two passages, I was relieved of watchkeeping duties and appointed to be his unofficial Naval ADC and look after his comforts. For an eighteen year old midshipman, it was a very remarkable experience to spend the best part of eight days in very close proximity to a very great man. He refused to have a batman and insisted on polishing his own boots and making his own bed each morning. In some ways he was a very lonely man (I believe that I had heard that his wife had left him and his daughter had run off and married somebody of whom he did not approve). He was, in fact, teetotal, but intentionally avoided being labelled as such by generally taking a glass of sherry before dinner and small amounts of alcohol on other suitable social occasions. After dinner he liked to take a "constitutional" for about an hour and normally had the company of one of his two ADCs, but while on board the ship they were very glad to pass this duty over to me, and I was equally glad to perform it. Nothing was beneath his dignity, and when I had the temerity to ask him if he would be good enough to inspect the nine men in my six-inch guns crew, he agreed with alacrity, and the following day spent over half an hour talking to them, both about their duty as guns crew and about their previous service in the Navy.

On the return voyage he even produced a chart of Iceland and asked my opinion on some of the defences of the various fjords. My opinion must have been entirely worthless, but the fact that he had asked for it made me feel about seven feet tall.

We landed him at Greenock, together with his two ADCs, and then proceeded on another patrol, on the return from which I was astonished to receive three very remarkable letters.

The first was a letter from Lord Gort himself, written in his famous green ink which was a well-known idiosyncracy of his. It was a plain simple letter of thanks, but what was so extraordinary was that a General at the height of the war had bothered to find time to write such a letter to a mere midshipman who had been appointed to act as an unofficial ADC for a period of some eight days.

The second letter was from the senior of his two ADCs, who in fact was a Peer of the Realm and a Major, and similarly it was really very gracious of him to write to me at all.

The third letter, from the junior ADC, also expressed thanks but went on to give a description of something which had happened soon after they had left the ship. He explained in his letter that the Field Marshal and his staff had been invited to stay with the Lord Lieutenant of Ayrshire, and he then went on to describe an incident which I recall quite clearly and can almost quote word for word as follows:

"An interesting thing happened yesterday (but keep this under your hat). We were invited by the Chief Constable of the County to view the contents of a German aeroplane which crashed near here a few days ago. The remarkable thing was that it contained a list of names and addresses of important people residing in the area."

Naturally I treasured these letters and put them away carefully in my room in Sussex when I was next on leave, and I did not come across them again until about a year after the war when I was going through some papers and the importance of this list of names and addresses in the aeroplane suddenly struck me, for it was in this very area that almost twelve months later Hess crash-landed his aeroplane and was subsequently captured and incarcerated.

The whole Hess business has always been surrounded in mystery, and even now it is one of the mysteries of modern history that he was for several decades the only one of the German top echelon who remained in prison in Berlin. In that letter was clear evidence that twelve months before Hess' arrival there had been a previous attempt to contact important people residing in that part of Scotland. The ADC's letter also mentioned that there had been no survivors from that first aeroplane, so that as far as is known, no contact had been made, but of course the possession of the list by our own authorities must have made them aware that there was a plan afoot to contact those people, and with hindsight it would appear likely that this was an endeavour to secure a peace between Germany and England prior to an all-out attack upon Russia.

Sadly, in the years between 1946 and the present day, my family house in Sussex was sold and the various papers and possessions that I had there went through a number of moves to different London flats, and finally a move out to Jamaica and back, and then through three houses in England. Somewhere along the line those three letters were mislaid or destroyed, and so it is not possible for me to produce them now as written evidence, but the words are written indelibly in my brain, and I leave others perhaps with more knowledge of the whole situation to make something more of the incident.

Both for amusement and to indulge in some form of exercise

during the cold weather, the younger officers of *Worcestershire* started playing deck hockey on what had been one of the promenade decks.

It started as a fairly gentlemanly and sedate game, using old walking sticks and a round puck made of wood, and was played in the dog watches between teams of four players.

Originally I suppose we started obeying the ordinary rules of hockey, about the details of which none of us were quite sure in any case, but gradually over the months the game developed a spirit and a set of rules of its own. Quite early on one or two of the walking sticks got broken and replacements were not available, so players carried on using the shortened version which was only about fifteen to eighteen inches in length. These proved so effective that eventually all sticks were shortened by accident or design to the same sort of length, and the round wooden pucks were abandoned in favour of square cork ones (cut from condemned lifejackets), which proved more effective in that they would not roll on edge and were easier to manufacture after a puck had gone over the side.

We had on board a vast number of cork-filled lifejackets built to the requirements of the Board of Trade before the war for passengers and crew. These had been condemned and declared unfit for use following the discovery that if you donned one of these garments and jumped over the side you broke your neck. They certainly provided a fairly suitable raw material for the rapid manufacture of deck hockey pucks.

The rules of the game seemed to get simplified as the time went by, and after a few months were rather similar to those for all-in wrestling, that is that the only things that were forbidden were tearing out of hair and gouging out of eyes. I certainly recall that the method of stopping a keen player who was " dribbling " up the wing close to the ship's rail was merely to push one's hockey stick through the rails so that the other player pushed your stick along until it came to the first upright, whereupon he landed flat on his face. In better weather, members of the crew off watch would foregather to observe our antics and cheer on their particular individual officers. Certainly my own six-inch guns crew provided a very vociferous supporting audience from time to time.

Probably the most violent game ever took place when we were transporting General Gort and an Army contingent into Iceland, and having persuaded some of their junior officers to join in our daily games, it was then we decided to hold an Army *v.* Navy match. Unfortunately only three Army officers could be mustered for a team, and in view of my temporary acting position as ADC to General Gort, I was roped in to play for the Army, and when the match was finally played in front of a most enthusiastic audience from both Services, feelings began to run rather unreasonably high, and enthusiasm overreached all bounds.

The game was finally abandoned when exhaustion and injuries had almost incapacitated both sides. One Army officer had broken two ribs, another had broken a leg and the Paymaster Sub-Lieutenant who was the Captain's Secretary had struck a steel stanchion with his head and had been knocked out cold to the extent that he did not recover consciousness for over ten minutes. I do not remember the score, but I am sure that the Navy did not allow the Army to win.

*   *   *   *

Worcestershire did a few more stints on Northern Patrol and was then ordered to Southampton for a refit. By this time the blitz had finished with London and had been directed at various other cities, of which Southampton was one, and we fully expected to be severely attacked while coming up the Channel from Lands End, but to our surprise we were not only escorted by two destroyers, but provided with fighter cover from a position North of Lands End all the way up the Channel into Southampton Water and up to the docks.

The city had been very badly battered, and wreckage was everywhere from bombed-out buildings all round the centre, but nevertheless one still was able to find pubs and hotels which managed to carry on serving drinks in at least one room, and even then one or two clubs that stayed open after hours. The Germans apparently thought they had destroyed both the city and everything in it, and they didn't return to attack it further while we were there.

Leave was granted, and it was a nice change to have a relatively short ride home instead of the long journey from Scotland, and just before going on leave I received two letters, the first advising me that my T124 appointment in *Worcestershire* as a midshipman RNR had come to an end and that I had been granted a warrant as a midshipman RNVR. The second letter told me that I had been appointed to *HMS Auricula* and for duty with A.S.C.B.S. and to report on board *HMS Auricula* at George Brown's yard, Greenock by January 15th. It

28

took me quite a long time to discover that A.S.C.B.S. stood for Admiral Superintendent Contract Built Ships and indicated that the ship was still in the builder's yard and had not yet actually commissioned. With further difficulty the information was unearthed that *Auricula* was one of the new anti-submarine corvettes that were building, and that she was a small ship of one thousand tons carrying five officers and around fifty men.

One of the first things to do on leave was go up to London and have my blue patches on the collars of my uniform taken off and replaced by red patches, these being the badges of rank of an RNVR midshipman. In fact this was all a bit of a cock-up at the Admiralty, and I had to get them changed back to blue ten days later when I was advised that I was, in future, to be a midshipman RNR and not RNVR. The only advantage that pertained to this short stay in the RNVR was that I was now able to boast that I had been in all branches of the Navy except the Wrens, for having started off in the RN, I then transferred to the T124 RNR and then the RNVR and then to the RNR, and of course there had also been the earlier period when I had supposedly been a member of the RNVSR. Long after the war I also became involved with the RNR (SCC) which is the Sea Cadet Corps of this country, but I never got round to changing my sex and joining the Wrens.

The other peculiar advantage of being in the RNVR was that while on leave at around one o'clock in the morning I was driving home in a car with two girlfriends after a very liquid evening and with the practically non-existent headlights that were required by the blackout regulations, the result of which was that I ran into a single-decker bus that had been taken over by the Army and painted the ubiquitous khaki. My car stopped suddenly on hitting the bus, and I smashed my nose against the steering wheel so that it was streaming blood, and on getting out of the car to survey the situation with a handkerchief to my face, I found myself surrounded by soldiers, some of whom were saying,

"You can't do that there 'ere to this 'ere. This is Government property this is."

Someone then produced a torch and shone it in my face, and I think the only thing that was visible to the soldiers was my red midshipman's patches which, in the Army, signify a member of the staff and possibly even a General. There was a great swishing sound as they all saluted and a clatter as their heels clicked together, and then they were all dashing round to pull my car clear and make sure that it was still able to move, and with a final salute, the sergeant rattled out,

"Sergeant Fitzgerald, sir, 4217 Third Wessex Rifles. Don't you worry about anything, sir."

And with that they drove off. It did not seem to be worthwhile to explain my somewhat junior Naval rank.

Chapter Two

HAVING REJOICED in the short journey home from Southampton to Sussex, it was once again the long night train north
to Glasgow and on to Greenock to find the little shipyard of George
Brown Ltd, which is not to be confused with John Brown Ltd, the
very famous Clyde shipbuilders who built the big trans-Atlantic
liners between the wars. As is always the case, *Auricula* looked a
complete wreck in an unfinished state in the middle of a very mucky
shipyard, but it was a very small shipyard with *Auricula* the only
vessel under construction, and so it was soon possible to get to know
everybody involved. It all seemed rather small scale after *Worcestershire* with only one thousand tons of ship and to man her, five
officers and fifty Petty Officers and men. The Captain was a
Merchant Navy officer who had obtained a commission as an RNR
Lieutenant on the outbreak of war and had been in command of a
trawler for some nine months, including some exciting times in the
Norwegian Campaign. The First Lieutenant was a yachtsman who
had become a Sub-Lieutenant RNVR at the beginning of the war and
had spent the previous eight months in the first corvette to be commissioned. The two other Watchkeeping Officers were Sub-
Lieutenants RNVR straight from the training establishment *King
Alfred* in Sussex with absolutely no experience whatsoever at sea,
and I had been added as an afterthought. The design of the
accommodation did not even include a bunk for me, but the very
willing people at George Brown's soon altered this and added a third
bunk in the Officers Cabin.

It immediately became apparent that we were incredibly short of
experienced watchkeeping officers, a situation which did not
improve much for the next twelve months, but we worked out a
system on board which would, I am sure, have horrified the Lords
Commissioners of the Admiralty if they had understood the shortcomings which existed. The system we employed was to go in three

watches in the Merchant Navy fashion, that is to say, all the officers kept standing watches every day and did not alternate around as is more normal in the Royal Navy. The First Lieutenant, who also acted as navigator of the ship, kept the morning watch (four a.m. to eight a.m.) and the two dog watches (four p.m. to eight p.m.) by himself; the Captain kept the first watch (eight p.m. until midnight and eight a.m. until noon) with the more competent of the two Sub-Lieutenants who he was able to leave on the bridge alone from time to time, and to a greater extent as he gained experience. That left me as junior boy keeping the graveyard watch from midnight until 4 a.m. and from noon until four p.m., with the other Sub-Lieutenant as my assistant and, so to speak, under instruction. In fact, our Sub-Lieutenants seldom seemed to stay with us very long — they either went sick or gained some experience and were appointed to other ships, or they went on long specialist courses, and in each case they were always relieved by an entirely inexperienced officer, once more direct from *King Alfred*.

Auricula was still some weeks from completion, and the Captain decided to make me the Anti-Submarine Officer and put me in charge of what was then called the ASDIC equipment (these days known by the American term SONAR), and to learn about this I was sent off to do a fortnight's course at the ASDIC Training School at Campbeltown, Mull of Kintyre. Since the vessel was built solely and entirely for the purpose of hunting submarines, the operation of the submarine detector gear was obviously extremely important, and I was pleased and flattered to be given this job. Later in the war, practically all officers on convoy escorts took this fortnight's course, but at this stage of the proceedings, it was possible only to send one officer from each ship to learn this trade.

The word ASDIC dated back to the 1914-18 war and stood for "Allied Submarine Detection Investigation Committee", and on the very first morning of the course, we were given a little rundown on the early history of that august body. Apparently all sorts of things had been tried in those days, including an attempt to train dolphins to find submarines, in the training of which they were rewarded by being given extra fish. The whole system apparently broke down because as soon as the dolphins were let out in the open sea, they dashed after what fish there were and forgot entirely about all the submarines, but it is interesting to note that in recent years dolphins have been trained to do a very considerable amount of work, both in finding underwater objects and in retrieving objects from the bottom of the sea.

Surprisingly there was still a very gentle peacetime attitude existing at *HMS Nimrod*, the school at Campbeltown, and all fully qualified A/S Officers (who were our instructors) were particularly keen to point out that this was a gentleman's occupation and was not to be confused with the nonsense that went on at *HMS Excellent*, the gunnery school, where all officers wore gaiters and everybody had to do everything at the double with all orders being given in the manner of the Regimental Sergeant Majors who have been made famous in many films. Our Instructor Officer apologised on the first day that there would be a few days when instruction would take place in the afternoon, and he realised that this was unpopular since it was so difficult to keep awake after a few glasses of gin at lunchtime, but he assured us that the course had been arranged in the main so that in the afternoon we did practical exercise on the submarine attack teacher which, on the whole, was more interesting and less likely to induce sleep.

The apparatus which we used was based on the discovery that very high frequency sound can be made to travel in a beam, and the other discovery that a sizeable metal object (such as a submarine) would produce an echo which came back along the beam path and knowing the speed of sound in water, it was possible to discover both the direction (by the bearing of the sound beam) and the distance away of an object from which one had received an echo. We were also told, incidentally, that the French used similar equipment, not for finding submarines, but for signalling between ships under water, and had spent years trying to get rid of the echo, without success.

It would seem, of course, that with this equipment, hunting, catching and subsequently sinking submarines would become child's play, but there were, however, a number of shortcomings. The first was that in absolutely ideal conditions, the maximum range in which one could possibly hope to get an echo was two thousand five hundred yards. In actual practice, conditions were so seldom ideal that this distance was considerably reduced. It was also possible to get echoes from shoals of fish or even individual whales, which sounded very similar to that produced by a submarine, and in coastal waters, wrecks would also give extremely good echoes, which only

33

became suspect when it was found that they were not moving, but of course a submarine lying doggo on the bottom would also not be moving.

A very ingenious simulator had been built, which enabled the situation of effective submarine hunting to be reproduced in a classroom. Some of the class would operate the equipment and endeavour to sink the submarine, while one member normally operated the submarine to see if he could get his mind into the attitude of a submarine Captain, while the remainder of the class could watch the whole thing take place on the plotting table and see what mistakes were being made. Towards the end of the course we actually spent three or four days at sea off Campbeltown in a small submarine chaser with a real live submarine for us to hunt. She was always referred to as a " clockwork mouse ". The main result of these exercises was to show how extremely difficult it was to find a submarine, and even more difficult to make an effective attack on her, and this when the " clockwork mouse " was normally steering a straight course and at relatively low speed, unlike our German friends who would be doing everything possible to avoid us.

Altogether it was a fascinating course, and we were left in no doubt by our instructors that we had become very important people indeed, and that our knowledge was of far greater value than pearls, rubies or gold. The same was true to a very great extent of the men who operated the equipment — the Seamen, who were ASDIC operators, the Leading Seamen, who had some technical knowledge to repair and maintain the equipment and the Petty Officers and Chief Petty Officers, who were very knowledgeable people indeed, and who were almost entirely employed on maintenance and repair and instruction. Since trained ASDIC operators were in such short supply for the vast number of ships that were being constructed, completed or converted for anti-submarine work, it was made very clear to us that one of our duties on return to our ships was to ensure at all times that when any of our ASDIC operators went on shore, they were to carry with them French letters, and it was definitely stated that it was our responsibility to ensure that this was done, since the Navy could not afford to have ASDIC operators withdrawn from duty merely because they had acquired that infection known as "Liverpool Measles".

Sunday Divisions was the nearest thing to any real formality that went on at *HMS Nimrod*, and we were advised somewhat apologetically by our Course Officer that we were expected to fall in for Sunday Divisions on the first Sunday of our course, since it was the custom for the Captain to meet all the officers taking a course at this time after the Divisions. We were fallen in in descending order of rank and seniority, so that as the first midshipman to actually take this course, I was the last in the line. After each officer had been introduced to the Captain, they had a few words and then the officer would turn right, dismiss and walk away back to the already open bar in the wardroom. I was thus the last item on a rather long menu, and the relief that almost all was over and the gins were getting nearer was visible on practically everybody's face as the Captain stood in front of me. Rather to everybody's surprise, the Captain took one look at me and said,

"By God, I know you," to which I replied,

"Yes, sir, you were Commander of the Royal Naval College, Dartmouth, when I was there as a cadet."

We then exchanged a few reminiscences, and much to everybody's surprise, he then said,

"Well, now, I think you're the first midshipman to become an anti-submarine qualified officer, so I think we'd better celebrate this. Come along and have a gin," and in this manner we left the parade ground together.

We probably would not have been very well acquainted, since he was the Commander and mixed only with the Captain, who was definitely superior to God, and I was one of five hundred cadets, but two days before the end of term a rather curious incident occurred, which assumed a disproportionately large significance in the rather enclosed community which existed. One of the civilian masters complained that on the Sunday night somebody had thrown stones at his classroom window with malicious intent. The Commander had ordered all the cadets fallen in on the quarter deck and stated that if the culprit did not own up by half past eight the following morning, he would cancel the end of term dance which was due to take place the following evening. This dance, which was organised by the cadets who were leaving the college that term, was a ball of some social significance, and practically all of us in the leaving term had invited two or three girl-friends and a number of parents and friends to attend the celebration which followed on the prize-giving and other shenanigans during the day.

During the rest of that evening and from six-thirty the following morning, all the Cadet Captains conducted a witchhunt in the hopes of finding the culprit, but by breakfast time it was evident that they had been unsuccessful. Since the crime was not particularly great and the punishment could also not be very large, and since, in my case, I was not carrying on a career in the Navy, I volunteered to confess to this crime if nobody else had done so before me, and watch was kept on the Commander's cabin to see if anybody should do so. Thus it was that as the college clock struck eight-thirty (one bell in the fore noon watch) I knocked on the Commander's office door and owned up to the heinous crime, and was promptly reprimanded for not doing so earlier. The situation soon became quite hilarious, because all the officers who knew me stated firmly that it was very unlikely that I would have done this, and anyway there was no particular reason for me to do so. To support my story I had carefully placed some gravel in the pockets of the blazer I had been wearing the evening before, and claimed that I had merely thrown away this gravel to get rid of it, and had not intended that any of it should strike the window of this master's study. The Commander placed me under a form of close arrest with the Captain, and I was then called before them again, and the comical charade ensued during which they tried to prove or get me to admit that I had not done it, and I furiously contested that I had. They were then in a "Catch 22" situation where they were convinced that they had not really got the culprit, but on the other hand could not prove it, and so could not carry out their threat of cancelling the dance that night. Towards the final stages, the Captain produced a bible from his drawer, but I had been warned of this ploy, so that as soon as he said,

"I want you to swear. . ."

I immediately stood back, braced my shoulders and said,

"As an officer, I expect you to take my word, sir," which brought them up all standing.

Finally I was required to promise that I had not meant any harm to the master, and agreed to go and apologise to him personally, and so the whole thing blew over and nobody ever did discover who the real culprit was, but after years of trying to talk one's way out of things one had done, it was rather amusing to be trying to talk one's way into something that one had not done.

The next amusement at Campbeltown was an air raid. Looking back on it, it was quite an intelligent thing for the Germans to do, and just surprising that they did not continue to do it, for it did not need much effort in the way of aeroplanes and pilots to disrupt the school and the harbour (which in our case was closed for three or four days), and it did considerably slow up the training of anti-submarine ratings and officers. Had it been seriously continued by the Germans, it would have been interesting to consider what effect it would have had on The Battle of the Atlantic. The raid started at about midnight and consisted in the main of dropping parachute mines on the harbour entrance, but one or two of these fell on bungalows on the other side of the harbour and exploded on contact. We all ran out to see what we could do, and for some time I found myself alone amongst the bombed out bungalows where I started moving debris to get near to voices that I could hear underneath. Eventually more people arrived and we managed to pull out one couple, shaken but alive, and another pair who unfortunately were dead. In the meantime, the aeroplanes had been dropping incendiary bombs on the rest of the small town, and made one or two passes with machine guns to interfere with the efforts of everyone to put out the fires. It was all totally disorganised, but to my surprise I found that my training with the ARP in the few weeks before I went to sea a year earlier came in quite useful, because I did actually know what to do with the incendiary bombs which nobody else seemed to have any idea about. My recollection even now is of it being a very exciting night which finally drew to a close around three in the morning when all the incendiary bombs had been dealt with and all the inhabitants of the bungalows accounted for one way or another.

We missed some of our sea days while efforts were made to account for all the mines that had been observed dropping by parachute, and at one time it was thought perhaps that they were experimenting with a new type of mine which was not magnetic, as there was some difficulty in accounting for all the mines that had been seen to fall.

Auricula was due to commission one day before the end of the course, and I was instructed to return to her for this occasion. Every evening was a party in the pub which we had taken over as a wardroom mess, and the last night of the course would have been an extra big party before the twenty of us all split up to go to our different ships, and as I was leaving a day early we had an extra " the night before the end of the course party ", at which it was certainly incumbent upon me to buy a round of drinks to start it off, and I rather fancy I bought another later on in the evening. It should be

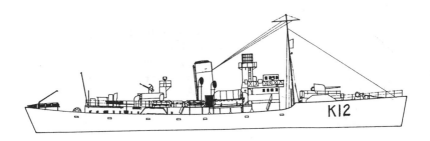

HMS Auricula
(late 1941)

explained that a local custom had grown up, whereby a round of drinks cost two pounds, and consisted of a bottle of whisky and an enamel bucket of beer holding about five gallons. Everyone present then helped themselves to whisky or beer (by dipping their mugs into the bucket) to their own desires, and when the bucket and the bottle ran out, somebody usually produced another.

It is difficult to recall who really started the idea, but somewhere around midnight we decided to take apart the upstairs room in the pub with remarkable precision, despite our somewhat unsteady manner. Firstly all the furniture was taken out of the room and the carpet lifted and turned upside down and relaid, then with great care every picture was carefully taken out of its frame and re-inserted upside down then re-hung on the wall, and after that, anything and everything (including the piano) that could possibly be taken apart with screwdriver, or whatever, was duly dismembered, and all the pieces piled in a heap in the centre of the room.

Feeling very much the worse for wear, I took a taxi out to the airport about seven o'clock in the morning to catch an aeroplane back to Glasgow and *Auricula*, and it was only some months afterwards when I met others on the course that I heard what had happened. The landlord of the pub claimed several hundred pounds' worth of damage and the class was duly paraded up at the school and addressed in a stern manner by the Commander, who told them that there would be a levy on everybody in the class to make good any damage. The Commander and the Course Officer had, in the meantime, inspected the damage and compared it quite favourably with other similar events which occurred regularly at seven day intervals as each course ended its period. Eventually our class returned to the scene of devastation and with great care and considerable effort managed to re-assemble everything as it was before the party, with the sole exception of one pane of glass which had inadvertently been broken during the evening, and this resulted in a levy of sixpence per head in order to provide the landlord with ten shillings to replace it. Nevertheless, what with one thing and another, I believe the final end of course party was somewhat subdued.

On arrival back at *Auricula*, it soon became apparent that miracles had been worked and the vessel was more or less finished, so with a trials party from the builders, we cast off moorings and steamed down-river to do full power trials, which involved, amongst other things, running for full speed along the measured mile and estimating the speed attained, and then at one stage throwing the engines into full astern from full ahead, always an interesting experience.

All went well, and the Captain duly signed the acceptance slip for the ship on behalf of the Admiralty and we then embarked all stores remaining, and sailed the next morning for the harbour of Tobermory in the Isle of Mull, where a working base had been established under the redoubtable Admiral "Monkey" Stephenson. For a full account of what went on during the war years in Tobermory, readers are advised to peruse the book entitled *The Terror of Tobermory*, written by Lieutenant-Commander Richard Baker, RNR (the well-known BBC newsreader). The nickname was well earned, and the ships were thoroughly put through it during the two or three weeks which they spent under his care and guidance, and no ship passed out of his hands to go on to convoy work until he had made a final inspection, during which everything and anything might happen, and usually it all happened at the same time.

He liked to create as much panic and confusion as possible and then see how the officers and ship's company managed to cope with the situation. Thus you might be informed by him or his staff of various situations requiring immediate attention, such as perhaps an air attack by Stuka dive-bombers, taking another vessel in tow, putting a collision mat over the side to stop the water coming into an imaginary hole in the ship's side, and in the midst of it all his favourite ploy: "Repel boarders". The word soon got round that he was never happy with the manner of dealing with the last order

*. . . He was never happy with the manner of dealing with
the last order unless the cook dashed out of the galley
with a carving knife, or the butcher's cleaver.*

40

unless the cook dashed out of the galley with a carving knife or the butcher's cleaver in his hand.

The stories about him are legion and probably apocryphal, but nevertheless it is perhaps worth recalling one or two. On one occasion he confronted a rather lackadaisical Sub-Lieutenant, threw his Admiral's cap on the deck and shouted at him,

"That's an incendiary bomb, what are you going to do about it?"

Whereupon the Sub-Lieutenant kicked it over the side. The Admiral was not in the least phased by this, he merely said,

"Man overboard. Away lifeboats crew, recover my cap," and then turning to the Sub-Lieutenant said,

"You'll be in charge of the lifeboat crew," while the message from his steely eyes poised between the tufts of hair on the upper parts of his cheek and his very bushy eyebrows indicated quite clearly that it was more than the Sub-Lieutenant's life was worth if he arrived back without the cap. On another occasion he is reputed to have thrown over a lifebuoy and shouted "Man overboard" on a Canadian vessel, then when nothing much happened in reaction, he leaped over the side himself, at which seventy per cent of the crew of the Canadian frigate also leaped over the side, and they had a considerable job getting them all back again. Any officer in a visiting ship who displeased him or whom he thought was not quite up to the mark would be re-appointed to his own headquarters vessel for a period of intense training, and one who had survived such weeks would be re-appointed to the visiting ship in his place.

Many years after the war I had the good fortune to meet Admiral Sir Gilbert Stephenson (as he had then become) when he was still a very active member of the Navy League, although he was then past his ninetieth year. At one of the annual tea parties following the meeting of the Navy League, I overheard one Admiral saying to another,

"I really don't know what to do about Sir Gilbert. He just shocked the eyebrows off the Cardinal and now he's telling rude stories to those two secretaries over there."

We finally left the meeting together and had to cross Northumberland Avenue to get to my car. While I paused to wait for a gap in the traffic, the Admiral stepped straight off the pavement and started walking across the road, saying loudly,

"I've been ninety-one years on this earth and if this is going to be my last minute, so be it."

41

"That's all very well, Sir Gilbert," says I, "but I've only managed my first fifty and I'd like to see a few more."

After we had completed our normal working up at Tobermory and done all our anti-submarine exercises and all the other ingenious tasks that were set for us by the Tobermory staff, we had to remain a further week to do our training in minesweeping. Most corvettes were not fitted for mine-sweeping, but since it was a belief at the Admiralty that the Germans would lay two lines of mines across the English Channel to protect their forces coming across from France to England during the invasion of Britain, twenty-four corvettes under construction had been fitted with Oropesa minesweeping gear to cope with this problem. No-one in our ship's company had ever served in a minesweeper or with minesweeper gear, and it was a very slow and difficult business learning to cope with it, despite the very able instruction received from Commander Crick, who had been involved in minesweeping for many years. Like many skilled jobs, it appears to be quite impossible at first, but is adequately simple once you know how to do it.

Eventually all our training period was over, and Admiral Stephenson gave us a final inspection and pronounced us fit for combat. We received our sailing orders and departed from Tobermory to Liverpool to join our escort group. At that stage in the war the Atlantic convoys were not escorted all the way across the Atlantic, but the escort groups from the United Kingdom took convoys out about one thousand miles west of the British Isles and then left them to do the rest of their journey unescorted, except possibly by an Armed Merchant Cruiser as a guard against German surface raiders. The anti-submarine escort group would then proceed to join an Eastbound convoy and escort them back into the British Isles.

With bad weather frequently preventing adequate observation of the heavenly bodies and the total ban on the unnecessary use of wireless transmitters, it was frequently very difficult to find the incoming convoy. Radar was beginning to become available, but *Auricula* was not to be fitted with this gadget for another nine months, and in the meantime we had to make do with what we had got. With breakdowns and other ship damage, the escort which normally consisted of six ships was sometimes reduced to four, and the escort groups normally steamed around ten to twelve knots, zig-zagging freely and widely to no particular pattern to reduce their actual speed of advance to the same as that of the convoy. If one was stationed on the beam (that is to say on one side of the convoy), one could steam away from the convoy at about forty-five degrees off their course for a quarter of an hour or twenty minutes, and then alter course the opposite way and steam back towards the convoy until it came in sight (if visibility was reasonably good) or until the ASDIC operator could report the range of the convoy on his machine. The line of ships of some considerable size, together with their wash, gave a very definite echo, and over and above that he could actually hear the noise of their propellers. From time to time human error crept in, and the Officer of the Watch would lose the convoy and would then be put in the embarassing position of having to call the Captain and advise him that this had occurred and incur his wrath, while attempts were made to find the convoy on the rather small amount of evidence available.

Life was not very comfortable in the corvettes for a number of reasons. Firstly, they had been designed only for coastal escort work and had originally been intended to carry a crew of around thirty-five to forty, but as additional equipment got piled into the ship, so did extra crew members arrive to handle it. Another problem was that the galley was right at the stern end immediately above the Petty Officers Mess, while the officers' accommodation was under the bridge and the seamen's accommodation in the fore-castle, which meant that in bad weather the only people on board who got a hot meal were the Petty Officers. Everybody else's food had to run the gauntlet along the upper deck, with the fair chance of being diluted by spray or even green water from the ever-present Atlantic waves.

The only refrigerator in the ship was a small domestic item somewhat tinier than I have in my own kitchen today, which could not do much to alleviate the situation for a crew of fifty men away from new sources of supply for fourteen days or more at a time. Depending upon the weather, fresh bread would last perhaps five or six days, if brought wrapped in greaseproof paper and if one was prepared to cut off the penicillin and eat the remainder during the last few days. Green vegetables lasted a bit longer and potatoes, with a bit of luck, the whole of the fourteen days. After that, it was tinned meat and tinned vegetables, tinned fruit and tinned milk, tinned soup and biscuits and tea and coffee, and of course that well renowned institution, " Admiralty Cocoa ". This was always known as Cai (pronounced "Kye"), probably the initial letters of "Cocoa Admiralty Issue".

It was a great favourite during the night watches, and came to the ship in large blocks resembling chocolate, which had to be scraped with a seaman's knife into powder and then mixed with hot water and Nestlés Condensed Milk to the consistency of porridge. It was sweet and sickly, but delicious and sustaining as long as one did not suffer from sea sickness.

Then again, every seaman had his rum ration, without which I think they would not have survived, and the officers still had their wardroom bar which enabled them to take a little reviving sustenance from time to time. Shovril — or sherry and Bovril — was an old established Naval custom and a great reviver during the night watches, since it was not quite so sleep-inducing as the Naval cocoa.

In the cod war of the 1970s, my son was a midshipman in a frigate on patrol off Iceland, and when I asked him what it was like, he said,

"It was pretty ghastly, Dad, the central heating on the bridge failed."

In *Auricula* we did not have any central heating on the bridge, and the protection from the winds and waves on the North Atlantic was somewhat limited. It consisted of an ordinary guardrail round the edge of the bridge, rising only some three feet six inches from the deck, and outside of this was lashed a canvas screen to which was also lashed some splinter mattresses, which were supposed to absorb machine gun bullets or splinters from bombs or shellburst. Having some idea of what we were going to endure, the Captain and myself had entertained the ship manager at George Brown's extremely well on two or three occasions, and persuaded him to add some tongue and groove boarding along the front edge of the bridge, which constituted a small amount of shelter from the wind and a little bit of wind baffle. This certainly improved matters, but hardly amounted to a central heating system.

In harbour fresh fruit was not easily available, especially in the winter time, and its benefits were not even realised until we and other ships on West Approaches convoy work began to find cases of scurvy cropping up amongst the crew.

It was very difficult for anybody to come out of the forecastle and go anywhere in the vessel without getting wet, and once clothes had become wet, it was very difficult to dry them. I think it was the

44

famous Dr Johnson three centuries back who said that going to sea was as bad as going to prison, with the additional chance of being drowned, and among some of the young crews, this philosophy was converted into action. They figured out that if they could punch an officer on the nose, they would be awarded at least seven days in cells, and that would mean that they would miss the next trip. Life in the Naval cells (prison) was not very comfortable, but at least it was dry and the meals came three times a day with regularity. There was nothing personal about this, and so anybody wanting to miss an escort trip never punched one of his own officers on the nose, but just chose one who happened to come by, whose face he did not recognise, but this did not make it any pleasanter if you were on the receiving end of the blow.

But life was not all misery by any means. It was an intense pleasure to me to find myself in charge of a one thousand ton ship with a crew of fifty for eight hours a day, and an even greater pleasure to be handed command of the ship when the ASDIC operators reported a contact with a suspected U-boat. The Captain very graciously admitted that he knew nothing about hunting submarines, and whenever I reported to him that I thought one was present, he would say,

" Very well, Scott, the ship is yours, " and I would then proceed to make an attack with depth charges.

Convoy work was monotonous, almost as monotonous as Northern Patrol, but it was enlivened from time to time by attacks from German aircraft and by submarines, while every fortnight or so found us back in Albert Dock in Liverpool for a few days' rest and relaxation. The First Lieutenant and I became drinking partners, and used the cocktail bar of the Adelphi Hotel as our early evening starting point, later on descending to a variety of legal, semi-legal or entirely illegal drinking clubs which abounded in the city which, like Southampton, had been severely battered by bombers. If we were going on " a quiet run ashore ", which was probably going to include a number of these less salubrious drinking establishments, we would leave any valuables behind, and I would carry the money for the two of us, probably five or six pounds. Then in the morning I would see what I had left in my pocket and we would split it appropriately.

On one occasion, however, on having had a few drinks on board just to get the corpuscles moving, we walked up to the Adelphi as usual, and there, as we went into the cocktail bar, he sighted a poster for the Royal Theatre nearby, and recognised the name of a young actress with whom he was acquainted who was appearing in the show as the juvenile lead under Jack Hulbert and Cecily Courtneidge. Plans were therefore changed, and after a quick drink at the Adelphi, we went to the theatre to watch the show, and then having sent a message to this girl in the interval, we nipped round to her dressing room after the show with the stated intention of taking her to dinner in the French restaurant at the Adelphi. I was not used to actresses, and was somewhat startled by the short conversation during dinner which went as follows:

She: "Have you hurt your wrist?"

Me (holding out both wrists and looking at them): "No, they're always like that."

She (smiling sweetly and fluttering her eyelashes): "Ooh, you must be frightfully strong."

And I couldn't really think of a reply to that one.

We had a magnificent dinner with wine and all the trimmings, sparing no expense, and then as time drew on, it became necessary to leave for the railway station where our actress friend was catching a train back to London for the weekend, this being a Saturday night. Carrying out my normal paymaster duties, I called for the bill in a grandiose manner, and found that I was just able to cover it with an adequate tip, using every last coin in my pocket, barring one shilling which was retained to retrieve our caps from the cloakroom. As we got our caps and I dispensed with the last shilling, I explained the situation to my drinking partner, and offered to go outside and ensure that the commissionaire — an old friend of ours — could *not* find a taxi. This done, we collected our companion and walked the odd three hundred yards to the station, dutifully carrying her bags. Once at the station we discovered which platform the London express was leaving from and approached it, chatting the while. At the barrier the ticket collector demanded our friend's ticket, which she produced readily, and he then glared at us and bellowed "Platform tickets". Platform tickets in those days cost a penny, and I was pretty sure I had not got even one penny left. Fortunately the light in the station was dim, so I drew off a short distance working around in my pockets and called out to Number One,

"You got any change, Number One? The smallest I've got is a half crown piece."

He quickly cottoned on and replied in a similar vein, whereupon

46

our charming guest produced two pennies and enabled us to avoid disgrace and accompany her on to the platform and up to her sleeping car. It was a narrow escape.

*   *   *   *

In March *Auricula* had to go into the Herculaneum Dry Dock in Liverpool for attention to some problem with the propeller shaft gland. Naturally when a ship is in dry dock it is not possible for the ship's company to continue to use the ship's heads (w.c.'s), and provision is made for such activity adjacent to the dock. Unfortunately some of these facilities were constructed many years ago at the same time as the dock, and it soon became apparent that Victorian standards of comfort and hygiene were somewhat primitive by the standards of 1941 and are worth describing, since they appear even more remarkable in 1986.

Essentially simplicity and economy were the keynotes. The central position of the facility was a thirty-six inch diameter pipe about a hundred feet long descending at an angle of about five degrees below the horizontal from a water supply point inland to a discharge point above the waters of the River Mersey. This pipe was pierced at five foot intervals like a flute by holes which, at one time in the distant past, had been ringed by something resembling a traditional wooden lavatory seat, but practically all traces of these had vanished, with the exception of the remains of some fixing screws or bolts which rose rustily from the metal flange. These residues interfered considerably with the almost non-existent "comfort" of the morning ruminative seat, the temperature of which on a cold and frosty March morning alone precluded any lengthy cogitation and encouraged fears of frostbite in very tender parts.

Privacy was also at a premium. A number of privy-like sheds had been constructed around each "flute hole" complete, at one time, with a door and latch, but the latches had long since disappeared and, in many cases, the doors as well, and frequently the roof.

Comfort was further interfered with by the geographical alignment of the River Mersey at this point, which ran roughly in a North Westerly direction, so that our pipe, being at right angles to the river, pointed South West, and was thus in a good position to receive the full force of the prevailing wind, making for an exceedingly draughty sensation around the private parts.

This sensation was altered slightly if one attempted to occupy the

47

only vacant position in this all-too-public loo in a strong wind. One then came to feel a bit like the ping-pong ball on the water spout that used to be the traditional target for air-rifle marksmen at country fairs.

As if all this was not enough to prevent one's peaceful contemplative enjoyment of one's daily morning duty, there was the occasional rippling crescendo of squeals and cries of dismay occasioned by some wit at the landward end lighting a newspaper and dropping it into the pipe, so that it floated slowly down to the Mersey causing no little pain and discomfort to anyone not quick enough in abandoning his seat of consideration.

Happily we were only two or three days in the dry dock, and those who could endeavoured to find some duty requiring their presence ashore where more comfortable facilities could be found. My own favourite for this was certainly the Adelphi Hotel, whose marble halls were by contrast almost the ultimate in lavatorial luxury.

Arriving there one morning in company with my shore-going drinking partner — almost too late — we dashed past the Commissionaire, through the revolving doors and across the thickly carpeted foyer at the run, to the astonishment of staff and guests alike.

In the multi-cubicled marble hall of hygiene we lost no time in dashing into adjacent compartments, thankful that fate had not dealt us a cruel blow by arranging none to be free at the moment of our arrival. Seated at last in warmth and comfort and breathing in the perfumed air, I heard a relieved and appreciative voice from over the partition,

"Aaah — excretia luxuria!"

❊   ❊   ❊   ❊

While *Auricula* was in Herculaneum Dry Dock, the furthest upriver of the Liverpool Docks, I heard that *Worcestershire* was in dry dock at Gladstone, the furthest downriver of the Liverpool complex, following her being torpedoed in the Atlantic.

Making the journey to see her and hear of the fun and games involved, I made the trip to Gladstone and stood on the dock side looking down at the damage before going on board. On the starboard side of her bow was a hole large enough to drive a double-decker bus with a single-decker alongside through the hull plating. There was room, too, to drive the single-decker out the other side.

It was a sobering thought to realise that, had I been at my action station at " A " gun on the forecastle, the torpedo strike would have been about twenty feet aft of where I normally stood, and consequently chances of survival would have been small. *Worcestershire* had been lucky. The hit so far forward was probably, in part, due to the U-boat over-estimating her speed. The U-boat men would be unlikely to believe that we would have Armed Merchant Cruisers with such a low maximum speed as thirteen and a half knots. A hit just a little bit further aft would have struck the forward magazine, and further aft than that the engine room, both of which would have been fatal. Finally those parts of her cargo hold not taken up with magazines were filled with empty forty-five gallon oil drums and these provided a lot of flotation in a hold penetrated by water.

The proof of the pudding was that *Worcestershire* had managed to steam well over a thousand miles after receiving this momentous damage and was, in this respect, more fortunate than many other Armed Merchant Cruisers and merchant ships.

* * * *

From the ship's company's point of view, one of the great advantages of the corvettes and the early frigates was that they were all steam driven, and one of the peculiarities of steam is that the boilers require cleaning every six weeks or so, and during this period the ship is entirely out of action. It normally used to take about five days, and it was customary to send at least half the ship's company on leave, and this was always a very welcome break. The other half was left on board with only a certain amount of maintenance work to do on deck during the day, plus the embarkation of stores as and when these arrived. That left the evenings and nights to enjoy the pleasures of Liverpool, a city which had been geared for many years to entertaining sailors. The corvettes normally berthed in Albert Dock, which was as near to the centre of Liverpool as you could get in a ship. Sometimes up to a dozen corvettes would be in port at the same time, and a good deal of inter-ship entertainment went on in the various wardrooms. The ASDIC Officer of *HMS Campanula* had been on the same course as me at Campbeltown and was highly entertaining, having been a barrister before the war, and he subsequently became a fairly well-known London magistrate in the years that followed. One of the other officers on board was Nicholas

Montserrat, who at that time was writing his first book called *HM Corvette* and who subsequently earned great fame and fortune writing *The Cruel Sea* and a number of other novels. I remember many incidents that subsequently appeared on the pages of these books.

There were inevitably a number of characters around, and the coxwain of *Auricula* was certainly one of these. He was an elderly Petty Officer who had completed over twenty years' service in the Royal Navy, but was a very small man with a great mop of red hair. He delighted in going off into long reminiscences of earlier life in the Navy, which inevitably started with " When I was doing my five years in China. . . " or " When I was doing my two and a half years on the West Indies station. . . " to such an extent that somebody with a statistical mind on board totted up all the figures and worked out that he had been in the Navy for at least one hundred and thirty-two years.

Normally the nights were fairly peaceful, being enlivened only by the occasional air raid, but sometimes the time of the tide caused a somewhat early start, and if the ship next to the wall, with two or three corvettes outside her, had to go to sea, there was a considerable amount of shuffling before everybody got re-moored, and I recall one such morning's activity being considerably enlivened by the appearance on deck of one of the ships of a most attractive blonde in a diaphanous nightdress enquiring what all the noise was about.

All the corvettes were named after flowers, and suddenly there was a great craze for every ship to have a " window box " each side of her funnel in which she grew her own flower. The salt water did not do them much good, and few would blossom throughout the year, while obviously some were easier to grow than others. Eventually somebody with a little bit of gardening knowledge from *HMS Marigold* chose the right time of year to plant their seeds in everybody else's boxes, which naturally produced a cuckoo in the nest situation, and after that, interest in horticulture seemed to dwindle.

In June 1941 I reached the ripe old age of nineteen, but it did not make any difference to my activities in *Auricula* where I carried on acting as " Instructor Midshipman ", knowing full well that I had another twelve months to do before I would reach the elevated rank of " Acting Sub-Lieutenant ". In August the monotony of working out into the Atlantic and back was relieved when we were ordered to accompany a convoy down to Gibraltar. We were lucky. *Campanula* went on the convoy before us, which was extremely badly mauled, this being one of the few occasions when the German submarines attacked the escorts, and having polished off most of them, proceeded to demolish the larger part of the convoy. It was particularly unfortunate that in this convoy were ships carrying the first batch of Wrens going over to Gibraltar, and a number of them were lost, but by good fortune we had a clear run out and the sunny warm weather was a welcome change.

On arrival at Gibraltar I discovered that General Gort was the Governor, and was advised to go in and put my name in his Visitors' Book. Despite the fact that I was still only a midshipman, the following day one of his ADC's was alongside with an invitation to go to lunch at Government House. The only other guest present was an Admiral from the Free French Navy, but General Gort could not have been more charming and considerate to me had I been an Admiral myself.

On our return to England we soon discovered that we were going somewhere warm, for the ship was fitted with awning stanchions and awnings and a normal household refrigerator for the ship's company. This latter was not of much value, since even before it was installed I discovered that it was not designed to work in temperatures over ninety degrees Farenheit, and even at sea off Freetown, where we were destined to go, it was quite normal for the temperature to exceed this throughout the twenty-four hours. The ship's company was duly issued with tropical uniforms, and officers had to go and acquire theirs at their own expense. We received a new Captain, a Lieutenant-Commander Royal Navy, who was a mine-sweeping expert, and the rumour was that we were going to form part of the minesweeping force for an attack on the Vichy French port of Dakar.

At this time our attitude to tropical climes and the effects of the tropical sun was still somewhat Victorian. Everyone was issued with sun helmets, and these were required to be worn between the hours of dawn and sunset, under pain of punishment. Even the tropical white shirts contained a reinforcing piece across the shoulders and down the middle of the back to protect the spine from the sun's rays. This was not quite so bad as some of the Army regiments, whose tropical tunics had a quilted back lined with red satin to give extra protection to the spine, and in fact were unbearably hot. Nowadays one never sees a European wearing a sun helmet, but it those days it was somewhat different, and rather in the fashion of one of Noel Coward's songs, the solar topis were definitely " de rigueur ".

The long passage with a slow convoy from England to West Africa was broken by a stop for fuel at Punta del Garda in the Azores. This facility was available on the basis of an alliance between England and Portugal which goes back several hundred years. In addition to fuel, we were able to purchase, for very small sums, large quantities of pineapples, bananas and other fruit which made a welcome addition to the normally rather monotonous diet on board, and of course these items had not been available in England since the beginning of the war. Pineapples, I recall, were about one shilling each, but by far the most interesting item to be embarked was a lovable white long-haired puppy, who inevitably became continuously dirty on board the ship and was nicknamed " Scruffy ". He was a most endearing pet, and although it is doubtful if he had any great pedigree, he was probably the most attractive dog I have ever met in my life, and gave everyone on board a great deal of pleasure during the next few months.

Eventually we arrived at Freetown, Sierra Leone. The ingrained memory in my mind is that we spent months, or even years, in this extremely boring place, but looking back on the sequence of events, it is apparent that we, in fact, arrived in September and had departed by February, and for a place as boring as Freetown, our stay was almost packed with incident.

There was evidence of the rumoured impending attack on Dakar in the shape of tank landing ships and other vessels destined for use during such an operation, and the atmosphere was further enlivened by the arrival at dawn two or three mornings a week of a reconnaissance aircraft from Dakar which flew desultorily round the harbour (presumably taking photographs) at a considerable altitude, pursued by equally desultory burst of anti-aircraft fire which never seemed to get very close to the plane. *Auricula* was employed on normal convoy work and patrol out of Freetown, but the lack of any enemy activity in the neighbourhood at that time made this even more boring than usual, and the lack of dockyard facilities there encouraged our engines to break down with a greater frequency than usual, which resulted in considerable time being spent in harbour.

The time in harbour was especially boring, since it was not

possible to go alongside, and the ships were moored or anchored separately out in a strong current, which made shoregoing in our boat impossible for this purpose, particularly as shore leave was granted only from 1400-1800 (two-six p.m.), and one tended to spend most of this time getting ashore or returning, and having arrived on shore there was precious little to entertain or amuse.

On one of the few occasions when I did venture ashore to enjoy the delights of Freetown, dusk found me on the main jetty in company with several hundred officers and men waiting for boats to take us back to our ships. Lying motionless on the stone jetty under the care of the Naval Patrol were half a dozen bodies who had been overcome by partaking of the local Palm Toddy. Time passed, and boats came and went, and the crowd thinned to some extent, and eventually after showing no sign of life for some twenty minutes, one of the bodies snored and rolled over, at which a great cry went up from those nearby,

"'E ain't drunk, I saw 'im move."

This was a definition of drunkenness which seemed to improve on the previous one I had heard from an American, which was,

"We reckon that if a guy can throw his hat on the floor he ain't drunk."

Apart from trouble with the main engines, *Auricula* was plagued by trouble with her steam steering gear to such an extent that we used to have the lights for signalling that we were "not under control" permanently hoisted at night and ready to switch on at a moment's notice, and on one occasion narrowly escaped being destroyed by the convoy we were escorting when the rudder jammed hard astarboard while we were zig-zagging to and fro in front of it at two o'clock in the morning.

When we came to investigate the problem, we found that it was a little more complicated than was normally the case, since the quadrant on the rudder head, which was toothed and driven by a cog connected to the steam steering engine, had managed to shear the limit stops at thirty-five degrees and gone over to an angle of about fifty degrees, with two of the teeth of the quadrant jumping past a shipside frame and jamming the rudder firmly in that position. It is not possible to tow a ship with fifty degrees of rudder on, nor do you get very far on your own engines, either astern or ahead, since your course is merely a series of very, very small circles. Work in the steering gear compartment was also virtually impossible until the

53

steam to the steering engine had been cut off for several hours and it had cooled down somewhat. It was not a very large compartment and filled with a fair amount of equipment, so that the number of people who could actually work down there at one time was severely limited. A considerable amount of force was going to be needed to spring the two cogs back over the shipside frame, and for some hours we endeavoured to apply this force by a Heath Robinsonian application of the bottlescrew slips, which were borrowed from the anchor cable on the forecastle. This was ingenious but unsuccessful, and it was unpleasant being on board a ship lying stationary in mid-ocean with the fear that she might be spotted by a German submarine and disposed of quite easily. The problem was only solved when the escort group leader returned to assist, and this ship was, in fact, an ex-American Coastguard cutter which had been made available to us on lease-lend, and her stores yielded up a remarkable assortment of useful equipment for our particular purpose, including lifting jacks of twenty ton capacity, and once these had been brought on board, we were able to solve our rather peculiar problem quite quickly and return to Freetown under hand steering.

Some weeks later, with steering gear at least temporarily operative once more, we were detailed to convoy a couple of ships down to Takoradi further down the coast and return independently. During the return journey a four-engine Sunderland flying boat, based at Freetown, approached us unexpectedly, flying very low, and to our surprise landed on the calm sea a short distance away. We approached the boat, and it transpired that they were suffering from engine trouble and wished to be taken on board, and for us to sink the flying boat and return to Freetown. The idea of sinking what appeared to be a first-class and viable flying boat in good condition, but with some minor engine trouble, seemed quite horrific to us, but acceptable to the Captain and crew. After some discussion, we decided to endeavour to tow the craft back to Freetown, although that was some six hundred miles distant. This was not an easy job, as the flying boat did not have a water rudder and was not fitted with anything suitable for attaching the tow rope to, but patience and ingenuity triumphed, and ten days later we brought our charge into Freetown Harbour and made the appropriate signal " Per Ardua ad Freetown ". Some three hours later the aircraft passed overhead, and we learned later that the only problem in the engines had been the failure of some oil pressure gauges.

54

One of the other corvettes stationed at Freetown at this time was *Myosotis*, commanded by a Lieutenant Commander RNR with a sharp and somewhat irrepressible wit, which was first noticed when he was ordered to sail from Freetown but broke down before reaching the harbour entrance, and anchored making the signal to the Flag Officer Freetown:

"*Myosotis* regrets she is unable to sail tonight," which evoked memories of a song about Miss Otis.

On a later occasion he was required to form part of an escort for the County class cruiser *HMS Dorsetshire*, commanded by a Senior Captain Royal Navy, who was particularly devoid of a sense of humour, causing an unfortunate clash of personalities. When *Myosotis*' ASDIC gear became partly inoperative, the Captain reported to *Dorsetshire* by signal lamp,

"My ASDIC 50% buggered," and received a ticking off for his troubles. Later on he made a second signal to say,

"For 50% read 100%", and as this was interpreted by the Captain of *Dorsetshire* as being somewhat cheeky, he received a second ticking off, but he bided his time for revenge. The following day, *Dorsetshire* fired off some of her four-inch anti-aircraft guns for practice, and on completion the Captain of *Myosotis* made the following signal to *Dorsetshire*,

"The base of one four-inch Mark XXIV shell has just landed on the port side of my forecastle immediately superior to the seamen's heads. One leading signalman previously constipated now completely cured."

To while away some of the boring hours out at anchor, I made an expedition to the fishing village near Freetown and bought there for a few pounds a beautiful dugout canoe, some eighteen feet long and pointed at both ends, hollowed out from a single trunk of wood and only about three-eighths of an inch thick. Unfortunately, unlike most boats, it had a negative stability, rather like a bicycle, and it took some time to learn to keep it upright. The locals used a very short, small single paddle to propel these craft with great skill, but I felt this could be improved upon, and manufactured from two ship's liferaft paddles a double-ended paddle of the type used by Eskimos and sporting canoists in this country. This not only made balancing very much easier, but it increased the power, speed and directional stability of the craft when paddling. It would be nice to return to Freetown today and find that all fishermen were using this type of double paddle for improved performance, but sadly I feel that it is unlikely to be the case.

Actually, while endeavouring to paddle back to the ship in this intentionally unstable craft, I capsized close to a one-time Brixham trawler flying the white ensign, which was moored fairly close inshore. They kindly rescued me and sent me on my way again without disclosing the nature of their occupation, which was obviously of a "cloak-and-dagger" variety. It was not my business to enquire closely, but I did meet them again a month or two later.

Others on board sought different forms of amusement, and our Captain, who hailed from Edinburgh, had been instructed by his wife and twelve-year-old daughter to bring home a talking parrot from his trip, and he accordingly expended much time and energy in combing the markets of Freetown for a suitable bird, finally returning on board with a villainous-looking grey parrot with a beady eye and sharp beak. As the unofficial carpenter on board, I was instructed to make a home for the beast and constructed a wooden T-shaped perch mounted on a copper tray filled with sand.

Whether he had been raised on a diet of local alcohol or not we never knew, but it soon became apparent that Polly enjoyed sucking gin, whisky or brandy from the end of a matchstick, and after consuming half a dozen drops or so, he would become decidedly inebriated. I can assure you that a drunken parrot is something extremely humourous to observe, sometimes losing his balance and swinging round so that he hung upside down on his perch, or even occasionally letting go altogether and falling into the sand underneath, accompanying his actions with loud squawks.

The Captain spent long, long hours patiently trying to teach the animal to speak, and it was many weeks before he condescended to utter a single word. When he did, it was that inimitable common expression which indicates "Go away", but which had been translated into language totally unsuitable for an Edinburgh wife and twelve-year-old daughter to hear. He did eventually learn to say "Away seaboat's crew" and "Pieces of Eight", but when the Captain taught him to say "Up spirits", the rest of the ship's company managed to teach him to add to that "Stand fast the 'oly ghost", and when the Captain further attempted to extend his vocabulary by teaching him to call "Wakey, wakey, wakey, wakey, show a leg", certain members of the ship's company delighted in teaching him to add to that "The sun's ascorching yer bleeding eyeballs out".

It soon became apparent that the returning mariner's traditional parrot was not going to be at all welcome in the genteel suburbs of Edinburgh.

After one long spell in harbour, and with the information that our repairs would take a further ten days, I actually volunteered to take a busman's holiday and went to sea for a seven day patrol as an additional officer in one of the one hundred and fifteen feet Fairmile ML's which were also based in Freetown. They only carried two officers, and the addition of a third for a seven day patrol greatly eased watchkeeping, and certainly was far preferable to lying in harbour in the hot sun with nothing to do.

The idea that one actually volunteered to go to sea on a seven day patrol demonstrates the extreme extent of the boredom encountered in Freetown which, it is reputed, was once described by Edward, Prince of Wales, as "the arsehole of the Empire".

Unbeknownst to us, big decisions had been taken in high places, and it had apparently been decided to cancel the operation for the invasion of Dakar in its present form, although as history will recount, it was reconstituted about a year later for execution by a largely American force, which brought the American army into North Africa. As an alternative amusement (although we were not to discover this for some time), a decision had been made to invade another Vichy French-held territory, namely Madagascar, and one of the minor decisions involved in the planning was that the minesweeping corvette *Auricula* would be required to assist in the minesweeping operations there.

We were therefore despatched from Freetown down the coast to Lagos, which used to be considered the centrepiece of "the white man's grave". There was a much-quoted rhyme which referred to the Bight of Benin, where few come out but many go in, but surprisingly enough we managed to do both without any particular problems. There was a small naval dockyard at Apapa which was immediately across the river from Lagos, and it was there that we were sent for some repairs before proceeding to Cape Town and thence to Durban and Madagascar.

Looking at photographs and films of Lagos today, with its busy streets and skyscraper buildings, it is difficult to recall that in 1942

57

there was not a building over two storeys in height, except for the Town Hall Clocktower, and furthermore the town was entirely without a normal sewage system. The sewage system was replaced by a light railway, which ran through the town every morning around dawn, and at this time a particular breed of refuse collectors, known as "abroushay boys", collected the earthenware pots from "the-smallest-room-in-the-house" of all Europeans' mansions and emptied them into the open trucks which, drawn by a small steam engine, puffed its way out on to the end of the pier at the harbour entrance and discharged its load on the seaward side of the wall.

All houses were built with their thunderbox at one end of the building, complete with a small doorway at ground level, which enabled the "abroushay boy" to extract the large earthenware pot and replace it with an empty one. It was necessary to be careful, if you were staying in one of these houses and happened to visit the smallest room around dawn, to ensure that you were not seated comfortably on the throne at the time that the "abroushay boy" arrived, as if so, you were in severe danger of losing the "family jewels".

It is also an interesting historical fact that the town of Lagos was bereft of its main source of defence while the "abroushay boys'" railway was operating for two or three hours every morning, since the same steam engine was also used to pull a specially adapted railway wagon containing a twelve pounder gun out on to the same pier, and the engine was obviously not available when it was otherwise employed, thus leaving the town defenceless. Hopefully this valuable piece of intelligence never reached the enemy.

The somewhat primitive life-style that existed there at that time was also demonstrated to me one evening when, driving with a local resident past the railway station and observing a large and somewhat unruly crowd, I enquired as to whether there was a riot about to start.

"Oh no," said my guide, "It is only that the train from Kano is expected in today. It is three days late."

Kano was the main town in Northern Nigeria and some five hundred miles distant.

Lying in Lagos at this time was an unusual sight. It was a ten thousand ton cargo vessel with rather peculiar bipod trellis work masts flying at her stern the White Ensign superior to the Italian flag. Moored nearby was the mysterious Brixham trawler which had rescued me on the maiden voyage of my dugout canoe at Freetown.

Rumours abounded concerning these two vessels, amounting to an interesting story which probably owes more to fiction than fact.

Apparently the cargo ship, with a valuable cargo of copper and other minerals, was lying at anchor in a neutral port when a bunch of piratical characters entered the harbour in a tug, berthed alongside, slipped her cables and towed her out to sea. It was further rumoured that someone had arranged a very alcoholic party for the officers of a warship moored in the port and for the officers of the protecting fort. It was even suggested that supplies of alcohol of doubtful quality were also supposedly smuggled out to the warship and the fort to divert the attention of the occupants.

When news of the disappearance of the cargo ship reached those in authority, a radio message was broadcast in some panic, stating that a Free French destroyer had entered the harbour and illegally carried off the Italian ship.

Supposedly, on receiving this information, the British Admiralty — knowing that no Free French warship was in the area — despatched a corvette to investigate. The corvette came upon an Italian cargo ship drifting in international waters, sent a boarding party on board and effected her capture. By coincidence a powerful tug happened to be only just over the horizon and she quickly took the ship in tow and proceeded to Lagos, escorted by the corvette.

It was even rumoured that the first message sent by the boarding officer to the corvette was,

"The Captain speaks very good English," but this was hardly surprising as it transpired that he was, in fact, a British officer.

In the Lagos Yacht Club I met again some of the crew of the Brixham trawler and one of their colleagues known as "Dickie", whom I encountered once more some two years later.

One evening, the Captain and officers of *Auricula* were invited to dine with the Governor of Nigeria, and we duly donned our full uniform and set off in a taxi for Government House. While the Captain sat on the Governor's right, as a mere midshipman I was way down the table, quite obviously below the salt. It was a truly colonial affair with some thirty people sitting down to dinner in a vast dining room, and the humid air being agitated by hand-operated punkahs, operated by cords disappearing through holes in the walls, and no doubt being langourously activated by some punkah wallah's foot as he lay on his back in the room next door.

The meal had several courses served by a multitude of Nigerian houseboys, all resplendent in white tunics, white trousers and red sashes. Eventually the meal drew to a close, and there came that magic moment when the Governor's wife rose to her feet and suggested to the other ladies that they withdrew, while the male guests shuffled up to the Governor's end of the table and proceeded to pass the port decanter. After a few glasses of port and some typically after dinner conversation amidst a cloud of cigar smoke, the Governor cleared his throat, rose to his feet and said,

"Well, gentlemen, shall we go and water the roses?"

We all dutifully trooped out the French windows into the gardens, only partly lit by lights from the windows of the Governor's residence behind us. Somehow in the confusion I found myself about to water the same rose as the Governor, and realised in that awful moment that no part of the curriculum in a young officer's education provided any guidance on what was the correct thing to do at this moment according to protocol. Should one assume that, as one who sat at the dining table well below the salt, one should proceed to the far end of the rose garden, or was this one of those jolly moments when rank held no privilege? Before I could decide on the right thing to do, the Governor engaged me in conversation, and at that I felt the only thing to do was to carry on with one's natural function rather than stand there and observe the Governor performing his with the air of an interested spectator. Sadly, this was a situation which those glorious Victorian books on etiquette and decorum did not cover.

A few days later we sailed for Cape Town, with neither a convoy to escort nor other Naval vessels in company.

Two somewhat unusual drawbacks were experienced on this long trip south, neither being discovered until we were well out to sea. The first surprise was that the ship's supply of salt had been stolen from the ship the night before. Salt is always considered very valuable in Africa, and in some parts is even used as currency. Our ship's supply consisted of one sack of rock salt, which was kept in the galley for ready use by the cook, and it transpired that one of the Nigerian workers had nicked this the night before we sailed.

It was really surprising what a problem it produced. Cooking for sixty-odd men without any salt whatsoever (any supplies of table salt on board must have run out very quickly) was really quite difficult, and certainly very tasteless and unpopular. My suggestion that at least potatoes and vegetables could be cooked in seawater (as is customary in yachts) was greeted with shrieks of protest and howls of derision, but eventually adopted against all the natural feelings of a seaman for salt water. Salt for other purposes was obtained by the engine room staff, who chipped it off various valves and joints where salt water leaked out and became encrusted on the outside of the fitting, and thus we survived somehow.

The second drawback was that the steam steering gear failed yet again less than one day out from Lagos, and we completed the rest of the journey in hand steering with a seaman down in the steering flat right at the stern receiving continuous orders by voice-pipe from the Officer of the Watch on the bridge, which was an extremely tedious business, although we did get relatively skilled at it by the end of the voyage. Due to being surrounded by steel, a magnetic compass could not operate in the steering flat.

For various reasons we put into Walvis Bay, originally a British enclave in what had been German South West Africa prior to the 1914-18 war and is now known as Namibia. Walvis Bay — a fine harbour — had been appropriated in 1815 for use as a supply port to St Helena when Napoleon Bonaparte was in residence. It was the only port on the long and barren coastline of that ill-fated German colony.

We had spent some nine months on the West African coast where, as the saying goes, women were few and far between, and those few were certainly beyond the reach of an impecunious midshipman on the odd occasions when he could get ashore.

Walvis Bay was not remarkable for its ladies, but we were advised that the nearby town of Swakopmund was very remarkable in this respect. It was some thirty miles away up the coast and was the scene of an unsuccessful German attempt to build a port during their occupation. The pier with its lighthouse was by then a mile inland, and is presumably even further from the sea today.

However, it was not this that was attractive. It was the discovery that, in this totally German town, all the men aged between eighteen and fifty had been taken away to internment camps in South Africa, and as a result it was a town of women with a few old men and some children added.

There was a small narrow gauge railway connecting Walvis Bay with Swakopmund, and with lustful intention George (the First Lieutenant), Harry (the navigator) and I boarded the train one afternoon with leave to stay overnight. We were seen off with many pieces of ribald information about the dangers of talking to blonde fräuleins and the likelihood that we would be uselessly weary on our return.

It was certainly an eerie experience. On dismounting from the train we found ourselves transported into the heart of Germany. Everyone spoke German, all the road and shop signs were written in German in Gothic script. Moustachioed old men in Bavarian style jackets sat at tables outside the Hotel Kaiserhof drinking dark Munich beer from lidded steins and reading the *Swakopmund Beobachter*. The sudden transformation was quite unnerving.

We took a short walk around the town feeling hostile eyes upon us and glad, at least, that we had each other for company. We entered the Hotel Kaiserhof eventually and booked rooms for the night. It was an establishment that had the air of a Victorian spa, doubtless in imitation of those hotels in the Fatherland at Baden-Baden and Königswinter. One expected any moment a detachment of Uhlans to come riding by in their spiked helmets or, possibly in a more modern vein, a band of SS men, belted and booted, to come striding into the bar.

To begin with we drank by ourselves, but gradually in broken English we got into conversation with the awe-inspiring " grande dame " who owned the hotel, and later her twenty-five year old daughter, Maria, appeared, and she was finally joined by two of her girl-friends. We soon forgot the warnings about consorting with blonde fräuleins.

It was, as I recall, a highly amusing evening, over the details of which I will draw a veil, and certainly it was a weary and rather hungover trio who boarded the miniature railway after breakfast the following morning to return to Walvis Bay.

We dozed fitfully as the carriage rattled and swayed down the track through barren country.

My sleep was disturbed every few minutes by a sleepy chortle from George, and as this continued throughout the journey, it began to aggravate Harry and myself, until eventually we could stand it no longer and demanded to hear the cause.

" Well, you will recall that I latched on to Maria last night, the daughter of the old harridan who ran the hotel. "

" Yes, yes, we know that, we were not that plastered, you know. "

" Well, " said George, " what you don't know is that around midnight we went for a walk along the beach in the moonlight. At one stage I said to her, 'Are you a Nazi?' and she said, 'Ja, ja', so I said to her, 'Would you tell Hitler that I am here? and she said 'I would if I could'.

"Well, after that we lay on the sand and quaffed Scotch from my flask — evidently a new experience for her — and then, well . . . things happened as things do.

"What is making me laugh is the thought that at this moment millions of people think it, thousands of people say it, but I'm different 'cos I've done it!''

* * * *

After the almost continuous entertainment by the South African army contingent in Walvis Bay (not to mention our visit to Swakopmund), it was quite a relief to get back to sea for the final seven hundred mile trip to Cape Town, which took us some three days and, by good fortune and good planning, was so arranged that we arrived in the early forenoon, being impressed by the view of Table Mountain and Cape Town Bay before berthing alongside.

Without doubt there would have been visits by technical people to take care of the repairs necessary to the steering gear and other parts of the ship, but forty years later what I really remember most is the detailed planning to look after the social life and entertainment of both officers and crew.

We had barely made fast mooring ropes before a message came for our Entertainments Officer to visit a lady in the offices of the *Cape Town Times* who, with extreme efficiency, arranged dances for the ship's company, beach parties, passes to go on leave and finally a party that night at the main nightclub in Cape Town for the officers of the ship. Having settled the time and place of the night-club party, our hastily appointed Entertainments Officer was then closely interrogated as to the type of girl that each of the officers would prefer to have for a partner that evening, and he finally arrived back on board clutching in his hand pages of notes regarding the various entertainments arranged and a slightly bemused and dazed expression.

Over a glass of gin in the wardroom, he attempted to describe his interview with this remarkable lady, who had explained that dealing with a single ship of five officers and fifty men was quite easy compared with arranging similar entertainment for a whole convoy of troops bound for the Middle East. As soon as we heard about the interrogation regarding our preferences in the matter of female partners, we were all agog to know what he had ordered up for us that night, and certainly on hearing his description of what he had prescribed for me, I had no difficulty in recognising my partner when we arrived at the night-club that night.

It must not be supposed that we depended entirely on the arrangements made for us ashore, and certainly we had shown some initiative and forethought in making plans to find female company for ourselves, since we were all suffering from a shortage of this facility after spending some six months on the West African coast, where women were certainly few and far between and definitely out of the reach, both financial and practical, of seagoing junior officers. George and I were particularly keen to follow up our success at Swakopmund, and had evolved an ingenious plan which resulted in the First Lieutenant's night order book for the night prior to our arrival in Cape Town containing the following paragraph:

"Item 5. Scruffy is to be washed, combed and brushed and provided with a collar and lead and to be in all respects ready for proceeding ashore under my charge at 1100. Midshipman Scott is to arrange for a taxi to be alongside the ship at that time to proceed into town."

Thus it was that at approximately 1120 George and I were entering the biggest and best hotel in Cape Town and wandering through the lounge and ascertaining the position of the bar, with the faithful and adorable Scruffy trotting along on his lead beside us. We had much more faith in the charm of Scruffy than in our own, and this faith was not misplaced. He was admired by one and all, and in particular by two charming Cape Town young ladies whom we had no difficulty in inviting to lunch. It is hardly worth reporting that between them and our partners at the nightclub that evening, we had a charming, eventful and busy time in Cape Town and were suitably heartbroken when it was necessary for us to sail to Durban some ten days later. The sad part of the story is that Scruffy's charm was so great that he was enticed away from the ship to some more luxurious home in Cape Town, where he no doubt led a more comfortable and pampered life than was provided for him in *Auricula*.

Four days' trip up the coast to Durban barely gave us time to recover from the frantic social life of Cape Town, which left very small portions of the night for sleeping, before we were arriving at Durban and found the situation starting once again, but here the tempo was further increased by that peculiar excitement of impending battle, because it now became well known that the reason for our presence was the imminent invasion of Madagascar, and preparation could be seen on every hand.

After the sexual deprivation which we had suffered while on the West African coast, we now seemed to be suffering from an *embarras de richesse*, but no-one was complaining, and certainly not me. George quickly found himself a charming young divorcee who fortunately had a very beautiful eighteen-year-old sister, so that our stay in Durban was all too short, and the strong rumours of the impending invasion meant that our forthcoming voyage was viewed with a certain amount of trepidation.

We sailed from Durban with a slow convoy, which was officially headed from Mombasa, but after forty-eight hours at sea the Captain was able to open the sealed orders and all the officers were able to read the detailed plans for the attack upon the harbour of Diego Suarez in the North of Madagascar, which was to be undertaken some ten days hence by the ships in our convoy and by a Naval force which was coming up behind us and would rendezvous to the West of the Northern tip of Madagascar the day before the invasion, or — as they have it in invasion parlance — on D-Day minus one.

During the slow passage from Durban to Madagascar we practised putting out our minesweeping gear and recovering it in total darkness. As has been explained earlier, although we were fitted with minesweeping gear, it was not our normal occupation, and in fact we had not even put out the gear for practice for nearly twelve months, so that a fair amount of exercising was advisable, especially at trying to do it in the dark. Naturally mistakes were made, and on one occasion we inadvertently dropped the kite while proceeding at full speed, and this very nearly had fatal results. The kite was a metal frame about four feet by four feet, which was towed behind the ship as part of the minesweeping gear by a one-inch diameter wire rope which, for handling purposes, led from the kite over roller fairleads at the stern of the ship through two large gin blocks to the warping drum of our fishing winch. The drop should not have taken place at high speed, but since it did, the strain it threw on the one-inch wire was very considerable indeed and in the dark the sudden jerk on the wire threw the two seamen straight over the winch and left the wire free to run out unrestrained for its total length of some eighty feet.

Most people knew the danger when they heard the shouts of alarm and explanation of what had happened and were aware that the wire was streaming out at high speed with a very heavy load of the kite on the end of it being pulled away from the ship at the ship's full speed. There were two possibilities: the first was that some tangle would be created to prevent the wire running through the blocks, and at this point the strain on the wire would cause it to break, with the ends flying in all directions well able to cut off a limb or kill anybody with whom it came in contact. The second possibility was that the wire would run free, but when the final end came lashing through the blocks it would be snaking from side to side like a bullock-cart driver's whip, and woe betide any person with whom it came in contact. Here again, it was likely to kill somebody or remove the odd limb. The only shelter was underneath the depth charge racks, and it suddenly seemed a bit crowded down there as we crouched in fear listening to the hissing of the wire streaming out over the stern. Eventually, with a terrifying clatter, the end came through the two blocks, lashed around in fearsome anger and disappeared over the stern, without hitting anybody at all. Suddenly there was silence, and in the silence a great sigh, as everybody let out their breath which they had been holding for the last few minutes.

As we were to be minesweeping in waters which were certain to be fairly full of mines and the likelihood of striking one was fairly great, I spent a good deal of time as the ship's unofficial carpenter constructing shores to support the bulkheads forward and aft in the event of the ship being damaged at the bow or stern, these being the most likely places of damage. This precaution subsequently proved of no value, but it was good for morale on board.

The principal target for the invasion was the capture of the harbour of Diego Suarez at the Northern tip of Madagascar with its entrance on the Eastern coast, but while a diversionary bombardment was to be undertaken on the East coast, the main attack was to take place on the West coast in Ambararata Bay, which was only some ten miles from Diego Suarez across the narrow part of the island. Ambararata Bay was protected by a chain of islands with relatively narrow entrances between them, the total area enclosed being very large indeed, and certainly large enough to contain the whole invasion fleet once they were able to get through the gap.

D-Day was finally fixed for May 5th, and the two convoys rendezvoused some thirty miles to the West of the Northern tip of Madagascar during the afternoon of the day previous, and the ships were then sorted out for the final approach to the attacking zone.

The cruiser *Devonshire* was to lead the four infantry landing ships *Keren*, *Karanja*, *Royal Ulsterman* and *Winchester Castle* in a single column preceded by the four small fleet minesweepers and the four minesweeping corvettes who were stationed sufficiently far ahead of the *Devonshire* to ensure that any mines swept by the sweepers would be carried away by the cross tide.

[For the list of ships comprising the invasion fleet, see Appendix A]

Unfortunately, due to some error in the navigation or the planning, the minesweepers passed over a shoal patch on the way towards Ambararata Bay which resulted in the carrying away of all the sweep wires. As soon as this happened, the second set of sweep wires were put out, but these were also carried away, and the result was that the invasion fleet steamed on without any minesweeping carrying on ahead of them, except for the presence of the fairly deep-draught corvettes, and in this fashion we entered Ambararata Bay between the islands and came to anchor in our prescribed positions, all this taking place in an eerie silence and complete darkness.

The first strike of commandos got away and actually surprised the French defenders still in their bunks, because they were of the firm opinion that it was impossible for any invading forces to enter the Bay at night due to the complexity of shoals and rocks and the absence of any navigational marks.

It was certainly a somewhat eerie feeling coming to anchor inside a harbour which one was planning to capture in a few hours' time and then calmly dropping anchor and turning in to await events. All was silent until shortly after dawn when a certain amount of supporting artillery fire from the destroyers took place and one could hear in the distance the rattle of machine gun fire of the army units, who were beginning to work their way through the countryside towards Diego Suarez. By this time all the vessels of the invading fleet, with the exception of the battleship *Ramillies* and the two aircraft carriers accompanied by some escorting destroyers, were all under way or at anchor inside Ambararata Bay. *Devonshire* and the destroyers were providing supporting artillery fire for the army ashore, and overhead a number of aeroplanes from the two carriers could be seen from time to time, while between the landing ships and the shore a constant succession of landing craft were dashing to and fro ferrying the troops and equipment to the beaches.

It was somewhat unnerving to remain at anchor doing nothing and feeling somewhat like a fifth wheel on a motor car, with the somewhat guilty feeling that one should have been doing something when everybody else was so busy. However, this matter was settled during the forenoon, when we were ordered — as half leader of the flotilla — to take two other sweepers under our command and sweep a particular section of the Bay where further mines were suspected, and which it was necessary to clear in order that the tank landing ship *Bachaquero* could land her tanks. *Bachaquero*, a vessel of some ten thousand tons, was one of the first tank landing ships, being a conversion of the special shallow-draught oil tankers that had been originally built to operate in Lake Maracaibo in South America. She carried the entire tank force of the invasion (about twenty-four tanks), and it was obviously necessary to get these ashore as soon as possible.

Corvettes were not ideal for minesweeping, but their particular shortcomings had been accepted in view of the "last ditch" type of work in the possible invasion of Great Britain for which they had been equipped. Ships designed as minesweepers are specially built with a shallow draught — perhaps eight or ten feet. Paddle steamers built between the wars for seaside trips on the South coast were also much used, since they had a draught of only six feet. Corvettes, on the other hand, drew seventeen feet aft and some fifteen feet forward, which made them somewhat susceptible to a mine strike.

It should also be understood that mines have a positive buoyancy, and are moored to the sea bottom with sinkers and a fixed length of wire according to the depth of water, and a corollary of this is that a mine's distance below the surface varies with the tide, thus the lower the tide the nearer the surface, with the worst situation being low water during a spring tide. Naturally, by Sod's Law, spring tides were running on that May 5th and low water corresponded almost exactly to the time we should start operations.

We commenced sweeping in the designated area in the usual echelon formation, and it was not long before we struck gold, the first mine breaking surface like a breaching dolphin once its mooring wire had been cut and landing back in the water to float in a sinister fashion with its horns clearly visible. Since there was no anti-submarine work to be done, I had been given a temporary job of being in charge of the four-inch gun's crew on the fore deck and, as an additional task, we were armed with rifles and armour-piercing

68

bullets to sink, by rifle fire, any mines that were visible, as and when this was possible.

Sinking mines by rifle fire is more difficult than it sounds, since there is only about one third of the spherical shape of the mine above water, so that unless a hit is obtained dead central on the waterline, the bullet will glance off (that is, of course, presupposing that you hit the mine at all). In our case our first mine was soon joined by a dozen more, and then by a further dozen which were swept by us and some by other ships in the flotilla.

Sweeping up a minefield is rather like mowing the lawn — one has to cut a swathe through the centre where you think the minefield is, and then swing the flotilla round to cut a further swathe parallel to and adjoining the first one, and carry on doing this outward from the supposed centre of the minefield until one feels that the whole area has been adequately swept. The only difficulty is that the water does not carry the marks in the same way as mown grass, and this makes for some careful navigation to ensure that the whole area is properly swept.

Each minesweeper has a sweep wire out on one side (in our case it was the starboard side), and each ship steams along in the swept water of the ship ahead in theoretical safety, while the leading ship endeavours to navigate so correctly that she is steaming down part of the previously swept water. The exception to this is at the first pass, when the leading ship is at risk, and this is always known as "Danger Lap". By good fortune we made our danger lap in water that was free of mines and so passed through in safety, and it was only on the second or third pass that we began to sweep mines which finally turned out to be somewhat thick on the ground.

All might have then gone well had here not been a slight gap in the training of the landing craft crews who were all undertaking their first real invasion, albeit after many months of practice. Sadly all their practices in Scotland had been done without the realistic presence of minesweepers, and no-one had thought to inform the crews of the landing craft of the sort of signals that minesweepers carry or of the effect created when mines are being swept. It was thus in entire ignorance that some of the landing craft were passing between ships of the minesweeping flotilla and directly over the sweep wires which were cutting the mines. Some of them must have been extremely frightened when a mine broke surface, bounced out of the water and splashed back only a few yards from them as they

they steamed along, but that at least was their problem and not ours.

Our problem was, when a landing craft full of soldiers motored across our bows extremely close, our Captain was faced with a difficult choice of three alternatives. Firstly, he could stop engines and go astern when the sweep wire would have become wound round our propeller and we would be overtaken by the other two mine-sweepers and thrown into considerable confusion. Secondly, he could alter course to avoid the landing craft and take the ship into dangerous unswept water. And thirdly, he could have taken no action at all, which would have resulted in our bow cleaving through the landing craft hull and inevitably wounding, or killing, a considerable number of soldiers. He took the second alternative, and thus it was that *Auricula* swept her seventeenth mine with her own keel.

*   *   *   *

There was no recollection of a bang, just a peculiar feeling of flying through the air, but certainly it was very obvious what had happened. I remember being particularly worried as to whether there was going to be any ship left when I finally came down again, and certainly my opinion was that if there was a ship underneath me, it was not going to be there for very long, so with this in mind my whole intention was to sprint to the stern, where the liferafts and other life-saving equipment were, as soon as my feet touched the deck. Unfortunately I had forgotten the second bump, and so as soon as my feet touched the deck, I was off up again for a second aerial trip. The impression was that one went up fifty or sixty feet, but I suppose in fact it was only something like ten feet, but it seemed to take an age before one landed back on the deck. In the air for the second time one's worries were considerably increased, since while there seemed to be a fair chance that their might be some ship down there when one landed the first time, the chances of there being any ship there the second time appeared remarkably remote. However, the only thing to do seemed to be to prepare for an Olympic sprint and hope for the best, but all plans were set to naught when I landed flat on my back on the deck and had every drop of breath knocked out of my body. I lay on the deck like a stranded whale gasping for breath and unable to move for what seemed something like hours before eventually being able to get to my feet and work my way aft in the ship. Naturally one assumed that the ship had only a minute or two to remain afloat, and on arriving at the stern I busied myself trying to release some of the life-saving rafts and generally prepare to abandon ship.

Unfortunately, since the mine had exploded almost directly beneath where I was sitting on the deck and thus its effect was fairly obvious to me, apparently the effect on those in the stern of the ship was entirely non-existent, and they had no idea at all that anything was amiss until the mast fell overboard, and a glance forward showed that the deck was no longer presenting the right appearance, since the ship had broken her back and the deck was somewhat bent downwards forward of the break.

It is a peculiar phenomenon that there is practically no difference in the sound or feel between an explosion at the other end of your own ship, a near miss, and a depth charge exploding a few hundred yards from your ship, but there is, of course, a considerable difference between that and the occasion when it explodes at your own end of the ship.

It soon became apparent that the ship was not going to sink immediately, and we set about lowering the boats with the wounded on board, including the Captain, who had been knocked unconscious by a piece of ironmongery falling on his head.

Seeing Able Seaman Macpherson, a dour Glaswegian, brandishing a large boat-hook with a villainous sharp spike at the end, I looked over the side with some apprehension to see what or who he was endeavouring to recover, and was in time to see him retrieve a large, comfortable, shady straw hat, which I had been wearing at the time of the explosion. As he swung it on deck, I retrieved it and placed it on my head, saying,

"Thank you very much, Macpherson, just what I was missing," to which he replied,

"My God, sir, I thought you was underneath it," and I thanked God that I was not. I really do not think he had any murderous intent in mind, just a somewhat naïve inability to understand what damage he could have done to my skull with the boat-hook.

Once the injured had been got away, we set about doing what was possible to determine the extent of the damage and figure out what were the next steps. The navigator checked that the light wind and rising tide were carrying us away from the dangerous water, and once we were assured that we were out of the mine area, I went onto the forecastle and dropped the starboard anchor to prevent our hulk becoming a danger to other vessels, and the next job was to go down below as Damage Control Officer to observe the extent of the damage.

It soon became apparent that the foreward boiler room bulkhead was intact and the ship was dry from there aft, and that the mine had struck below the bulkhead dividing the officers' accommodation under the bridge and the after lower sleeping mess deck. Stationing a Leading Seaman outside the watertight door (to help me open it in a hurry if necessary), I entered the mess deck and closed the watertight door behind me, and then went forward to see if the forward lower mess deck had been flooded. On opening the valve in the hatch there was no air pressure and no water, so I gently eased off all the clips and, still finding no water coming in, finally opened the hatch and went down to inspect the forward side of the bulkhead in this compartment.

Even now, thinking about it makes the hair rise on the back of my neck, for if the bulkhead had burst my chances of getting out would have been very small, and looking back on it, I realise that my nerves were not all that they should have been after the double bounce up on deck. However, the bulkhead seemed in good condition and on examination even the compartment below was dry, but it was obvious that the next two compartments aft were entirely flooded. Coming back up into the mess deck, I closed the hatch to the lower mess deck and replaced all the clips tightly, and then with no small relief made my way aft to the main mess deck door and started knocking off the clips, in which I was soon assisted by the Leading Seaman outside. It was certainly a very wonderful feeling to emerge once more into the fresh air and close the watertight door behind me before finding the First Lieutenant and reporting to him that, in my opinion, the vessel would not sink any lower in the water and that it might be possible to beach her.

Freesia — with Commander Crick, the minesweeping flotilla commander, on board — approached shortly afterwards, and we were able to give him a complete report on the situation, and he ordered us to make all preparations for being taken in tow. There was not a lot more that could be done, and fortunately with the galley right aft of the ship, the cook was able to prepare a scratch meal of corned beef sandwiches which appeased the hunger which somehow made itself felt at this time.

We had a grandstand view of the main attack which continued throughout the afternoon, and we were able to observe that our minesweeping efforts had been successful and that *Bachaquero* had duly put her bows on the beach and landed a couple of dozen Valentine tanks to give substantial support to the infantry who were already ashore. I spent some time smashing up the ASDIC set in case the ship should suddenly sink, and managed to put aside a stopwatch and a broken pair of binoculars (both of which I have to this day) as my own personal souvenirs of the ship which I did not think would be missed.

It transpired that everyone was too busy with the attack to bother any more about *Auricula*, and finally around five o'clock we were given orders to abandon the ship for the night, and boats were sent to take us to the landing ship *Keren*. We were a pretty bedraggled scarecrow-like bunch that boarded *Keren* just before dusk, and I was greatly cheered and considerably surprised to be met at the head of the gangway by Johnnie Jukes, a Paymaster Lieutenant RNR who had previously served in *Worcestershire* and who, knowing that I had been on *Auricula*, had taken the trouble to come and welcome me on board.

We were all issued with a couple of shirts and a couple of pairs of shorts and some socks and shoes, and then Johnnie took me away to find me a cabin and a bathroom, for which there was a fairly urgent need. I remember well that in those days passenger ships did not carry fresh water sufficient for all washing purposes, and it was customary to have a bath in hot salt water and fill an enamel washing tub with fresh water from a nearby tap, and this was put on a board which stretched across the bath in which one did the actual washing with soap before sluicing off in the salt water. I filled the bath with salt water and filled the tub with fresh water, and then to my astonishment found that I was unable to lift the tub off the floor onto the board across the bath. Presumably this was some effect of shock, but I did not really understand it; I only remember being dreadfully embarrassed when I had to find the steward and ask him to lift the tub off the floor on to the board, and the look he gave me signified that he was thinking,

"Cor blimey, some officers can't even lift their 'andkerchief to their nose," so eventually I mumbled something about having just

73

been blown up, at which he became very sympathetic and in fact offered to come back a few minutes later and pour the tub of fresh water over me to wash off the salt, which was the normal drill.

Bathed and dressed in clean clothes I felt considerably better, although still somewhat dazed, but Johnnie came down to find me and take me to the wardroom for a few glasses of gin before a very civilised dinner in this ex-passenger ship's dining room. After dinner the other two uninjured officers and myself went down to visit our crew in the Petty Officers' mess and on the mess deck to make sure they were all properly looked after, and then after that, bed suddenly seemed an extraordinarily good idea.

It seemed only minutes later that I was being woken, and it turned out to be seven o'clock in the morning and I was required to go back to the ship for attempts to tow her to a nearby beach. We crossed Ambararata Bay in a motor boat and went aboard to stand by to receive the towing warp and to slip the anchor cable, which had been made all ready the day before. The towing wire was brought aboard and I took the precaution of fixing this to one of the anchor slips, so that it could be released quickly in the event of the bulkhead failing, a precaution which seemed prudent at the time.

The starboard anchor cable, which had been unshackled the previous day, was duly slipped and the tow commenced, but it could have been only a few minutes later when *Auricula* started to move forward at two or three knots that there was an unpleasant bang from below, and the sound of water rushing into the boiler room. The ship, which had already sunk lower in the water overnight, now sank down two or three feet until the point of her bow was under water. I ordered the towing wire to be slipped and waved to the motor boat to come alongside, which he managed to do just in time to enable us to step off the after part of the forecastle of *Auricula* before the water reached our shins, enabling me to say for many years when asked about the sinking,

"I had a pretty easy time of it, I managed to step off the ship without even getting my feet wet."

The motor boat withdrew a short distance, and at my request stopped her engine, and we lay there in the smooth water of Ambararata Bay in the early morning sunshine and watched *Auricula* sink.

No seaman can watch his ship sink without a feeling of sadness, and certainly as the only officer to sail in her from commissioning to

74

sinking, I could not restrain the odd tear as she sank below the waters of the Bay, her White Ensign at the ensign staff on the stern being almost the last thing to be seen above the surface.

* * * *

Some years later, just after the war's end, when being entertained to dinner in France at a sumptuous château, my hostess gushingly remarked,

"I expect you had a very exciting time during the war, and were sunk lots of times," to which I replied,

"Oh no, only once — by the French."

Chapter Three

A FTER A FEW DAYS on *HMS Keren* the worst of the invasion of Madagascar was over, and I was appointed to the destroyer *Duncan* and carried to her in a motor boat across Ambararata Bay clutching all my worldly possessions that I was not actually wearing, which consisted of one white uniform shirt, one pair of white uniform shorts, a towel, a toothbrush and the only two items I had saved from *Auricula* which were, in fact, a stopwatch and a pair of broken binoculars. Everything else I possessed out of England had gone down in *Auricula* with the exception of the clothes I was wearing, which had had to be destroyed. No-one had been able to provide me with a Naval cap, so I was forced to shield my head from the sun with my straw hat which had been so valiantly saved for me by AB Macpherson.

I arrived aboard *Duncan* as she was weighing anchor, and went up to the bridge to report my arrival to the Captain. Although he knew where I had come from, he was not very sympathetic, merely looking over his shoulder and saying in a very superior voice,

"Haven't you gor a cap, Snottie?" to which I could only reply with the factual remark,

"No, sir."

This was a ship which had, by remarkable chance, seen practically no action during the war, and the same went for all her officers, with the result that there was a very inadequate *esprit de corps* on board.

The next few weeks which I spent on board until I was transferred to another destroyer were probably the least happy of all those I spent between 1939 and 1946. The only remarkable incident which I have had the pleasure of boasting of ever since was that the following morning we passed through the very narrow entrance to the large harbour at Diego Suarez, and there was some doubt as to whether the Marines or the Army had actually managed to capture the forts on

HMS Griffin

either side of the entrance. According to our intelligence, these forts were armed with twenty-four inch bore stone-shot firing, muzzle-loading cannons, which had been constructed in the middle of the nineteenth century. Since the entrance was not more than half a mile across, nobody had ever thought it necessary to replace these weapons with something more modern, and it did make the hackles rise a bit at the thought of a destroyer which was built only of quarter-inch steel being hit by a twenty-four inch sphere of stone propelled by some ancient, but still efficacious, charge of gunpowder.

However, all was well and no shots were fired, and after a few days lying at anchor in some confusion after the invasion, we sailed from there up to the Eastern Fleet's base at Mombasa, where I was transferred to the destroyer *Griffin*, which was a very different cup of tea indeed.

Griffin had been in the thick of things from the beginning of the war. She had been at Dunkirk, she had been in Norway (where she had captured a German Naval trawler with a boarding party), and then since the Autumn of 1940 she had been in the Mediterranean, extremely actively engaged, taking part in the battle of Matapan, being one of the ships that ran stores up to Tobruk, and had also been in Greece and in various other little sideshows like fighting the Vichy French in Syria.

The day after I arrived on board, we were inspected by Admiral Somerville, the Commander in Chief of the Eastern Fleet, and as the nine officers lined up on the quarter deck to be introduced to him, I was the only one without a beard, which caused him to make the inevitable remark about a piratical bunch. He gave a cheerful; talk to the ship's company, pointing out that we were becoming part of a fleet assembled to deal with the "little yellow bastards". Then, in an aside, he remarked that it seemed to be generally conceded that, while the Italians were referred to as "poor bloody wops", the japanese were always referred to as the "little yellow bastards".

A short while after he had left the ship, his Flag Lieutenant came scurrying back and asked to speak to the midshipman. To my surprise he gave me Admiral Somerville's apologies, and explained that the Admiral was not aware there was a midshipman serving in *Griffin*, but now that he had discovered this was so, he would be pleased if I would accept his invitation to a party given at his house ashore that night. Such a Royal Command was not to be refused, and I naturally proffered my thanks and began to wonder what I should possibly wear, since my wardrobe was still limited to two shirts and two pairs of shorts, but I need not have worried, for *Griffin*'s wardroom rallied round immediately, and I went to the party that night dressed in full mess kit, wearing my own handkerchief and some loaned piece of clothing from every other officer on board.

It was a most extraordinary party, since the menfolk consisted of either Admirals or midshipmen (there seemed a plentiful supply of both), and the ladies of the party consisted of all the presentable young women aged between eighteen and twenty-five that could be gathered from a radius of twenty-five miles. There is a very extra-ordinary uncle/nephew, or maybe even managing director/office boy, relationship between Admirals and midshipmen which does not seem to exist in the other services, presumably because they do not have an equivalent rank to midshipman outside their training college. My clearest recollection is being seated in the front of the Admiral's Rolls-Royce beside his coxwain, who was driving, with a girl squeezed in beside me as we returned to get our boats off to our ships some time around midnight. In the back of the majestic machine were a number of midshipmen and some of the girls, and at one stage there was a strangled cry from one of the girls with a very fruity accent,

"No, no, no — not in C-in-C's car!"

* * * *

One of my multifarious duties was Searchlight Control Officer, an unenviable task rather akin to that of a picador in a bullfighter's team. It did not seem to matter what I and my team did, somehow it always came out wrong.

The searchlight — a massive device with a lens and reflector some three feet in diameter — was situated fairly far aft in the ship, and manned by a team headed by a Petty Officer Torpedoman. In those days, Torpedomen (for some obscure reason) looked after all the electrics in the Navy, and searchlight was their pride and joy. It used phenomenal quantities of electricity, and produced a brilliant light by creating an arc between two carbon rods similar to the more common practice today of arc-welding. The carbon rods became burnt away when the light was on and had to be fed together by small electric motors. Sometimes these were too slow for the rate of burning and sometimes too fast — in either case, the light went out.

Just occasionally they could be fed at the correct rate, and then the light would stay on for a few minutes, sending out a powerful rod of brightness which would illuminate another ship several miles away on the blackest night.

There were several other complications which need to be explained. The first is the shutter. The searchlight had a retractable shutter operating like the stop control in a modern camera, which enabled one to get the arc burning without showing any light to the enemy or illuminating one's own ship. The order for this to be done was:

"Burn the light behind the shutter."

When (or if) the Petty Officer Torpedoman succeeded in striking the arc and getting the light burning — quite an art in itself — he would report,

"Light burning behind the shutter." Thereafter, if the pencil beam was required the order would be:

"Open shutter," and when no longer needed,

"Close shutter."

So much for the searchlight itself. Now we come to the business of ensuring that it is pointing in the right direction. To achieve this, the searchlight mounting was connected to the bridge at least one hundred feet away by a complex and Heath Robinson arrangement of rods, bevel gears and universal joints. The bridge end of this clamjamfry was connected to what looked like a gun mounting without a gun but with a sight. Two seamen manned this gadget, one turning the handle that swivelled the light around, and the other endeavouring to keep the light pointing horizontal as the ship rolled or heeled. There was also a voicepipe (nothing so modern as a telephone) connecting this position with the searchlight itself, and nearby stood the man of the moment — the Searchlight Control Officer — within earshot of the Captain, who was further forward on the bridge.

The theory about the whole thing was that if one was involved in a night action with enemy surface ships, the searchlight could be pointed at the enemy ship and the arc light struck and then, lo and behold, when the Captain gave the order, the enemy would be unmasked and bathed in glorious light (much to his surprise), so that the Gunnery Jacks and the Torpedomen who were actually manning torpedoes (which they did in their spare time when not looking after electricity) could fire off their weapons and destroy the enemy.

Fortunately — at least while I was on board — *Griffin* never became involved with the enemy at night, but we did take part in one or two exercises which highlighted one or two drawbacks in the theories of the business.

One such exercise took place on an extremely dark night in the Indian Ocean with some of our fleet deployed to play the part of "the enemy". During this exercise, the successful use of the searchlight by any destroyer was to be interpreted as a successful torpedo attack and any vessel illuminated was to be considered sunk.

After ploughing around the ocean at high speed for a couple of hours, the bridge sighted an "enemy" ship through their high-powered binoculars and indicated that it was forty-five degrees on the starboard bow. The two seamen operating the searchlight control swung their mechanism on to the bearing and the Searchlight Control Officer stared myopically in the same direction. Unfortunately these three appeared to be the only people on the bridge not supplied with binoculars or other aids to night vision, and

80

having dutifully reported "Searchlight on" to signify that we had put the device on the right bearing, we continued to stare out and see nothing but blackness.

Despite our failure to see anything, the order came:

"Burn the light behind the shutter," and this was duly passed down the voicepipe.

"Burn the light behind the shutter." From afar eventually came the report,

"Light burning behind the shutter," and this was duly reported to the Captain,

"Light burning behind the shutter, sir." At about this time, our two searchlight controllers felt that they could discern a dark shape in the night and duly pointing their device at it shouted,

"Searchlight target, sir."

"Very good," replied the Captain. There followed a series of helm orders and others to the Gunnery Jacks and the Torpedo Tubes, and then came the moment of truth,

"Open shutter."

"Open shutter, sir," I replied with great pride, and bending to the voicepipe, bellowed down it,

"Open shutter."

Sadly, instead of a great illumination, nothing happened at all. After about five seconds, the Captain's testy voice came,

"Searchlight Control Officer, what is the delay?"

I bellowed frantically down the voicepipe,

"What is the delay?" and was rewarded with a weary voice saying,

"Light's gone out, sir." This news I passed efficiently to the Captain, but he did not seem pleased and commented somewhat sharply on my perspicacity, general efficiency and even made some rather unkindly comments on midshipmen in general.

No reply was really needed.

A few minutes later another "enemy" was sighted, and the same drill carried out, except perhaps that in this case *Griffin* made even more alterations of course than before between the proud report "Searchlight target" and the fatal order "Open shutter".

This time the Petty Officer Torpedoman had done a fine job with his carbon rods, and immediately I shouted "Open shutter" down the voicepipe, a blinding beam of light shone out into the darkness and illuminated a large vessel nearby.

To my horror, even I recognised the ship instantaneously as the Flagship of the Eastern Fleet, but before I could say or do anything, angry cries of,

"Put that bloody light out" came from all over the bridge.

With considerable sang-froid, I managed to translate the varied instructions before calling down the voicepipe "Close the shutter", and once more all was darkness.

"Snottie, you miserable worm, you have failed to sink the enemy and now you have sunk our Flagship. Whose side are you on?"

*   *   *   *

Following the Allied invasion of Vichy French Madagascar, it was decided to "mop up" the similarly-held Comoro Island group to the North West and establish there a small anti-submarine force to prey on Japanese submarines which were becoming active in the bottleneck of the Madagascar Channel between that island and the coast of Africa.

The base was to be established in Mayotta, an island encircled by a coral reef with a fine natural harbour and a miniature airfield. The force comprised two destroyers (one of which was *Griffin*), several Catalina flying boats, a flying boat tender and a Merchant Navy tanker, loaded with aviation fuel for the flying boats and fuel oil for the destroyers.

Although somewhat primitive in facilities, it was an idyllic island, highly suitable for use as a film location for a re-make of *Treasure Island*, *The Blue Lagoon* or any similar "wind-soughing-through-the-palm-trees" epic.

We landed a small force of King's African Rifles shortly before dawn and lay off ready to give artillery support if necessary, finally entering the harbour through the gaps in the coral reefs with full daylight to assist us, after radio messages had been received to say that the pongos had overcome what resistance there might have been. It had not been much.

During the day we made a fruitless sweep to the South and returned to our anchorage before dusk. Two of the Army officers who had been our passengers just previously came aboard for some liquid sustenance at sundown, and invited us ashore to dine in their "mess", which had been set up in the one and only hotel which the small island boasted.

We judiciously raided the destroyer's stores for raw materials, in

HMS Duncan

the fervent belief that even in this far-flung outpost of the French Empire, the culinary expertise in the kitchen of the only hotel was certain to be considerably superior to that of a Naval Leading Cook, and in this we were by no means disappointed.

Despite the fact that they had been in residence for only about twelve hours, it was remarkable with what success the Army had changed the character of this seedy tropical French hotel into a distinctive British Regimental Mess of apparently long standing.

HMS Griffin's officers and the two ex-passengers arrived in the mess only just in time to pour a glass of sherry on top of the other liquids already consumed aboard before dinner was formally announced, and we all trooped into the dining room at the Adjutant's nod of command.

The French chef did wonders with the Naval rations, neatly interspersed between various local delicacies hastily garnered for the liberators (or invaders, depending upon one's point of view), and there was certainly no shortage of something with which to wash down the banquet.

With traditional ceremony the Loyal Toast was drunk, smoking commenced and the Colonel concluded a short amusing speech of welcome to the guests by proposing a toast to the Royal Navy " upon whom we frequently depend and on whom we have learnt to rely ". *Griffin*'s First Lieutenant replied with equal wit, and in due course we raised our glasses to the Army " who had this day carried out an invasion of hostile territory which, we all hoped, would be followed by many more in the near future".

At this, the Colonel rose again to acknowledge these stirring thoughts and called upon Second Lieutenant Ponsonby to give his account of the part he had played in the dawn attack. He recounted in detail.

" Well, actually we were met on the beach by this Free French froggie fellow with all sorts of secret passwords and all that nonsense, and then he led us up to the Governor's Residency so I could capture the jolly old Governor.

" When we got there about oh five hundred hours, I had my sergeant surround the house and all that, and then I knocked on the front door, which was opened by a black man in a nightshirt.

" ' Are you the Governor? ' I asked in my best French.

" ' Mais non, monsieur, I am ze butler. 'Eez Excellency is not at home. Ee is visiting a friend, monsieur, the other side of town — I show you, monsieur.'

" Well, I suspected a trap, so I left a corporal and four nuggets guarding the Residency, and had the sergeant and the others follow me, while I followed the froggie agent, who followed the butler, and a comical sight we must have looked, trudging through the town in the dark.

" Eventually we arrived at another house in a charming garden, and the butler said, ' This eez 'ouse, monsieur', and so I had the sergeant surround it and I knocked on the door for the second time.

" The door did not open, but after some minutes a night-capped head appeared at a first floor window, demanding in angry French to know what we were about.

" ' We are the British. We have come to capture the island. Are you the Governor? ' Actually my sixth form French was only just about up to that, and fortunately the Governor's English was better than my French.

" ' Mon Dieu, mon Dieu, why did you not come at a raisonable time of day? We 'ave been expecting you for tree months. I am in bed wiz ze wife of ze Chief of Police. I will see you in ze morning'.

" With that, the head disappeared and the window slammed shut.

" It was deuced embarrassing actually. I mean, what could a fellow do? We had to wait in that damned garden for four hours before he condescended to let himself be captured.

" Maybe this is the ' done thing' in a French colony, but — dash it all — it's hardly the sort of behaviour one expects from an Englishman abroad. ''

* * * *

During our passage between the coral reefs I had aired my knowledge of the French language while interpreting the French charts to such an extent that, when the Army ashore called for the assistance of a demolition party, I was sent along as interpreter. The fact that the patois spoken by the local natives was entirely incomprehensible to me was of no import.

The demolition party landed the following morning consisted of the Warrant Gunner (T) (the " T " standing for Torpedoman), plus myself and two seamen torpedomen with several large boxes containing standard Royal Naval demolition charges with associated fuses, detonators, primers and other necessaries.

Guns was one of the old school who had served at least twenty years (not including time as a seaman boy) and he could — and did — recite long passages from various gunnery and torpedo manuals. In fact, in retrospect, his conversation seemed to consist of little else.

He was also full of convenient proverb-like sayings with which he would intersperse his instructional quotations, and his message for this day was,

" Hexplosives his not dangerous huntil you forget that they his. ''

Guns had no doubt received and probably delivered numerous instructional lectures on the use of demolition charges, but I strongly suspected he had never actually seen or heard one explode — or should I say, " hexplode".

On arrival at the little jetty, we were met by one of the officers from the King's African Rifles, who had formed the invasion party, with a cheery,

" Hallo, there. I suppose you are the safebreaker wallahs. ''

" We are the demolition party requested by the OC troops," I retorted, " but we don't know anything about safebreaking. ''

" Oh, jolly good show. Looks like you will have some fun finding

85

out. Your objective is to blow the safe in the old froggie Governor's Residence. Collar all the secret codes and all that, what? Earn yourself an OBE and the thanks of Parliament, et cetera, et cetera. Better pile your stuff on this one horsepower velocipede here. Sorry, chaps, but it's the best we've got, there being no jolly old petroleum on the island."

Behind him stood a rather tired four-wheeled horse and cart, with the horse looking the older of the two.

"All right, lads, smartly now, git those boxes hup into the transport provided and for Gawd's sake take care of they detonators or we'll all have a non-stop trip to 'eaven or, more likely in your case, 'ell."

"Nobby" Clark and "Snowy" White, aided by the motor boat's crew, soon had the boxes loaded, and then we all climbed aboard for the short ride to the Residency. As it hove in sight, our guide explained,

"At the back of the study there's a mighty big safe which is locked tight, and none of the frogs will provide the combination, so the Colonel said 'Let's get the Navy to blow it open, they're good at that sort of thing'. Follow me, I'll show you."

While Nobby Clark and Snowy White unloaded the boxes from the cart, the subaltern led us into the house through the well-furnished rooms to a comfortable study and opened an ordinary door to reveal what was obviously a safe door some six feet high and three feet wide.

Guns surveyed it with a professional eye and then, desperately trying to give the impression that he blew open safes of this sort twice a week, muttered,

"Ah, yerse. Well, I reckon a couple of bits of our tin opening compound 'ere, and we'll soon have this 'un open."

He rapped out orders in quick succession. The Army was to clear the Residency and the grounds for at least a five-hundred yard radius and post sentries to prevent the unwary entering the danger area. The cart was unloaded at a safe distance and a native working party set to dig a trench stowage for the explosives — a task which taxed my limited French to the utmost — and another native party was set to filling sacks with earth.

Guns, meanwhile, paced around the Governor's study sucking his teeth and saying,

"Ah, well, yerse. Let me see," and occasionally making calculations in a small notebook with a short stub of pencil which he licked from time to time in the hope perhaps of in this way making his writing legible.

Nobby, Snowy and I stood around watching the man of the moment, fearful of interrupting his train of thought. Eventually he ordered,

"All right, then, listen 'ere." We listened.

"Away you go to the Magazine" — a rather high sounding name for the hastily dug trench — "You, Nobby and Snowy, bring back each of you one demolition charge one and a quarter pound. Right? You, Mid, can bring back nine and a 'alf feet of black fuse hand the higniting pistol, complete with one cartridge. For safety's sake, Hi will deal with the detonators."

We duly collected the items and reassembled in the study, and were sent off from time to time to collect pieces of timber and usher in natives with filled sandbags.

Slowly and methodically, as if building one of the great Pyramids, Guns positioned the explosive charges and held them in place with filled sandbags, until the safe looked more like a machine gun emplacement or an atomic shelter.

After several hours' work, Guns pronounced himself reasonably satisfied and went to fetch the detonator, a small copper tube containing (if I remember rightly) a nasty, unstable explosive called fulminate of mercury, which was easily exploded by a fuse or by dropping. With exaggerated care, Guns inserted the detonator into one of the charges and clamped one end of the fuse into the end of it, explaining every detail.

"We now carefully inserts the detonator and crimps one end of the fuse like so." (After all, you could hardly have put both ends of the fuse in the charge).

"The hother hend of the fuse we secures firmly hin the muzzle hof the higniting pistol hand then we loads the pistol. All right, now what do we do next?" Fire the pistol, thinks I, but craftily I said nothing.

"Fire the pistol, sir?" says Nobby.

"Hah, yes, that's wot you would do, but not me. Wot I does is to look at me watch hand take the time. Hand wot do I do that for, Nobby?"

"To see what time it is, sir?"

"Hand I surpose you fink the hobject of that is to see how long it is ter go till yer gets yer tot? Well it ain't. Hits so you can calculate hat wot time the hexplosion will hoccur. If you recalls the instructions wot I gave you afore we came ashore, this 'ere fuse burns at the rate of ten inches per minute, and we, 'aving nine hand a 'alf feet, 'ave now got hexactly heleven minutes to get clear hof the danger area afore it all goes orf. Course hactually we 'ave four inches hextra of fuse 'ere wot gives us a small margin for error hin the shape of some twenty-four seconds hextra.

"Right now, Nobby, you and Snowy set off for the hobservation trench and make sure that working party of wogs gets clear, and walk now, don't run. Mid, you go 'oist the Red Flag hup the Governor's flagstaff and rejoin me 'ere and we'll detonate the charge."

On my return to the study Guns looked me in the eye and said, "All right then, take the time," and as I did so, he held out the igniting pistol at arm's length and with great drama pulled the trigger.

It was really rather a let-down after all the build-up, since instead of a loud report, the pistol gave off a small "phutt", and shortly afterwards the burning fuse fell away from the muzzle.

"Right now, Mid, we shall now take a walk. Slow and sedate now, cos we don't want to trip and we don't want no-one to think we is scared."

So we walked. We walked out of the Residency across the garden, through a gate and along an overgrown path for a full ten minutes until we came to a shallow trench in which we crouched with our heads below ground level.

"'Ow long ter go?" Guns asked me.

"About a minute — it's difficult to tell really. My watch hasn't got a second hand."

"Well, it's better 'an mine," said Guns gloomily, "mine's stopped."

We sat and listened. Eventually we heard a small bang and the tinkling of broken glass.

"Right then, we best go and collect them codes and stuff the pongos want," and we set off to trudge back to the Residency. The tropical sun beat down on us, and the sweat trickled down our backs and legs.

In the study not much had changed. I laid the Red Flag on the desk and noticed that all the windows were blown out and the walls were speckled with earth from the dissipated sandbags. The only thing that appeared to be entirely undamaged or unmuddied was the safe door, which gleamed smugly at us from its alcove.

Guns rattled the handle, but it showed no signs of opening.

"Hah, well, we 'ad better give it a little bit more of the tin opener," he said with confidence, only slightly tinged with disappointment.

The whole operation was repeated — rather more quickly this time as we all knew what to do — but the result was the same.

The third time I timidly suggested that we might double the amount of T.N.T. and use four charges instead of two. Guns looked at me suspiciously and said,

"Two bleeding hexplosions and now you're an expert at safe blowing, eh?"

"It was only an idea, Guns," I said.

Guns said nothing, but he surreptitiously increased the charge to four.

This time the noise, as heard from our observation post, was slightly louder and the damage done to the study slightly greater, but the door of the safe stood firm.

The charge was increased yet again, with proportional increases in noise and damage, but still that safe door remained firmly closed.

"Guns, I know you are the expert and all that, and that you have been doing this all your life, but I really think this safe is somewhat stronger than the ones you have practised on before. It is now late in the afternoon and will soon be dark, and we are both hungry and thirsty." (His eyes lit up at the thought of the pink gins that would soon be served in *Griffin*'s wardroom). "Furthermore, we don't want to tell the pongos that we can't open the bloody thing. So why don't we put all the charges we've got left against that bloody door and tamp it with a double dose of sandbags and then retreat to our trench and offer up a quick prayer to the God of Safe Blowers?"

Guns started muttering under his breath, ". . . contrary to para. 9, sub-section (iv) of the Demolition Manual, Chapter 4. . ." and made further muted references to the King's Regulations and Admiralty Instructions, and even to the Articles of War, but eventually the thought of having to admit defeat to the pongos stirred him into staking our all on a last effort.

Nobby and Snowy toiled back and forth with demolition charges, and the native working party — sensing that a great moment was coming — redoubled their activity and encouraged their numerous relations to assist. A veritable Hadrian's Wall of sandbags half-filled the somewhat ruined study and held the mass of explosive against the safe door.

The working parties were dispersed. I ran up the Red Flag for what I hoped would be the last time and returned to the study to nod to Guns who, even more dramatically, if that were possible, fired the ignition pistol, stuffed it in his belt like a pirate, and took my arm saying,

"Shall we take hanother walk, then?"

We wearily trudged the now familiar and tiresome path, which somehow seemed longer than ever and exceedingly pointless, since we always had ended up almost out of earshot rather than danger.

As we passed a larger overhanging rock which offered what seemed an ideal shelter from any blast, I dug my heels in and told Guns,

"You can keep going until you can't hear the bang if you like, but as for me, I am taking shelter here," and with that I sat down, back to the rock and the coming explosion.

"You are not following the regulations, Mid. It says quite clear that all personnel should retreat to a minimum distance of five 'undred yards and take cover."

"Yes, I dare say, Guns, but we went so far we nearly fell off the edge of the island."

"It's not right, it ain't."

Guns stood in front of me, shifting from one foot to the other.

"'Ow long till the detonation now then?"

Automatically I looked at my watch, and then realisation dawned,

"Oh Christ, I forgot to take the time of ignition." (He even had me talking like a manual).

Guns started swearing and continued for what seemed like several minutes, and when at last I was able to get a word in edgeways, I reminded him,

"Maybe, Guns, but may I remind you that our bumper pile of T.N.T. is due to go up quite soon, even if we don't know when exactly. May I suggest that you contravene your beloved Manual of Demolition in one of two ways. Either come into the cover of this rock, improper though that may be, or run like hell, even if the book does say walk, but for God's sake, don't just stand there swearing."

Continuing the swearing in a lower voice, Guns sat down beside me, occasionally adjusting his curses towards midshipmen in general, amateur demolition experts and me in particular.

The seconds ticked past slowly, and it seemed to be a quarter of an hour later that we both jumped at the sound of an ear-splitting explosion. Seconds later, pieces of wood and masonry started raining down through the trees around us as we cowered against our protecting rock — safe, but only just.

Eventually silence returned, and standing up I endeavoured to cheer Guns up with,

"Well, let's go and see what the safe looks like now."

We trudged back to the Residency garden, and it was some minutes before we realised what was wrong. The Red Flag was not there, neither was the flagstaff. As we got closer, it transpired that the Residency was not there, either.

In the centre of the garden was an area of devastation where the Residency had once stood, and in the middle of this, sticking up unbowed like a telephone kiosk, was the Governor's safe.

On closer inspection it was found to be not entirely undamaged. The lock was actually broken and the door was open by about half an inch. With the aid of a crowbar it was forced open, and I was inside quicker than a flash, already seeing in my mind's eye the imposing ceremony at Buckingham Palace — Guns and I in our best uniforms stepping forward to meet our monarch and receive his words of thanks and the deserved award.

But now, as I searched the shelves of the safe, they were as bare as Mother Hubbard's larder, and the vision faded from my mind. Then my fingers closed on an envelope, and gathering it up I opened it and emerged into the daylight to examine the contents.

To my surprise the contents consisted of a selection of photographs of a number of ladies — some white, some half-caste, some dark-skinned, but all totally nude.

It later transpired that they were the Governor's "friends", and I realised that sending these back to London would be unlikely to earn me an OBE. Instead it cost me a great deal in gin pacifying Guns over the next few days.

* * * *

My only other recollection of Mayotta Island was going ashore to the local distillery and bringing back a bottle of lemon grass oil. Lemon grass is the basis of many scents and was in ordinary times a

91

profitable local crop which gave the evening breezes a rather Hollywood type of smell. Because of the war, the local distillery had not been able to export any of their product and had it coming out of their gills, so they were quite pleased to give us quantities of it if we could provide the empty bottles. These were fortunately not in short supply in the wardroom. As I recall it, to make scent you mixed six drops of this lemon grass oil with a litre of medicinal alcohol, which was fine, but due to the absence of ambergris it did not keep, and soon went sour and produced a most disgusting stench which was not quite so popular with any girlfriends we could manage to find in those parts.

After a few more days in this tropical paradise we were ordered back to Mombasa, and from thence Northward up to Aden, through the Red Sea and then through the Suez Canal to Port Said and subsequently Alexandria. There was to be a temporary weakening of the Eastern Fleet and a temporary building up of the Alexandria force in order to run a convoy to Malta. In fact, Malta was very hard pressed at this time, and there had just been a failure to relieve it, so on this occasion the idea was evolved to send a convoy from Gibraltar and another from Alexandria simultaneously, in the hopes that at least one of them would get through. The general feeling was that the Italian Fleet would probably try to attack one or the other, but could not manage to attack both, while the German Airforce operating from Crete and from North Africa airfields was able to harry us all the way with fairly short flying time. This was in the period shortly before El Alamein, when the German forces had advanced within some fifty miles of Alexandria. These convoys were named HARPOON and VIGOROUS.

For this little sunshine cruise to Malta I was relieved of my duties as Searchlight Control Officer and given the high-sounding title of "Close Range Weapons Officer", and sent to take a course at the gunnery range outside Alexandria for some five days. The course enabled me to learn a little of the theory and practice of shooting at airborne targets — although not at real enemy aeroplanes, and brought me up to the position of knowing about one-twentieth as much as all the chaps who manned the various anti-aircraft weapons in *Griffin*. All the guns crews were very old hands, with experience picked up in Norway in 1940 and in the Mediterranean over the previous eighteen months, and they really needed no guidance from such a tyro as myself, but occasionally they did need a little restraint.

The official close-range anti-aircraft armament of the vessel consisted of four 20mm single-barrelled Oerlikons, which fired explosive shells and were controlled each by one man, together with two four-barrelled 0.5″ machine guns which were a peace-time invention and the bane of my existence. These guns each had to be operated by two men, one swivelling the gun from right to left and the other elevating it up and down, and the chances of getting these two men to work in unison was very small indeed, added to which the guns jammed seriously after each burst of fire unless somebody dashed round and took up the slack on each reel of ammunition.

What, however, was far more interesting, amusing and to some extent dangerous, was that in her various travels and exploits in evacuating Army personnel from Norway, Greece, Tobruk and other glorious retreats, she had acquired a number of unofficial .303 machine guns of various types. Failing the manpower to incorporate these in the ship's armament, they were distributed in a friendly fashion (or perhaps acquired in this way) amongst the different non-gunnery departments in the ship. Thus, the torpedomen had two ex-Army Bren guns mounted on top of the torpedo tubes, which they used when they were not busy torpedoing; the stewards kept a couple of Bren guns in the Officers' Pantry, which they used when they were not serving meals; the stokers had a couple more guns hidden away somewhere, which they brought out from their murky recesses whenever they felt so inclined; the signalmen and wireless operators formed a joint union to man some more machine guns on the bridge wings; and even the doctor and the sick berth attendant kept a machine gun in the Sick Bay, which they utilised when they were not engaged in life-saving and general repair of flesh and limb. As I recall it, we had a total of fifteen machine guns that were entirely unofficially carried on board and utilised to some effect. Actually, by this stage of the war the .303 machine gun was not of much value in actually bringing down aeroplanes, but I think its morale effect amongst those members of the crew who did not normally fire guns was something tremendous, and it certainly helped to maintain the superb *esprit de corps* which existed.

Contrary to the standard opinions of all the chair wallahs and non-seagoing experts at this sort of thing, our enthusiastic volunteers never managed to shoot away any part of our own ship, despite the fact that there was no mechanical device to prevent them doing so. The after two Oerlikons did, in fact, have devices to prevent them shooting away the mast, bridge and funnels, and also limited each gun to firing on its own side of the ship but, somewhat to my surprise, some way had been found of circumventing this equipment, and on certain occasions both of the after guns would fire towards one side of the ship, which was a little upsetting to me, since my action station was to stand in between the two guns and endeavour to direct them.

Our convoy never in fact reached Malta, although fortunately for the inhabitants of that island, the convoy coming from Gibraltar did manage to do so. Our convoy, consisting of some eleven Merchant ships escorted by six cruisers, twenty destroyers and a dozen other vessels, ran perilously low of ammunition before getting three-quarters of the way towards Malta, and after suffering numerous air attacks, motor torpedo boat attacks and submarine attacks, and even a scare from the Italian Battle Fleet, which did not materialise, we eventually returned to Alexandria minus three destroyers and one cruiser sunk and the cruiser *Newcastle* extremely badly damaged.

My own two most vivid recollections of some eight days of continuous action stations were the sight of an Italian aeroplane carrying a torpedo entirely disintegrating some three hundred yards off our port side when flying amidst a hail of fire from all our guns. Presumably something eventually detonated the torpedo and the plane just disappeared in one blinding flash, while the other memory is of dismantling one of the 20mm Oerlikon guns, stuffing a ramrod down its barrel and striking it with a sledgehammer to remove a cartridge which had become jammed in the breech. This was a treatment which was not laid down in the handbooks for the gun, but seemed highly practical at the time when otherwise the gun would have been out of action, with possibly fatal results for the ship.

It was a slightly unusual fault in the gun which occurred at the height of the action. The gun stopped firing and failed to re-cock. It was re-cocked manually and fired with no result, so the magazine was removed and found to be empty. A new full magazine was immediately fitted, but when fired the cock only went partially forward. Aggravated by the continued trouble the gun was re-cocked and the new full magazine removed and then the fault became obvious. One cartridge, which had failed to fire, was jammed in the breach and an effort had just been made to put another in behind it. This second cartridge had the bullet rammed into the cartridge case

94

and was hastily thrown overboard, and we then had the problem of extricating the cartridge in the breach which had been hammered in somewhat violently. Gentle pushing of a ramrod down the barrel produced no results and the technical Petty Officer did not care for using any more force as the bullets were explosive and had very delicate fuses which were supposed to explode upon going through a sheet of paper. I called for a sledgehammer, whereupon everyone near found a pressing need to be elsewhere quickly, but after a sharp blow from the sledge on the end of the ramrod, the offending cartridge popped out of the breech and was hastily thrown over the side.

Within a few minutes the gun was re-assembled and in action again.

On return to port, Guns unfortunately mentioned the incident and bureaucracy got into motion. A full report was required and deprecatory remarks were made about midshipmen undertaking weapon repairs in a crude and ignorant manner, but the real crux of the matter was to discover the "Lot Number" (manufacturer's batch number) of the offending cartridge which had misfired and started the whole chain of events. Frankly it had seemed too hot a potato at the time it was consigned to the deep, but bureaucracy must have its way and dire penalties were threatened if the Lot Number could not be produced. Eventually in despair I went down to the magazine and selected a Lot Number at random and, presumably, in due course orders went out to condemn and destroy all ammunition bearing that innocent Lot Number.

There was, at this time — and for most of the war, in fact — a bone of contention between the Navy and the Royal Air Force. We in the Navy tended to fire at any aeroplane which approached us in an aggressive manner without bothering to spend too much time trying to decide what make of aircraft it was and whether it was friend or enemy. The Royal Air Force contended that we should all become experts in aircraft recognition and be able to recognise every aeroplane — friend or foe — in an instant and act accordingly, and to this end the charts of silhouettes and drawings of enemy and allied aircraft were normally posted up on the inside doors of the ship's heads, as w.c.'s are known in the Navy. At one stage during this convoy we had to leave our station and stop the ship to send away a boat to pick up a pilot who was in the water with his parachute and who, when recovered, turned out to be an RAF Flight Lieutenant, who — to his very great annoyance and indignation — had been shot down by his own Squadron Leader. It was always a pleasure to quote this incident afterwards when entertaining Royal Air Force officers in the wardroom and they started on their hobby-horse.

What is perhaps difficult to realise for those who have never been in a big air/sea battle and have only been nurtured on Hollywood epics is the very small number of aeroplanes which are shot down in the course of a number of hours of action, and the very small number of bombs which actually secure a hit on ships, even when the Germans were using — as they still were at that time — their highly renowned and very successful 87B Stuka Divebomber. Times without number one would observe groups of these aeroplanes attacking a single ship, sometimes a group of twelve separating out and diving from four different directions in groups of three, and completely obliterating the ship in water splashes. From a distance the ship would entirely disappear in a fog of water, and then one watched with some anxiety to see if she would emerge unscathed or with flames and smoke coming from her hull. Surprisingly enough, it would seem that nine times out of ten the ship would emerge unscathed, a sight which would usually be greeted with cries of,

"Lucky bastards!" or if some visible hits were observed the cry would change to,

"Bugger me! The old *Stupendous* has copped a packet."

As a matter of interest, it was also impossible to tell the difference between a depth charge going off, and explosive near-miss and a direct hit on the other end of your own vessel, as has previously been remarked upon during the loss of *Auricula* at Madagascar. This sort of effect resulted in a curious incident related to me by a midshipman in one of the other destroyers.

He was walking along the afterdeck of his own ship and came across the figure of the Chief Stoker, who was standing waist-high in the boiler room hatch observing the battle so that he could retreat from time to time to keep up the spirits of those down below. At this point, his ship was passing close to a short bow section of a destroyer which had been cut off just forward of the bridge by a bomb or torpedo. Smoke was rising from this severed portion, and some survivors were preparing to abandon ship. As this piece of wreckage passed by, the Chief Stoker called out to the midshipman in a cheery voice,

"Cor blimey, sir, some poor bugger's copped a packet," to

96

which the midshipman was forced to reply with some asperity, "Don't be such a bleeding idiot, it's us."

And it was indeed their own bow which had been cut off and was slowly passing astern down the port side.

*   *   *   *

Back in Alexandria, a certain amount of celebrating went on in the light-hearted mood that always seemed to follow a serious piece of action. Trade at Mary's House was brisk, both at the bar and in the secluded room upstairs, and it so happened that we arrived just in time to be included in Operation EP7.

Several of these "Operation EPs" had already taken place, and the officers from *Griffin* had taken part in some of them, so we were quickly enrolled to join in the latest effort, EP7. If all the effort and organisation which went into Operations EP1 to 7 had been devoted to the war effort, I think the war in North Africa might have been over several months earlier.

As it was, the mystic letters stood for "Extract Palm", and it should be explained that in the Mediterranean at this time it was fashionable for any officer worth his salt to have a small palm tree in his cabin, and every wardroom had a large palm tree, it being an obvious corollary to this that these palm trees had to be stolen, usually from bars or restaurants in Alexandria or others adjacent ports.

There was, however, one particular restaurant which had an entrance down a few steps through a revolving door into a foyer where the cloakroom lay, and from thence to some further doors into a long, low-ceilinged room with a bar down the left-hand side, and a number of three-feet diameter fans on pedestals to endeavour to keep down the heat in those days before air conditioning. In the foyer stood an immense palm tree some fifteen feet high, and this was the object of all our attentions.

The operation orders for these expeditions ran into a dozen pages of typewritten foolscap, and sometimes as many as sixty or seventy officers were involved from the Navy, Army and Air Force, but mainly from the Navy. Various plans and manoeuvres were adopted of great complexity, and those involved were divided into ship-wrights parties, transportation parties, transportation defence parties, diversion parties, and protective diversion parties — to name but a few.

97

EP7 was the most complicated one of all, and involved a ship-wrights party jamming the revolving door and the door into the bar with wedges, while an inside transportation party stole a trolley from the nether regions and produced it on the balcony round the foyer. An inside riggers party hoisted the palm tree with specially prepared sheer legs and lowered it on to the trolley, which was wheeled to an outside balcony where the outside riggers party had a second set of sheer legs with which they lifted up the palm tree and lowered it down onto the roof of a taxi. Needless to say, the taxi had been brought round by the outside transportation party.

Meanwhile, down below in the bar and restaurant the diversion party (of which I was one) were hard at work. Some of us had acquired bowls of custard and were flinging this around, while four of us had smuggled in several feather pillows which were slit open behind the big thirty-six inch fans and caused a veritable snowstorm. These efforts were intended to attract the attention of the bunch of heavies employed by the management for the protection of their establishment (and to a certain extent of their palm trees), and their efforts were hindered as much as possible by the protective diversion party, who placed chairs and tables in their way to gain a little time for their colleagues engaged in the real object of the exercise. Sadly EP7 failed, since the heavies managed to get wind of what was going on and beat a retreat from the bar restaurant through the back door and raced round to capture the taxi just as it was about to take off for the docks with its precious cargo.

It was all really very good natured and no harm was done to anyone, and since all those taking part in the various operations were extremely good customers for the rest of the time, I do not think the management regarded the whole thing very seriously, and in some ways seemed to enter into the spirit of the competition.

* * * * *

In those days, every destroyer carried a Warrant Officer, normally a Warrant Gunner (T), and this unfortunately is a rank which has disappeared from the Royal Navy, and the nearest equivalent perhaps is the modern Fleet Chief Petty Officer, but the essential difference being that the Fleet Chief Petty Officer wasn't an officer while the Warrant Officer was, and he lived in the wardroom and stood a watch at sea and carried his badge of rank in the shape of a half gold stripe on his sleeve. Apart from looking after the torpedoes on board, and incidentally other equipment of a similar sort, like the depth charges, he also had to look after the gunnery stores and the technical side of the guns generally was his responsibility.

Trying to keep the books straight as far as the ammunition on board was concerned was an impossible task in those days when the ship's complete outfit of ammunition might be fired off in eight days, and a complete new stock taken on board and likewise expended in the next eight days. The poor fellow even had to account for all the empty brass cartridge cases, not only from the 4.7 guns but from the 20mm, the half-inch and the .303. So important was the book-keeping of the empty 4.7 shell cases that it was necessary to have a crew member stationed behind the guns when firing on a low angle abeam with an overgrown baseball bat, and his job was to try and whack the shell cases as they shot out horizontally over his head and keep them from flying over the side. It was not for about another twelve months that the regulation finally came in that said cartridge cases should merely be returned when possible and were not required to be accounted for on paper. All this is to explain a happy scene which occurred on board *Griffin* a night or two later, when a German air raid was taking place on the harbour and some bombs struck the ammunition ship which was responsible for supplying the Naval ships with ammunition of all sizes.

It was a real Brocks benefit, better than the 5th November any year, but while most of us were enjoying the spectacle, suddenly a brilliant idea came to Guns. He dashed down to his cabin, stuffed some paper, carbon and copy paper into his typewriter and quickly wrote a letter to the Ammunition Stores Officer in the ammunition ship which was presently providing us with such a spectacle, and in this letter he declared that he was returning all his ammunition accounting books for checking. Then, carefully preserving the carbon copy dated the previous day, he dashed up on deck, threw overboard all his ammunition accounting books and ceremoniously tore up the original of his letter.

※　※　※　※

A few days later we were on our way back to the Eastern Fleet, and had a hot passage down the Red Sea. At Aden we paused for fuel, and found there the cruiser *Newcastle* (a similar ship to the *Belfast* now preserved as a museum by Tower Bridge), and she was showing the results of our recent Malta convoy effort. She lay at anchor with the most enormous hole right through her hull under the foremost turret. It was such a large hole that, while exercising a whaler's crew under oars, we actually rowed right through the ship from one side to the other without touching our oars on the damaged portions ahead or astern of us. In the next few days we steamed down to Mombasa in company with *Newcastle*, who went ahead in good weather, and then when the Southerly winds blew strong she turned round and went fifteen knots astern into the steep sea. Subsequently she steamed across to Bombay, where she was repaired and put back into service. It said a good deal for the strength of construction and design of these vessels that she was able to steam so many thousands of miles at relatively high speed with this enormous hole right through her without suffering any further damage.

Once back in Mombasa, we were again put through various exercises with the Eastern Fleet, which was then in the course of formation. The nearest thing to being under fire from the very heavy guns occurred when we were used as a target ship for what was described as a "throw off shoot". On these occasions, the battleship's deflection on her guns was set so many degrees to the right or left, and they then aimed at us and fired off their salvoes so that they landed astern. We would take bearings of the shell splashes and the range of them with a small portable range finder and pass this information back by radio, and the clever mathematicians could then tell whether the shells would have hit us if they had been correctly aimed. The noise of a salvo of fifteen-inch shells passing overhead, even when not directly aimed at one, was rather like an express train coming through a small village station at maximum speed, and certainly made us glad that they were not for real and were not genuine enemy shells being aimed at us with malice aforethought.

*   *   *   *

My movements from one ship to another since stepping off *Auricula* in Madagascar had rather defeated the paymaster system, and it was difficult for me to get hold of any of that useful stuff called money which was handy for buying things. In any case, a midshipman's pay in those days seldom was sufficient to meet his mess bill, let alone deal with other essential items, so one day I walked into the branch of Barclays Bank in Mombasa and asked to see the manager. I explained the situation to him, and after listening to me very sympathetically, he agreed to cash a cheque immediately, although I had no form of identification and no cheque book and no means of guaranteeing to him that I had any money in my bank in England. He also made arrangements to transfer further sums from England as and when I would require them. Jubilant at this financial success, I was dashing out of the bank and ran into a Wren officer who was coming in, and — standing back to apologise — discovered that she was a girl whom I had met while sailing on the Clyde before the war.

We had lunch together, and then spent the afternoon trying to find the Mombasa Yacht Club, of which we had both heard, but which nobody we knew had found. It took some considerable detective work and a very expensive taxi ride, but eventually we found a small hospitable club, where the secretary agreed to us both becoming members as long as we did not declare the whereabouts of the club to anybody else in the Eastern Fleet.

One of the members we met announced that he was going down to South Africa for six months and would be pleased if we would take over his sailing dinghy and look after it and use it as much as we like. All this seemed too good to be true, and that night when I got back aboard *Griffin* I was very smugly saying to everyone that I did not care how long we stayed in Mombasa; I, at least, would be happy there. The others who were celebrating to some extent looked at me in astonishment, and then said,

"Do you really mean you don't want to come back to England with us tomorrow?"

We sailed at dawn for Cape Town. Yet another example of Sod's Law.

We passed a few days at Durban, where I had a happy reunion with Paddy Russell, and then on to Cape Town. We stopped long enough to embark fifty ingots of gold in their little numbered wooden boxes, which were stowed in the torpedo magazine below the officers flat, then on to Saint Helena, Bermuda and New York, acting all the way as escort to one of the old wobbly "R" battleships which was going to America for refit.

My promotion to Acting Sub-Lieutenant, which should have occurred on my twentieth birthday, was now somewhat overdue, and due to lack of communication with the Admiralty in London, had not taken place. However, we were fortunate enough in having a full Naval Captain on board (being the Captain in charge of the flotilla of destroyers), and as soon as he heard of this situation, he officially ordered me to purchase my Sub-Lieutenant's insignia and take up my post as one of the watchkeeping officers on the ship, which had not been possible up to that time in the more "by the book" organisation which existed in destroyers. I still had not got any proper uniform of the normal blue serge and brass button type. but was given an Army battledress in Durban, so that by the time we ran into New York I was to be seen walking the streets with Naval shoulder strap badges of rank on an Army battledress and a Naval cap.

Ashore in Cape Town I encountered, by chance, the S.B.A. (Sick Berth Attendant) from *Auricula* who had, after *Auricula*'s demise, been drafted to the "Wobbly R" (*Ramillies*) which we were escorting. He recounted to me the sad story of the Captain's Parrot.

Amidst the alarums and excursions that followed the explosion of the mine and accompanied the evacuation of the wounded and, finally, the able-bodied members of the ship's company, Polly had fastened upon the shoulder of the only representative of the medical profession on board, who held the lowest rank in that department in the Royal Navy, Sick Berth Attendant (S.B.A.) and who was, of course, known to all aboard as the "doctor". There is no doubt about it that the piratical appearance of the survivors, many of whom were black from head to foot due to the bursting of one of the oil fuel tanks, was much enhanced by the parrot clutching firmly to the shoulder of the S.B.A. (and sometimes with his beak to his new master's ear), while intermittently rending the air with suitably salty lower deck expressions of disgust about the situation in general, not to mention "Up spirits" and "Away seaboats crew".

In due course the S.B.A. was drafted to the battleship *Ramillies*, the Flagship of the Fleet, and although no direction came from My Lords of the Admiralty to that effect, Polly chose to adopt the same drafting instructions. On the battleship's mess deck he soon became a great favourite, and many of the thousand or so men used to vie with each other to be allowed to give him part of their daily rum ration, and he certainly never failed to amuse them in return.

It should be explained here that pets were very popular in Royal Navy ships and in peacetime were sometimes very exotic. *Malaya* had a large bear, about whom many stories are told. On the outbreak of war, all animals had to be landed and the mess decks were sadder for their loss. The arrival of a parrot, therefore, was a cause for considerable joy and the discovery that he was a natural alcoholic caused much hilarity. A few drops of wardroom gin every week did not do him much harm, but the daily scene of several hundred men attempting to give him a droplet of rum was rather a strain on his constitution.

Whether parrots can suffer from cirrhosis of the liver or not I do not know, nor do I know whether it was his over-indulgence in Nelson's blood that caused his illness, but after some weeks it became apparent that Polly's health was not all that it should be. Polly was definitely sick.

Fortunately this was obviously a medical problem, and his master was not now a mere Captain of a ship, but a member of the "Profession". Since Polly was definitely off his grog, the S.B.A. offered part of his own tot to the Leading S.B.A., the next highest man up the medical ladder. In view of Polly's popularity with the whole ship's company, the Leading S.B.A. did not delay, but immediately went to see the Petty Officer S.B.A. bearing with him, in his turn, part of his rum ration. Realising that a serious situation hd developed, the Petty Officer S.B.A. immediately reported it to the Chief Petty Officer S.B.A., stressing the importance of the matter with a full tot of "neaters" out of his emergency bottle.

The Chief appreciated the alarming state of affairs instantaneously, and approached forthwith the Surgeon Lieutenant. Such was the gravity of the matter that all this occurred between 1100 (the time of the rum issue) and half past noon on the same day. The Surgeon Lieutenant was, therefore, appraised of the details while taking a glass of gin before lunch, and he lost no time in offering the Surgeon Lieutenant Commander a larger portion while they discussed their first impressions of this medical problem. After a few minutes it was obvious that they needed another opinion, and together they approached the great man himself, the Surgeon Commander. After a few more glasses of gin to thoroughly survey the matter, the message was passed down that a full examination would take place in the Sick Bay at 1430, and on the strength of this the medical profession fortified itself with the midday meal.

At 1430 all those on board who had taken the Hippocratic oath were assembled in the Sick Bay, where Polly was by this time lying on his back with his claws in the air looking very seedy indeed. No stone was left unturned, no avenue left unexplored, no possibility left uninvestigated. Polly was given a thorough medical check-up, and after a short consultation they came to the conclusion that the only solution was to operate.

"Sir, about anaesthetics?" hesitated the Surgeon Lieutenant Commander.

"Well, don't just stand there, look it up in the book."

"Aye, aye, Sir," said the Lieutenant Commander.

But a few minutes later it became obvious that neither the Naval nor the civilian medical books on board went so far as to inform the uninitiated as to how much anaesthetic to give a fully-grown male African grey parrot.

"Well, we shall have to do it from first principles," said the Surgeon Commander, so they weighed Polly on the dispensary scales and spent the next hour or two trying to calculate mathematically how much anaesthetic to prescribe. A further hour or two were spent adapting the equipment available to administer the stuff. Finally all was set for the great moment, and they all duly attired themselves in white coats and masks, scrubbing up in the manner to which we have become so accustomed following those endless television dramas of the hospital.

Then the operation commenced.

All those that were there that day were unanimous in the opinion that it was a magnificent operation and a masterly piece of surgery on the part of the Surgeon Commander.

The operation was a brilliant success, but as the Surgeon Commander stood there receiving the plaudits of his team with a suitable professional modesty, the Surgeon Lieutenant-Commander had to break the spell with the sad news that Polly had not recovered from the anaesthetic.

He was buried at sea with full ceremony, and hardly a dry eye on board.

* * * *

After a few hours in Bermuda for fuelling, we pressed on to the entrance to Chesapeake Bay where we handed over our battleship to the American coastal escorts and proceeded independently to New York, where we arrived just after dawn on a misty morning.

Even then, in 1942, the skyline was stupendous, and seeing it emerge out of the mist as one had seen so often on film was really unbelievable. We berthed eventually in Hoboken on the West side of the Hudson River in a rather dirty, industrial slum not very different

104

from the dockland of London. We really were not meant to stay very long in New York, but a few of the officers had not had a lot of fun for the previous three years and so all connived with the Captain to cook up a very lengthy list of essential repairs, on which all held the opinion that to endeavour to cross the Atlantic without having them attended to was nothing short of suicide. In this we were unwittingly aided by the engineers in the shipyard who were frankly astonished at the slack in her A bracket propeller shaft bearings which our engineer officer had considered quite normal in reality, but which was something like two hundred per cent over the slack allowed in similar American vessels.

The really prize item on the repair list was the rewiring of the officers' accommodation in the stern, since as soon as this was accepted as being necessary, it also resulted that it was essential to evacuate this portion of the vessel, which resulted in all officers being billeted ashore in that hotel which the Royal Navy had substantially commandeered — The Barbizon Plaza. This was all rather too good to miss, and I managed to persuade the Paymaster to allow me to draw considerable sums of pay in advance on the excuse that I needed to buy new uniforms which, needless to say, I never did, since there were far more interesting things to spend money on in New York at this time.

Eventually we spent about ten days in harbour, but it seemed to me that valuable time was being wasted when I found that, as Junior Officer aboard, I was on duty for the first twenty-four hours, only able to observe the bright lights of Manhattan across the murky waters of the Hudson River.

Shortly after our arrival the Paymaster had been ashore and acquired a considerable quantity of American dollars, which he handed over to me with instructions to pay twenty dollars per man to all those on board who wanted it. With that he dashed back down the gangway with his overnight bag on the way to the Barbizon Plaza.

When I opened the parcel of money which he had handed over, there immediately arose a small problem. All the money was in one-hundred dollar notes, and I did not think the ship's company were going to enjoy going ashore in groups of five trying to share the hundred dollar note between them. It did not take long to find out that all the banks were closed by this time, and in my innocence I then proceeded to tour the bars adjacent to the shipyard, asking the bar-keeper in each one how many hundred dollar notes he could change. As soon as my English accent was heard, it seemed that everyone in each bar wished to purchase me a drink, and since it was necessary to visit at least ten bars before I had broken up all the hundred dollar notes that I had started off with, my arrival back at the ship was extremely unsteady.

The Good Lord protects fools and innocents they say, and He certainly seemed to do so on that occasion, for not only was I not robbed or mugged, but I was not even cheated in my change in the latter stages of the expedition, and to everyone's surprise (not least mine), when all the grubby dollar notes of various denominations below twenty were extracted from all the pockets of my battledress and counted up, the total came to two thousand dollars, which was exactly the figures with which I had set off, and one hundred members of the ship's company thirstily took their twenty dollars and signed for it and dashed off ashore to see who could be the first to spend it all. I do not think any of them were as well entertained by strangers in the various bars they visited as I had been earlier that day.

*　*　*　*

The following morning I had to make another foray ashore for some purpose and it being the sort of area where taxis were not commonly to be found cruising around, it turned out to be quite a long walk. On the way back I was very glad to be offered a lift in a U.S. Naval car being driven by a Petty Officer, and having in the back a Vice Admiral and a "four ring" Captain. Sitting in the front with the driver, the Captain and the Admiral asked me what ship I was from and how long I had been at sea, and finally whether I had seen any action. Looking over my shoulder I referred to being blown up in *Auricula* while minesweeping in Madagascar and taking part in a Mediterranean convoy in such a way that they probably got the impression that never a week went by without some deeds of derring-do occurring. Their eyes were open wide and their mouths almost equally so, to such an extent that the situation reminded me of the picture of "The Boyhood of Raleigh", only in this case it was the boy who was recounting the adventures and the old salts who were listening spellbound.

In the afternoon I was able to take a ferry across to Manhattan and a taxi to the Barbizon Plaza, where I was rapidly installed in a most luxurious bedroom. It was only a matter of a ride in the lift to arrive at the U.S.O. (Officers Entertainment Office) situated in the hotel, where I had barely time to give my name before receiving two tickets for *Die Fledermaus*, an invitation to a cocktail party being given at a "Ladies Only" hotel, a free voucher for dinner for two at a first class restaurant, and the assurance that if there was anything, absolutely anything, that I wanted in New York "I was to be sure to come back and ask".

They were indeed as good as their word, and in the days that followed they arranged for me to spend an evening in El Morocco with its famous zebra hyde banquette, a VIP tour of the Radio City music hall, where the film was viewed from Rockefeller's private box and the stage show from the front row of this five thousand seat auditorium. They even made the necessary arrangements with the local Captain of Police for me to go to Abercrombie & Fitch and purchase a .32 Savage automatic pistol, and finally they even made arrangements for our wardroom glee club to visit the RCA building to record some rather obscure old English folk songs.

* * * *

It has been said that the only true folk songs are those that are passed down from generation to generation without ever being written down, and on this basis, probably the best known in the English language are "The Good Ship Venus", "The Harlot of Jerusalem", "Caviar Comes From the Virgin Sturgeon" and "The Ballad of Kirriemuir", and there are, of course, many others of a similar style.

Today they tend to be sung by Rugby clubs and other predominantly male gatherings late in the evenings — or very early in the morning — and they are occasionally to be heard in Naval wardrooms.

In *Griffin* we had one officer who was pedantic about the lyrical effects and he typed out the words of all the songs and reproduced them as a form of songbook. In fact, he became a sort of maniacal collector and would get most excited if a rare song appeared, such as the first occasion on which he heard the minuet from W. S. Gilbert's lesser known "Bugger's Opera", the manuscript of which is said to reside in the "Private Case" at the British Museum. Incidentally, Sir Arthur Sullivan would probably spin in his grave like a gyroscope if

107

he knew that the music from his minuet in "The Gondoliers" was used as an accompaniment for this ribald song.

Over the years the songbooks became somewhat tattered, and our pedantic lyricist became gradually more and more disgruntled with the sloppy musical rendering of these fine old ballads. Volume of sound rather than purity of note appeared to be what most singers were striving for, and alcohol undoubtedly aided their endeavours.

A solution to the problem fortuitously came to hand when, by chance, our avid song collector discovered a building nearby the Barbizon Plaza owned by the RCA Company, where one could insert some coins — quarters, if I remember rightly — in a machine which would then reproduce one's voice on a standard gramophone record. This was too great a chance to miss.

An extempore choir was assembled one Saturday morning at the bar of the Barbizon Plaza and a strictly limited — but adequate — intake of alcohol was partaken. Then, with each member of the choir firmly clutching his songbook, our leader carrying a sipply of quarters, and everyone bearing a filled flask in his pocket — lest thirst should overcome us in the long afternoon ahead — we made our way to the building housing the mystical machine, where a booth had been booked by the ladies from the U.S.O. Committee.

There was a certain amount of organisation required to adjust the lengths of our songs to the records, and great arguments as to which verses should be included and which omitted, but gradually we worked through the songbook in the course of the afternoon, pausing, only occasionally, to refresh ourselves from the flasks.

The pile of completed records grew slowly, but we gradually managed to tick off the many well known titles.

Following "The Good Ship Venus" and that attributed to Robbie Burns — the famed "Ballad of Kirriemuir" — we sang of the caviar that comes from the virgin sturgeon and then recounted the sad history of little Angeline — poor but honest — and that rather more wealthy young lady who lost it at the Astor, although she knew she had it when she came.

We recounted the meeting of Deadeye Dick and Mexican Pete with that remarkable lady Eskimo Nell, and sung a lesser known version of "The Girl in the Alice Blue Gown". The unfortunate predicament of those three old ladies locked in the bathroom ran to many verses, and this was followed by a detailed description of a

108

gigantic engineering wonder with a revolving wheel driven by steam, and, in turn, this led to the more manual expertise required to dig up a parent's grave to build a sewer. As a finale we finished up with the odd adventure of a tinker and a duchess.

It was dark and cold when the happy band of choristers descended to the ground floor, clutching their many recordings of these famous songs and left the building to return to the bar of the Barbizon Plaza.

Outside the building and spreading out across Fifth Avenue, a tremendous crowd had collected, all staring up at the face of the building. We turned and stared up too, expecting to see some lunatic poised for a spectacular jump, but there was nothing to be seen, and an expectant hush silenced the crowd.

Eventually my curiosity overcame me, and I asked one of the gazers what was going on. He pointed up to a horn-like decoration about fifty feet up.

"Hell," he said, "there's a bunch of guys in there singing songs, and boy-oh-boy, what songs they are, and they're all coming out of that loudspeaker there."

＊　＊　＊　＊

It was, of course, my first visit to the U.S.A., and the memory of the occasion on which their extraordinary insularity and ignorance on matters outside America was brought home to me is still as clear in my mind as the evening it happened.

At another delightful cocktail party arranged by the ladies of the Barbizon Plaza, a South African midshipman from another destroyer in harbour and myself were talking to a very charming twenty-year-old resident of New York. She opened the conversation with the inevitable "Where do you come from?" to which the midshipman replied,

"I am from Johannesburg."

"Say, but where is Johannesburg?"

"Well, it's about a thousand miles inland from Durban."

"Well say, where's Durban?"

"Well, Durban is about fifteen hundred miles up the coast from Cape Town."

"Well say, where's Cape Town?"

At this point I realised that the poor chap was running out of patience and further directions, so I stepped in with a polite remark of,

"Do you really mean to say that you don't know where Cape Town, Durban or Johannesburg are?"

She turned to me, smiled sweetly, blinked her eyes twice, and said, "Well I'm sorry, I really don't know my England very well."

        *   *   *   *

Sadly, the shipyard — working at astonishing speed — rebuilt the ship from stem to stern and even completed the rewiring of the wardroom and officers' cabins and many other jobs besides to such an extent that nobody on board was able to think of anything that needed repairing anywhere in the ship, and so our excuses for staying ran out. We had received orders to form part of the escort for the support convoy for Operation "Torch" (the Allied landing in North Africa, which was the first deployment of American troops this side of the Atlantic).

We kept with the convoy until a few hundred miles from North Africa, when we turned North and went into San Miguel in the Azores to fuel before returning to Greenock.

Apart from Molly in Mombasa, who I was able to see for only one day, it comes to mind that I was extremely well entertained in Durban by Paddy, and even better entertained by Barbara in New York, and even during our limited twenty-four hour stay in San Miguel, the charming daughter of the British Consul was most hospitable. Surprisingly, I did see some of them again. Paddy visited England in 1950, and I visited New York in 1954 and was able to look up Barbara there, but somehow, whether it was the absence of the uniform or the absence of the magical excitement of a wartime meeting, the later encounters did not have anything like the same piquancy.

        *   *   *   *

Greenock was only a short stay, and as the first port back in the United Kingdom I was duty officer automatically once again. My solitary evening in the wardroom was enlivened by the arrival of a very suave gentleman in a pin-striped suit and bowler hat carrying the inevitable umbrella, who explained that he was from the Bank of England and he had come to collect "the small parcel of gold".

Actually, in my ignorance of international affairs and especially international finances, I had been expecting the gold to be landed in New York to form part of the payment for the vast quantity of

110

lease/lend equipment which America was sending over to England at this time. Originally, in fact, the whole wardroom had suspected that this was the reason for us being sent to New York, and we had all been expecting it to be unloaded there, with all the razzmatazz of American police and FBI action with Thompson machine guns and everything else to the fore, so it was really rather a disappointment when we sailed from the U.S.A. with it still on board. By converse now, all we had at Greenock was one pin-striped suited gentleman with his umbrella and bowler hat, one lorry driver and one very disinterested ordinary policeman.

We unlocked the torpedo store and turned out the duty watch, and it did not take a very long time for the fifty blocks of gold to be passed out on to the jetty and into the lorry. Each block of gold was encased in a wooden box with sealed metal bands going round it in two different directions, and on each box was stencilled a number which I recall was in four figures. Pin-stripe had a list of all the boxes and all the numbers stencilled thereon, and each box had to be checked against his list. All went well, and the fifty boxes were duly loaded into the lorry, or at least that was what I thought. At this point, Pin-stripe pointed out that he was one block short, and I had visions of myself as a white-haired, white-bearded old man working for the next fifty years without any pay trying to repay the Bank of England for this solitary block of gold which had gone astray. We searched the torpedo store and no blocks of gold were there, and finally, in desperation, we took all the boxes out of the lorry and checked all their numbers against Pin-stripe's list once more, and this time he had to concede that all fifty blocks were there, and I heaved a great sigh of relief and went back on board and fortified myself with a large gin. In fact, I was so relieved I even offered Pin-stripe a large gin as well.

The next day we set off on a round Britain trip, going North up the West coast of Scotland, East around the North end of the islands, and down the East coast to the Thames. The passage from some-where near the Humber to the Thames was carried out in darkness, and used to the open Atlantic rather than the hit-and-run habits of the East coast, we spent the whole night at action stations, convinced we were going to be attacked by German bombers and E-boats, but in fact we did not see a thing, and as dawn broke we were heading into the Thames and up the river to the shipyard at Tilbury to undergo a refit, since as far as My Lord's Commissioners were concerned, the refit in New York just did not count.

Having been away from England and my home for about eighteen months, it was a great pleasure to pack my bags, catch a train to London and from there back to my home in East Grinstead. I had missed the last train to East Grinstead, and had in fact to take a train to Three Bridges, some ten miles short of my destination. My luggage was still extremely skimpy, since apart from some tropical uniform and a spare shirt or two, everything else was on my back, but fortunately I had a dozen pineapples in my kitbag, and with one or two of these was able to bribe somebody in the Station Hotel at Three Bridges to drive me the last ten miles home. After all, pineapples were almost as valuable as gold bars at that time in England.

Chapter Four

CHRISTMAS, 1942 at home. Victory did not seem to be in sight, but at least the idea of possible defeat seemed to have receded, and I felt I had really reached manhood with my single intertwined RNR Sub Lieutenant's gold stripe quickly applied to my best uniform, which had fortunately been left at home.

Gieves, that most Naval of Naval institutions, continued to cope with most difficult wartime situations in a manner befitting its ancient heritage. When the Charles Laughton film *Mutiny on the Bounty* was made in the 1930s, it was said that the producer visited Gieves in Bond Street and enquired whether they had ever made a uniform for an officer named Bligh.

"About what date would that be, sir?" the Gieves man enquired.

"About 1788," replied the producer.

"If you would care to take a seat, sir, I will enquire," came the unruffled reply, and it is then said that some minutes later Mr Gieve himself appeared to speak to the producer, followed by a minion holding open an ancient ledger, and he said "Would that be Lieutenant William Bligh, sir? We have here the full details of his uniform outfit."

"Fine," said the producer, "I would like you to make me a complete duplicate outfit. Here are the measurements of the man they must fit," and he handed over a small sheet of paper. Thus, the story goes, Charles Laughton was correctly outfitted for the film, and no doubt the same applied to other officers as well.

My own experience was not quite so dramatic, but while in *Griffin* in Alexandria I had visited his temporary establishment there and placed a fairly large order for a complete outfit of uniforms, both tropical and European, not expecting at that time to be returned to England so rapidly. Now on leave I hurried up to London to have my badge of rank put on my existing uniform, and to order a complete new kit. I explained that I had ordered a similar kit in Alexandria some three months beforehand which I no longer required, to which the Gieves man replied without the quiver of an eyelid, "That will be quite in order, sir, we shall cancel that request, and supply you with everything you require from this head office."

There was a small matter to check all my measurements to see whether these agreed with those they had on record, and to make adjustments where necessary, and when I removed my battledress blouse for the measurements to be taken for my new uniform jacket, the cutter's eyes did not rise a millimetre when he observed the .32 automatic pistol in a shoulder holster under my left arm. He merely said to his assistant, who was writing down the notes, "We shall make the jacket a little full under the left shoulder."

In the piping days of peace it was always said that one heard of one's promotion from three sources in the following order. Firstly, a telegram of congratulations from Gieves, secondly by reading a notice in *The Times*, and thirdly by receiving a letter from the Lords Commissioners of the Admiralty, while Gieves' service to the cadets being enrolled in the Royal Naval College at Dartmouth was something to be seen. It certainly paid off in my case, for I have maintained my account with them for a period of over fifty years, while my son has had an account with them for nearly twenty years. I have always felt that if, while one was having a suit fitted, one remarked to the cutter "I am thinking of buying a steam yacht,", he would reply, "Really, sir, about what size?" and a few minutes later he would return with particulars of suitable craft for one to peruse. Not being able to afford a steam yacht I have never tried it, but still, the idea continues to amuse.

It was the first time since the war started that I had been able to spend Christmas at home on leave, and even though I was not to know that it would not happen again until 1946, I applied all my efforts to make the most of it. Most of the girls that I had known in my home district seem to have managed to get themselves married or firmly engaged, but there did not seem any shortage of supplies in that direction, and I discovered a particularly good source of supply when my cousin, who had become the local vicar, invited me to read the lesson in church on "Sailors Sunday". I duly donned my uniform on the Sunday morning and walked with some difficulty the mile to the church, hoping that it would clear my head from the excesses of the Saturday night in the local pub, and duly stood up at the appropriate moment to read the lesson to the largely elderly and female congregation. It was only after the service that I began to get the first inkling of the benefits that my lesson reading would bestow on me, when I received two invitations to tea from members of the congregation who happened to mention that they had a niece or daughter expected home the day in question. Several more invitations came by telephone during the ensuing week, and at the ensuing meetings I was happy to find that the younger generation to whom I was introduced were not necessarily quite so puritanical as their church-going elders probably hoped. It certainly broadened my education, and on all future occasions when I came back on leave, I always made a bee line for the church to read the lesson on the first Sunday that I was there, with generally speaking similar fortunate results.

On December 30th I received an appointment to HMS *Moyola* and for duty with ASCBS and instructions to report to Middlesborough. With my previous experience of *Auricula*, I knew that this indicated that I was joining a vessel that was not yet complete, and therefore I had no qualms about putting my telescope to my blind eye and remaining on leave until January 2nd, being prepared, if necessary, to blame the late arrival of my letter of appointment on the Christmas and New Year mail rush. It certainly was a wise decision. The New Year celebrations in my home town with my bevy of new-found friends was infinitely more amusing that it would have been in Middlesbrough, a somewhat drab northern town, and as I surmised, *Moyola* was far from complete even when I arrived on January 2nd, and in fact she did not finally commission until the beginning of February, so that my presence over the New Year was certainly not missed.

Moyola was one of the enlarged twin screw corvettes (later designated as frigates) designed and built to supercede the single screw corvettes of the *Auricula* type. They were 1500 tons instead of 1000 tons, they had twin screw instead of single screw, although of the same type and they were 300 ft. long instead of 200 ft. long, and carried a crew of about 130, with considerably increased range and habitability and a moderate increase in armament. They were equipped with the latest radar and ASDIC gear and devices for detecting U-boars making wireless transmissions, and they carried nine officers instead of the corvettes' four or five, including a doctor and an engineer officer. Of the six watchkeeping officers, two had similar experience to my own, one Lieutenant had only some six months' experience at sea, and the other two Sub-Lieutenants were new arrivals from *King Alfred*, but both had considerable experience at sea on the lower deck, including one who had been a leading ASDIC operator and naturally inherited the job of anti-submarine officer on board. I found myself appointed as Torpedo Officer, which gave me the task of looking after some 150 depth charges and 8 depth charge throwers, together with a new device which had been invented for throwing bombs ahead of the ship while still in contact with the submarine on ASDIC. This was called a hedgehog, and of course by the old Naval system, I also inherited the responsibility for all the electrical equipment on board the ship, which was relatively sophisticated. Fortunately the radar, ASDIC and wireless equipment were outside my province, since I already had more than I could really cope with, as my knowledge of electrical equipment was entirely limited to some rather primitive instructions received in the engineering shops of the Naval College at Dartmouth resulting in practical skills not much greater than those required to change a fuse or put in a new electric light bulb.

Eventually the shipbuilding yard put the final touches to the vessel, and we ran the builders trials, whereupon the Captain accepted the ship on behalf of the Admiralty and we steamed out of Middlesbrough Northabout round Scotland to Tobermory to undertake the working-up ritual under Admiral " Monkey " Stephenson, which I had already experienced once before in *Auricula* almost exactly two years earlier.

The menu was much the same but two years' ceaseless effort by " Monkey " Stephenson and his staff had honed the system to a fine edge. Depth charge and gun crews were trained in reloading and the staff were more helpful and less likely to harry and shout merely to increase confusion.

Just occasionally something of the old devilment came out. Our motor boat had developed an annoying fault with the engine producing only some ten per cent of its proper power, so to land nine tenths of our crew for an exercise ashore we requested a base boat stating that our motor boat was out of action. The Captain, all officers except myself and the doctor and all bar some ten members of the crew disappeared ashore and I prepared to hoist the useless motor boat. At this moment the doctor asked for a man to be sent to " Monkey " Stephenson's flagship *Western Isles* for treatment and as she was only a hundred yards away, I stupidly agreed to send him over at slow speed in the motor boat while arrangements were being completed to hoist her.

The transfer was effected and the hoisting of the motor boat, using the anchor windlass for power, was almost completed when a signal was received by lamp from *Western Isles* saying " Send boat to Morag Tarn jetty forthwith ".

With suspicion growing in my mind and memories of the redoubtable "Monkey" Stephenson's energy and antics, I went to the bridge to look at the chart and discover the whereabouts of the jetty while calling for P.O. Taylor, the only seaman Petty Officer aboard, to meet me there.

The jetty was on the opposite side of the harbour to the town and nothing useful was nearby but I guessed the reason. The Petty Officer was shown the jetty and instructed to find five men (stokers, stewards or what-have-you) and get them dressed as seamen and ready to tow the whaler (our other boat which had no engine) to the jetty. Meanwhile I got hold of the doctor — the cause of the trouble — and made him help me to lower the whaler, which was a difficult task for two. Once the crew was embarked, P.O. Taylor was told to take the whaler to the jetty where, unless I was much mistaken, he would find an angry Vice-Admiral with large tufts of hair sprouting from his cheek-bones. "When you get there," I told Taylor, "you do absolutely anything he tells you and I mean anything."

I watched discreetly from the bridge through binoculars as the whaler approached the jetty. Taylor stood up and saluted and I saw the stocky uniformed figure step into the whaler, which then rowed to *Western Isles*. The crew, consisting, in fact, of two stokers, a Sick Berth Attendant and a wireless telegraphist, rowed pretty well under Taylor's instruction, and when he returned alongside there was a broad smile on his face.

"You were dead right, sir, there was a Vice-Admiral on that jetty. How did you know?"

"I've been here before, Taylor, that's how I knew; but tell me what did he say to you?"

"He just said 'Take me to my ship' and got aboard, so I did."

"Very well done," I replied, "you have probably saved this ship and her crew a great deal of hassle and possibly a lot worse. Now let's get the whaler hoisted and afterwards there will be a bottle of beer apiece for you all."

117

* * * *

Eventually our period in purgatory came to an end with the inevitable final inspection. We prepared to take in tow stern first, we placed a collision mat, put out fires, beat off air attacks, bombarded shore positions, picked up survivors and repelled boarders more or less all at the same time. I thought I detected a flicker of amusement when the Admiral glanced at me as we repelled boarders as our two cooks clutching butchers cleavers led the howling mob.

I was defeated in one thing, for I had believed for some reason that we would have to construct a raft and had secreted all the suitable material in a handy place, but this task was never set. Perhaps "Monkey's" spies had informed him of our readiness.

Passed as fit and ready for war we joined Escort Group 40 with our Senior Officer in *Landguard* (another ex-US Coast Guard cutter) and proceeded across the Atlantic without a convoy to St. John's, Newfoundland to pick up an Eastbound task.

On April 21st *Hastings* claimed a submarine "kill" and the Escort Group Commander signalled the group to splice the mainbrace. In fact carrying this out at sea — while good for morale — did little for our fighting efficiency, especially as he followed this with a signal " Men old enough to fight are old enough to drink. Issue rum to men under age forthwith."

Now that the daily tot of rum is fast receding into history, perhaps I should digress to give some details of this honourable and ancient custom and some of the diversifications connected with it.

Firstly the daily issue. Every man on board (but not the officers) was designated "G", "T" or "U.A." standing for "Grog", "Temperance" and "Under Age", the latter being fixed at twenty years, those below this age not being entitled to an issue. Those above the magic age could declare whether they wished to receive their tot or receive a small sum of money each day in lieu — threepence in old money, if I remember correctly. Most elected to take their tot, since this was a major currency on the lower deck and worth more than the financial alternative. Although it was strictly against all regulations, the trade in tots was widespread and the giving away of a tot or portion of it was the recognised way of repaying a favour or purchasing a boon.

The tot could be divided into "gulpers" and "sippers" with the mathematical formula:

118

Three sippers one gulp
Three gulpers one tot
and the tot itself consisted of a full gill — that is to say three pub measures and this of a rum which was a much higher proof spirit than is legally sold in a bar in Great Britain today. To drink a tot in one swallow — as was traditional — was therefore equivalent to swallowing about five glasses of whisky at once.

When a birthday occurred it was normal for the lucky lad to have "sippers all round" — a sippers from the tot of each member of his mess.

The daily issue had to be very carefully measured out and distributed to each mess under an officer's supervision, with Chiefs and Petty Officers receiving theirs neat while the remainder had theirs diluted with two parts of water. Apart from diluting the spirit this had the added advantage from a disciplinary point of view of making it impossible to keep for any period. Needless to say, all Chiefs and Petty Officers kept a bottle at least partially full of "neaters" for their own benefit and occasionally for the benefit of others.

Incidentally, to be accurate the term "grog" should only really apply to the mixture of rum and water since this dilution was introduced by Admiral Vernon in 1740 and his nickname was Old Grog from his habit of wearing grogram breeches.

The paperwork of accounting for the rum was complex, too, and woe betide any officer responsible for the rum if a sudden audit caught him with too much or too little stock as against his books. Too much indicated that he was diddling the crew of their rights and about to sell the surplus and too little signified that he had already done do. A real Catch-22 situation.

In fact the only way to keep the books straight was to rectify the figures every time a barrel was opened. It must have been a nightmare in battleships and cruisers — I was never involved — since it was bad enough in a frigate.

The rum came to the ship in barrels containing about ten gallons and having the exact quantity carved in the end of the barrel, i.e. ten and five-eighths gallons. Roughly every seven days a barrel had to be broached and using a rum pump and one gallon measure the first ten gallons was withdrawn and decanted into basket-covered stone one gallon jars. The remainder was then extracted and carefully measured with the aid of the set of copper measures provided.

It never, ever came to the stated quantity. It was always less.

But there was a let-out. It was known that some rum escaped from the barrel with time and there was an "allowance for seepage". There was a further allowance for losses incurred in issuing the rum known as "spillage". Juggling with these two allowances the paper quantity could be made to agree with the actual quantity and all could be made well.

One thing was impossible, and that was strict honesty. However hard you tried you always ended up with too much or too little and only recourses to fiddling the amounts for "spillage" and "seepage" could restore your accounts to pristine rectitude.

Returning to the question of "Splicing the mainbrace", further complications ensued. By regulation this could be undertaken only at the order of the monarch or after sinking an enemy warship and consisted of issuing a full tot of rum for *every officer and man on board excluding those under age*. Those who were registered as "T" were supposed to drink their tot or throw it over the side. (Some hope!) No financial alternative existed. It is only at splicing the mainbrace that officers ever receive an issue of rum.

Going back to the occasion of the sinking of the submarine by *Hastings*, it should be realised that approximately half our crew were under age. The ordinary rum issue had taken place in the forenoon as usual and at supper time the mainbrace had been spliced when those under age had certainly had "sippers" of not an equal share. Then came the Group Commander's second signal so that what amounted to a third issue of rum was made that evening.

As has been said before, it was good for morale but the general state of the ship's company — especially the younger ones — was hardly sober that evening.

As for myself I had managed, as Rum Officer, to have a crafty tot while "testing for salt" at each issue and then was able to go to the wardroom and have my official mainbrace tot as well. So I certainly was feeling no pain by then.

The term "splice the mainbrace" goes back of course to the old sailing ship navy, when this task was a particularly arduous one, on the completion of which it was usual to reward the crew.

Incidentally, if anybody should think that this custom of issuing a tot of rum was likely to cause insobriety among the crew, I should mention that in the eighteenth century the daily issue was far greater. For example, during Admiral Anson's voyage of circumnavigation in 1740 to 1744 the daily issue was a half-pint of brandy or rum and a pint of wine *or* a gallon of beer for every man and there was no mention of anyone being registered as "T" or "U.A.".

"Testing for salt", which was mentioned above, was another delightful custom that merits explanation. According to the strict regulations, each time a rum barrel was emptied of its contents a handful of rock salt was to be inserted before the bung was replaced. This was to prevent anyone putting a pint or two of water into the barrel and rolling it around to draw the rum out of the wood and make an alcoholic beverage for their consumption.

The barrel was eventually returned to Naval Victualling Stores ashore, where supposedly it was washed out before being refilled with rum and re-issued to another ship. Since those lazy rascals in the Victualling Store might be less than careful in washing the barrel before refilling, it can be seen it behoved the prudent officer who was for ever zealous in guarding the well-being of his crew to test the rum from time to time — and certainly whenever a new barrel was broached — to ensure that no salt was adulterating the purity of the rum. Sometimes there was some doubt in the matter, and it then became necessary for the officer, the coxswain and the Petty Officer Storekeeper to make a second test to be absolutely sure that it was pure.

* * * *

The system of escorting the Atlantic convoys had also changed since 1941 when *Auricula* was involved. More escorts were available and these were formed into Escort Groups of six or more vessels which worked together as a team for considerable periods. They would also normally stay with a convoy all the way across the Atlantic, spend a few days in port on the American side and then bring an Eastbound convoy all the way back to the U.K. If necessary they would refuel at sea from an accompanying tanker and even occasionally re-stock with depth charges or other essential material. For the first half of 1943, *Moyola* and her group worked the North Atlantic route based in Londonderry and recuperating in St. John's, Newfoundland on the Western side. All the convoys were numbered and had a lettered prefix to indicate their route. "OG" for example meant "Outward Gibraltar" and "HG" was "Homeward Gibraltar". "HX" signified a convoy starting from Halifax (Nova Scotia) heading for the U.K. and occasionally a third letter "F" or

121

" S " was added to signify " Fast " or " Slow ". Sometimes convoys would merge and thus we will find later SL 139/MKS 30 which was convoy from Sierra Leone to the U.K. numbered 139 to which had been added a Mediterranean to the U.K. slow convoy.

Occasionally a special convoy would be put together which might receive a codeword instead of a descriptive number.

Throughout the war the fight between the U-boats and the escorts oscillated to and fro with the initiative changing from side to side. Actually Germany started the war some years too early for the German Navy, and initially she had very few U-boats in operation and long distances to traverse from German harbours to reach the operational area of the Atlantic. Fortunately for them we suffered from a great shortage of escorts and lacked skill in U-boat hunting.

The Norwegian campaign provided forward bases for U-boats in Norway and very soon after the conquest of France gave them the bases in the Bay of Biscay which brought in the first " Happy Hunting " period from September 1940 to the end of 1941. Few of our ships had radar (R.D.F. as it was called then), and those that did have had only a somewhat primitive and unreliable type. This meant that at night the U-boats could operate on their diesel engines with just their conning towers awash and gain the advantage of higher speed.

The revolving aerial scanner radar began to be introduced in 1941 and by mid 1942 was to be found in every convoy escort, making operating on the surface unsafe, and forcing the U-boats under water when attacking.

The U-boats for their part commenced operating further and further West which in turn was countered by our providing escorts all the way across the Atlantic and the Caribbean, as well as all the way to Freetown and further South.

On shore the Admiralty established high frequency direction finding stations which could pinpoint U-boars with remarkable accuracy and could issue warnings to Escort Groups, estimating the number of U-boats thought to be in contact and the positions of those ahead which might be avoided. By 1943 the larger escorts were fitted with their own High Frequency Direction Finders (generally nicknamed Huff Duff) and the ahead firing weapon for attacking submarines named " Hedgehog " (*Moyola* carried both these items). This was even later superseded by a more effective weapon called LIMBO.

ASDIC sets were much improved and techniques for U-boat hunting were improved and developed, especially by the famous Captain Walker.

On the other side, the Germans developed a homing torpedo which could direct itself into the propeller noise of a hunting escort and we had to find an antidote to that, too. It was a continuous ding-dong battle, and meanwhile the losses of merchant ships mounted.

The major overall statistical turning point of the war was when the combined monthly production of merchant ship tonnage by the Allies finally exceeded the tonnage being sank by U-boats but for us, at sea, it was when the escorting of a convoy changed from being a defensive operation to an offensive one, where the convoy was routed towards the biggest concentration of U-boats (rather than away) and the objective changed from defending merchant ships to sinking U-boats.

This happened to us with convoy SL 139/MKS 30.

However, before we get to that particular episode in November 1943, other incidents were to occur.

Returning eastwards, it was normal to go very far North to skirt the edge of the icepack if possible, and sometimes, on leaving St John's, we would steer North-North-West for a few days until we came to the icepack, and then turn to the Eastward, completing the final few days by steaming South and coming down the West Scottish coast inside the Hebrides.

Our watch-keeping system was to have two officers on watch at night and, in good conditions, only one on during the daylight hours, for as in many ships, we followed Merchant Navy practice of keeping standing watches. Thus, for some two years, I found myself on the middle watch (midnight to four a.m.) every night, and with every other afternoon watch (midday to four p.m.). The big advantage of keeping these somewhat horrendous hours was that one was seldom disturbed, as others (including the Captain) normally slept at these times.

In *Moyola* we managed to adopt a routine during the middle watch, which both added to our material comfort and helped to pass the time, and in this we were aided and abetted by the young Canadian engineer officers under training whom we were carrying at that time. David and I kept the middle watch on the bridge, while Chuck, one of the Canadian engineer officers, kept watch in the engine room, although part of his duties included examining hatches and electric ventilation fans outside the engine room, and a visit to the bridge to see how the other half lived.

Our middle watch was highly organised. As soon as we had taken over and things had settled down, we broached some coffee from a thermos flask filled at dinner the previous evening. This was "improved" with a small addition of rum, for it was not to no purpose that I attended the traditional rum issue each forenoon. At 2 a.m. Chuck would arrive on the bridge carrying three large potatoes (which had been perfectly cooked in their jackets by placing them on the top of the main steam condenser in the engine room for an hour or more), while we produced a packet of salt and a packet of butter, and simultaneously the bridge messenger arrived with three mugs and a steaming jug of Bovril. This was the moment for David to make his contribution to the proceedings, which was a travelling flask filled with sufficient dry sherry to improve, vastly, the three mugs of Bovril.

Connoisseurs of food and drink may prattle on about caviar and champagne, graven lokks and aquavit, stilton and port, or other famous delicacies, but I can assure you that in mid-Atlantic, in the middle of the night on an open bridge, "baked buttered potato and Shovril" take a great deal of beating.

On one occasion, however, disaster struck. Our midnight feast was interrupted by a report from the sonar operator: "Echo bearing two seven zero. One thousand eight hundred yards. Believed submarine."

With practice borne of several years' experience, we coped with the situation automatically. The ship was pointed at the echo; we listened to the sharp ping and confirmed the operator's opinion; the guns crew was alerted; the depth charges were set; the Captain was called, and finally the alarm bells for action stations were sounded.

In a few minutes David and I were relieved and went to our action stations. Chuck had returned to the engine room, and for the next sixty-odd minutes we endeavoured — without success — to destroy the U-boat, falling some miles behind the convoy but, at least, preventing his making an attack.

Eventually we were recalled to our station astern of the convoy by the senior officer of the escort, and on standing down from action stations, David and I returned to the bridge to take over our watch

124

again. We found the Captain, the navigator and the First Lieutenant all complaining bitterly as they continually slithered around the compass platform.

We professed ignorance of the cause, and tried to claim that we did not find it at all slippery, but once they had left, we had quite a task getting the deck scrubbed silently during the remaining hour of the watch without disclosing our activity to the Captain in his sea cabin directly below.

More importantly than that, however, we bemoaned, bitterly, the loss of our buttered potatoes and "Shovril", which had been scattered around the bridge in the excitement of going to action stations.

But the next night they were doubly delicious.

* * * *

Apart from being designated "Torpedo Officer" (without any special training or experience), which included bearing responsibility for the depth charges and their gear in the stern and the hedgehog and its gear at the bows (necessitating some pretty sharp sprinting at times) as well as the electrical equipment in the ship, I was also given the hilarious task of Submarine Boarding Officer.

Even these days I am sometimes accused of being a trifle piratical and it may have been some sign of this in those days that resulted in my being selected for this task.

Every escort group was required to have a Submarine Boarding Party trained and ready for action in the hopes of capturing yet another U-boat.

On August 27th, 1941, the Royal Navy had managed to capture a complete German submarine — U.570. She was subsequently refitted and commissioned into the Royal Navy as HMS Graph and did some yeoman service before she was wrecked on Islay on March 20th, 1944. She was salved but was scrapped in 1947.

There were some fringe benefits from this capture. Firstly, the capture of some code books and codes and a number of rotors for an ENIGMA machine. (Presumably there was an ENIGMA machine on board but there was already one in operation at Bletchley Park.)

Secondly, the discovery of the capabilities of German submarines which we had innocently believed to be similar to our own. For example, as late as January 1941 officers on ASDIC courses were told: "Never use the five hundred foot setting on any depth charge as no submarine can go nearly that deep". After the capture of the U.570, the story was altered and the depth charge pistol was introduced which took charges down to — if I remember rightly — some fifteen hundred feet, and it may have been more. The capture had shown that U-boats *normally* went to nine hundred feet and could go even further. Presumably newer U-boats would go even deeper than that.

Thirdly, we obtained a U-boat which it was possible to operate under the White Ensign — perhaps someone else will write that story one day.

Finally, the capture provided the knowledge necessary to train Submarine Boarding Parties. Today it is hard to believe that such a task could be seriously considered as an objective meriting regular training and planning, but it was.

After the passage of over forty years, it is difficult to remember exactly when the party was formed, but I feel that it cannot have been in existence when we went to do our stint at Tobermory under "Monkey" Stephenson, for I am sure he would have delighted in evolving some hair-raising exercises for us, but I certainly remember our early training in a warehouse in Greenock.

In this warehouse there had been built a full-size replica of a U-boat's control room, engine room and the accommodation section forward of the control room, together with the complete conning tower above the mid-ship section of outer hull and the deck.

We spent a considerable time touring this complex and endeavouring to remember where everything was before practising boarding many times, finally doing it in complete darkness wearing gas masks.

The various valves in the control room did, in fact, open and shut and we were required to locate the correct valves and close them during the exercise, as well as doing many other things, as will be seen. Then the lights would be put on and the "wash-up" begin. Gradually we reached some measure of success.

Let us look at the general plan and the composition of the Boarding Party.

First the composition, including the gear carried and duties to be performed.

Rank/Rating	Armed With	Gear Carried
1. Sub Lieut RNR	Automatic pistol Lead cosh	Tin helmet Gas mask Plastic grenade Safe-blowing charge Life jacket Torch Mills bomb

Duties to be performed:

Gain access to control room
Subdue enemy crew
Close vents (forward)
Organise closing of Kingston valves
Blow Captain's safe
Evacuate code books, etc
Prepare for towing
Disarm crew
Take command under tow

Rank/Rating	Armed With	Gear Carried

2. Petty Officer	Lanchester carbine
	Lead cosh
		Tin Helmet
		Gas mask
		Life jacket
		4 x 50 round
		    Lanchester
		    magazines
		20 ft. short-link chain
		    with snap hook
		Torch
		Plastic grenade
		Mills bomb

Duties to be performed:

Assist officer in charge
Provide and secure chain
Gain access to control room
Close vents aft
Assist in reminder

127

Rank/Rating	Armed With	Gear Carried
3. Signalman	.45 Revolver Lead cosh	Tin helmet Gas mask Life jacket Aldis lamp & battery Heaving line G.P.O. mail bag

Duties to be performed:

Communicate with ship
Evacuate code books

Rank/Rating	Armed With	Gear Carried
4. ERA or Stoker P.O.	.45 Revolver Lead cosh	Tin helmet Gas mask Life jacket Valve wrench Large Stillson Torch

Duties to be performed:

Operate valves to blow all tanks as necessary
Deal with valves from which wheels had been removed

Rank/Rating	Armed With	Gear Carried

5. Seaman	Lanchester
	Lead cosh
		Tin helmet
		Gas mask
		Life jacket
		4 x 50 round
		  Lanchester
		  magazines
		Torch
		Mills bomb

Duties to be performed:

Assist in subduing crew and other duties as necessary

6. Seaman — as above

7. Seaman — Coxwain and crew of pulling whaler, all armed with revolvers, rifles or Lanchesters.

It can be imagined that it was advisable to take care when getting from the boat onto the submarine, as swimming with all this gear was not going to be easy.

All the special gear required was kept in a locker from which it could easily and quickly be carried to the whaler in the event of exercises or a real operation. All the members of the Boarding Party were volunteers and, in fact, one of the Seamen was a steward who had very keenly volunteered for the Navy long before he was conscripted and who had been "conned" by an unscrupulous recruiting officer into becoming a steward. He was the first in the whole ship's company to volunteer, was easily the keenest and was very proud of his unique position.

Now, the drill for this operation.

Firstly, one assumed that the U-boat had broken surface after hull damage or severe depth charging and that her conning tower hatch would immediately open and disgorge her crew, eager to abandon ship and surrender. Possibly scuttling charges had been laid and fuses lit while probably many vent valves had also been opened.

The frigate was supposed to approach at full speed and endeavour to deter the crew from coming out of the U-boat with Oerlikon fire while the whaler was being lowered with the boarding party embarked. As the whaler neared the U-boat, the frigate would cease firing and the "anti-abandon-U-boat-fire" would be taken over by those in the whaler. Once alongside the U-boat, the Boarding Party was to board in numerical order, force their way to the conning tower and drop a plastic grenade (possibly two) down the hatch.

These grenades, made of Bakelite, had no killing power but they were *supposed* to frighten any enemy crew members still in the control room into retreating forward or aft beyond a water-tight bulkhead, thus giving time for one or two members of the Boarding Party to enter the control room unmolested.

It was also supposed to persuade them to disarm any scuttling charges that had been set, since these would ensure their own death now that they could no longer abandon ship.

It was a nice theory anyway.

We were even told that these plastic grenades were not even

129

designed to kill anyone. For this reason our party carried Mills bombs as well, which could and did.

Having subdued the crew below by dropping the Bakelite grenade (or Mills bomb), the Boarding Officer climbed down the conning tower through the upper hatch but not through the lower one. At this point, the Petty Officer lowered one end of his chain down as far as the lower hatch while the Boarding Officer knelt down, reached through the lower hatch and snapped the snap hook on to the top rung of the ladder below, calling up to the Petty Officer to haul taught and secure. This sophisticated move was designed to stop any nasty enemy crew members from closing both hatches and submerging the U-boat with the Boarding Party on board!

The Petty Officer then descended to the lower hatch, and after a short prayer, the Boarding Officer and he descended into the control room.

I am sure most readers can realise that if any U-boat crew members were still below and were not cowed by the bang of the Bakelite grenade, they might well take steps to prevent the entry of foreigners, quite apart from the fact that they were probably keen to abandon ship up the conning tower hatch while we were coming down. It is also fairly obvious that when climbing down the hatch into the control room, all of one's body would be visible and vulnerable for several seconds before one's head entered the compartment, when one *might* be able to take the odd pot shot at the enemy. Quite how you take a pot shot while climbing down a ladder encumbered with a gas mask, life belt, tin hat, safe blowing charges and lead cosh I am still not quite sure, but this again was the theory of the operation which it was not for us to question.

Working on the principle that it will be all right on the night, we can ignore all these possible difficulties and consider the next necessary moves.

When the Boarding Officer and Petty Officer had established themselves in the control room, the ERA and one seaman followed them down. If any enemy crew remained, they were already (?) either forward or aft of the control room, and it was assumed they would not interfere further. The Boarding Officer and the Petty Officer and the ERA then worked in unison to close all the ballast tank vents and to blow all tanks, including those emergency tanks known as "Q's".

If reasonably confident that the U-boat would stay afloat for a few minutes, the Boarding Officer then entered the Captain's cabin (just beyond the forward bulkhead of the control room), placed the safe-blowing charge on the safe and ignited the ten-second fuse. He retreated to the control room while this went off and returned to collect the contents of the safe, code books, etc. which were passed back to the control room. By this time, the Signalman should have lowered the G.P.O. mail bag down the conning tower hatch on the end of his heaving line and the books would be hauled up to the upper conning tower and then lowered outboard down to the whaler's crew alongside.

At this stage the main mission was considered accomplished.

However, if the U-boat was not showing violent signs of sinking, there were some more options to be carried out.

Firstly, the Kingston valves in the bottom of all the ballast tanks, which normally remain permanently open, could be closed. I remember this was done with a T-spanner (stowed in clips on the forward bulkhead of the control room) which fitted square valve spindles recessed into the control room deck. Once this was done, it was difficult (if not impossible) to flood the ballast tanks. After this the U-boat's own emergency towing hawser was made ready and signals made to the frigate to prepare to take in tow.

If all went well, another U-boat would shortly fly the White Ensign.

Every time we were in port with all the crew on board for a day or two, the Submarine Boarding Party would muster and proceed to the warehouse for another practice run. On one winter's day, the transport failed to arrive and we boarded a corporation bus for the journey, complete with all our arms and gear. It raised a few eyebrows, but not too many. The public was fairly blasé about unusual things in those days.

Once, after a day's exercise at sea with a Netherlands Navy submarine, our Captain decided to send us off to capture her as she surfaced at the end of the day. I like to think we did it rather well, but the Dutch Captain was somewhat surprised when we all clattered aboard in a very aggressive manner, as he had not been warned that the boarding exercise was to take place. He even gave me a gin before we disembarked.

After all this arduous training the nearest thing we got to putting it into practice was to be called away in earnest as *Moyola* increased to full speed to approach a submarine brought·to the surface by another escort.

We manned the whaler clutching our numerous items of gear with not inconsiderable trepidation and awaited the slowing of the ship and the subsequent order to lower the boat.

I had not before believed a lot in the power of prayer, especially prayers made by my piratical boarding party, but I was convinced of its efficacy when the call came down from the bridge, "Secure Submarine Boarding Party. Return gear and secure seaboat".

It transpired that the submarine had disappeared beneath the waves before we even got within several miles but that did not prevent some of the boarding party bemoaning our aborted venture in loud voices once their blood pressure returned to normal.

Our sojourns in St John's, Newfoundland were usually enlivened by some inter-ship visiting and occasional forays to the officers club in the upper storey of a warehouse entitled "The Crows Nest". We also purchased various items ashore which were in short supplt in the U.K. and made useful "ground bait". My memory is of purchasing Chanel 5 and silk stockings in almost wholesale quantities. Taking home the latter had a selfish motive for the donating of these items of apparel were always contingent on receiving old laddered ones in exchange since these worn next to the skin under thick woollen sea boot stockings were very effective heat insulators, although we did get some queer looks before explaining the reasons for what appeared to be a kinky habit. Nylon stockings were as yet a thing of the future as fas as I can recall.

On one occasion it was decided to hold an Escort Group party on board the Group Commander's ship which, being an ex-US Coast Guard cutter, had a large and palatial wardroom suitable for the event.

All ships in the group were berthed in the Naval Base on the seaward side of the harbour to which civilians were not allowed admission. It was arranged, therefore, for all ships' motor boats to ferry the female guests across the harbour to circumvent the regulation.

One sloop was commanded by one of that delightful band of Naval officers whose fame had spread far and wide and who proved such a tower of strength between 1939 and 1945 despite having been somewhat shabbily treated during the inter-war period. They

132

belonged to that age group who were cadets at the Royal Naval College, Dartmouth in 1914 and who were all sent to sea as Midshipmen on the outbreak of war — often in old vessels commissioning from reserve — and some were as young as fifteen. In 1919 the Lords of the Admiralty decided that their education had been cut short by the war and arranged for them all to go to Oxford or Cambridge, where their exploits are talked about to this day. Then in the late nineteen-twenties the greater part was tossed out of the Navy, under the infamous "Geddes Axe", into a depressed environment where jobs were difficult to find in any case, and naval officers unqualified in anything but naval warfare were a drug on the market.

However they all came back in 1939, and their experience and training proved invaluable once more. For the most part they were a wild bunch, brought up in wardrooms where a pound would buy two hundred and forty glasses of gin and only rich people drank whisky because you only got one hundred and sixty glasses of that for the same amount. The captain of the sloop in question also had another great claim to fame, which was engraved on a small silver-plated cup on his day cabin mantelpiece. It read:

H.M. Prison Wormwood Scrubs
1937 Sports
FIRST PRIZE
HIGH JUMP

Apparently the husband came home unexpectedly and during the struggle that followed had fallen down the stairs and broken his neck which resulted in a verdict of manslaughter and a sojourn in "The Scrubs" for the visitor.

On the day of the party he had entertained continuously in his day cabin throughout the midday drinking period and the afternoon and he had a most entertaining fund of stories and reminiscences.

Guests were due to be ferried across the harbour from six o'clock onwards, and at about this time the gallant Captain decided to venture across the harbour in his "skimming dish" (a small high-speed motor boat carried principally for the Captain's use) to acquire for his own entertainment a small selection of female guests. Two or three were as many as the boat could accommodate in addition to himself and the one-man crew.

Setting off across the harbour at high speed in the direction of a bunch of guests, all might have been well had not the Captain sighted what appeared to be a choice selection at a different jetty. He shouted to the coxswain, who failed to hear him above the engine noise, so he attempted to climb around the little shelter behind which he was standing to tap the crewman on the shoulder and redirect him. Somehow he missed his footing and fell into the harbour, but by luck managed to catch hold of a rope as he fell. His eighteen-odd stone acted as a sea anchor and reduced the little motor boat's speed instantaneously to about three knots. These boats were notoriously unreliable, so that the coxswain suspected nothing other than some form of engine failure and swearing furiously he jiggled with accelerator and choke and prayed that at least the engine would not stop while in mid-harbour. The Captain's cries for help as he was towed along behind half under water were drowned by the engine noise until they arrived at the jetty and the coxswain slowed the engine to idling speed and stood up to salute as his Captain disembarked. It was only then that he found that the Captain was no longer in the stern and his voice could be heard from the water directing in choice words his future recovery. Sadly there was no-one on the jetty to render assistance and the coxswain was well aware that he lacked the strength to lift aboard an eighteen stone man in wet clothes even if he was the Captain, so he found some more rope, put a lashing round him and towed him back across the harbour to his ship where sufficient manpower was available to extricate him from the water.

In less than twenty minutes the Captain, wrapped in several towels, was entertaining all comers (and especially some wide-eyed female guests) to strong beverage and salty stories and was in no way the worse for his immersion in the ice-cold harbour which would probably have killed off a lesser man or certainly one with less alcohol in his system.

One peculiar — and frightening — incident occurred during one middle watch when *Moyola* was stationed to the north of a west-bound convoy. The ASDIC operator reported an odd noise on the starboard bow and this could be heard on the bridge loudspeaker sounding like a giant glass of Eno's Fruit Salts fizzing in a glass with some occasional animal-like squeaks. It was a dark moonlight night and nothing could be seen on the bearing with or without binoculars. The radar likewise reported nothing and everyone was mystified. Just as calling the Captain was being considered, the starboard lookout yelled "Jesus Christ!" and this somewhat unorthodox report caused me to look up from where I had been listening to the bridge ASDIC loudspeaker and observe an iceberg reaching well above eye level on the starboard bow. Looking up to the top at an angle of about thirty degrees above the horizontal meant that it was either a very large iceberg, or it was very close, or both.

"Hard-a-port" followed an agonising few seconds later by the somewhat astonished helmsman's reply from the wheelhouse below "Wheel's hard-a-port, sir" then gradually at first and later more quickly the berg drew aft on the starboard side. We waited anxiously for the sound of our hull striking the extended underwater portion of the berg, but by a miracle it never came.

The Captain came on the bridge demanding to know what was going on and an explanation was given as far as was possible. The failure of the radar to give any indication of its presence was found to be due to the face of the berg sloping away and providing a poor reflecting surface while the noises heard on the ASDIC were later described by a message from the Admiralty to warn other ships of the danger inherent in such sounds.

After the war I recall reading that U.S. Coast Guard cutters on iceberg patrol used to fire harpoon-mounted radar reflectors into the bergs to make them visible on radar.

Apart from *Hastings'* success with a U-boat early on and a near brush with a wolf-pack when bringing back HX 299A, we seemed to have little trouble with the enemy despite having only six escorts to cover between sixty and a hundred merchant ships. We did lose a few by ice due to being routed North-North-West from St John's until we met the ice.

In July 1943, for reasons quite beyond our comprehension, the powers-that-be decided to take us off North Atlantic convoy work and away from the Escort Group 40 and send us down to join the Freetown Escort Force — not a prospect that appealed to those of us who had been based before in that outpost of the Empire so devoid of charm.

For the passage out we were to be part of the escort of a miniature fast convoy that was designated by the codeword "FAITH" and consisting of three merchant ships only. They were SS *California* and SS *Duchess of York*, two North Atlantic passenger ships of around seventeen thousand tons each, carrying together about fifteen hundred mixed service personnel and a number of civilians, including thirty-five women. Also in the convoy was the Port Line cargo ship *SS Port Fairy*.

They were routed South somewhat nearer to the Iberian Peninsular than was usual, keeping approximately to longitude 15° West and proceeding at the relatively high speed of sixteen knots.

At a time when convoys of eighty to one hundred ships would normally be escorted by a single escort of five or six Naval vessels, the escort of this mini-convoy was unusually strong, comprising *Moyola* and the "between the wars" destroyer-leader *Douglas*, supported, for the first part of the trip, by the Canadian Tribal Class destroyer *Iroquois*, which was to return to Plymouth when the convoy reached latitude 40° N.

In the pleasant summer weather the convoy made good time Southwards in smooth seas. After years of haphazardly and slowly zig-zagging to and fro, shepherding large convoys struggling to maintain six knots, it was quite exhilarating to be one of six ships keeping accurate station at sixteen knots and following one of the regular zig-zag patterns that would make all turn together perhaps sixty degrees to starboard with the precision of a guards regiment on the parade ground at Aldershot.

All went well and without incident until we neared the position where *Iroquois* would return Northwards and leave us to continue on our way to Sierra Leone. After the boisterous weather of the North Atlantic which we — in *Moyola* — had been enduring for the previous six months, the Mediterranean-like conditions of calm seas and warm nights were a pleasant change, but the peace was shattered somewhat unexpectedly in the early part of the first watch on the evening of July 12th, only four days after sailing from the Clyde.

Three high-flying aircraft were observed approaching, mere specks way beyond the vertical range of our somewhat agricultural 4-inch guns. (Experts later established their altitude at around twenty thousand feet). We watched — there was not much else we could do — and went to anti-aircraft action stations. Normally my action station was on the quarter deck looking after the eight depth charge throwers and two rails of depth charges manned by a crew of some thirty-five men — reloading in those days was a pretty manual affair — but with depth charges being unsuitable as anti-aircraft missiles, my station changed to being Officer-of-Quarters of *Moyola*'s after 4-inch gun.

136

We expected the aircraft to follow the usual Focke-Wulf Condor method of attack which was to come in low over the sea and drop bombs from little over mast head height, usually approaching merchant ships from bow or stern to provide the biggest target. It was thus to our considerable surprise that the first stick of bombs descended from twenty thousand feet odd, and straddled the *California*. A few minutes later another stick arrived throwing up great plumes of water on each side of *Duchess of York* and accompanied by an audible report and a puff of smoke, signifying a hit amidships. This sort of accuracy from this sort of altitude was not only miraculous, it was thoroughly offside and against the ground rules. Dive-bombers and torpedo bombers scored hits off ships, low-flying and shallow glide bombers sometimes managed also, but high-level bombing against ships was but a mess deck joke. It just was not fair.

By this time *Douglas*, *Iroquois* and ourselves were loosing off a long-range barrage towards the German planes which probably did not even succeed in spilling their coffee, but which improved our feelings and, hopefully, encouraged the folks on board the troop ships.

In the midst of this, a third stick brought up a raft of splashes fairly near *Port Fairy* without managing to achieve a hit.

Surprisingly, the clearest memory of the barrage our gun put up is the sight of one of the ward room stewards whose duty it was to carry the 4-inch shells from the top of the magazine hoist around to the gun and hand them to one of the loading numbers for subsequent insertion into the breech. The gun used fixed ammunition — that is, the shell and the cartridge case were fixed together like a very much enlarged rifle cartridge about thirty inches long and weighing some thirty pounds. Fitzgerald was a highly experienced steward with some fifteen years' experience in the Cunard Line before joining the Navy, and most of that time had been in the first class saloon of those incredibly luxurious trans-atlantic liners, some of this time as wine steward.

He carried those 4-inch shells with superb dignity, treating each one as of a prime vintage and mentioning the fuse setting as he handed it over in the same hushed tone as he no doubt used to indicate the year of the bottling. Nothing disturbed his equilibrium, the excitement made him move no faster, nor did any thought of danger slow him up. Possibly his eyebrows rose a trifle at the rate at

Naval Message
S. 1320c.

50M Pads of 200
7-41-(1212-3)
N.S. 815-9-1320C

For use in Signal Department only	CALL SIGNS, DISTINGUISHING SIGNALS, SERVICE INSTRUCTIONS, ETC.

Sunday 11th Jany.   4

TO: FROM:

Text and Time of Origin.   (Write Across)   from Green 90. Ht. 10,000.
                                                              Speed ? 200.

2110 :	Attack commenced 41°20'N 15°26'W.	5 / 10
	First bombs dropped — direct hit on "Duchess	15
	of York". Engines crippled.	20
2112 :	2nd F/W Green 90° — bombs dropped.	25
	direct hit "California" — down by bows.	30
	3rd F/W circling.	35
2120.	3rd attack, near miss "Duchess of York"	40
	All 3 planes circling around	45
2140	4th attack Port Fairy — near miss.	50
2141.	Only one a/c forced.	55
2145.	a/c circling overhead. "Duchess of	60
	York" + "California" on fire.	65
		70
		75
2205.	"Swale" missed by bombs (5th attack)	80
		85
2220.	Alongside "Duchess of York".	90
		95
0145.	DY + PF located by Douglas	100

System or Wave Frequency	P.O. of Watch	Ldg. Hand of D.O.	Time Rec'd. in D.O.
Type of Code or P/L	Reader	Time of despatch	Time Rec'd. in Coding Office
Cabinet No.	Sender	Time of receipt	Date

Note made on a signal pad during the attack by MOYOLA'S Navigating Officer Lieutenant, Ken Clark, R.N.V.R.

138

which his servings were being consumed, but he kept them coming at a steady rate.

We kept the barrage going in the belief that this would prevent the aircraft coming any closer and improving their accuracy, but it soon became apparent that they did not need to come any closer.

A second run by each of the three aircraft (which again seemed to pick a ship apiece) produced hits on both *California* and *Duchess of York* and another near miss for *Port Fairy*. The two passenger ships were soon burning fiercely with columns of smoke betraying their position as the sun set, after which their bright fires lit up the scene like a Guy Fawkes night celebration.

The three aircraft continued to circle high above us, well out of range of our guns and watched warily by us until darkness fell, when they flew away and we began the sad and laborious task of picking up the survivors.

Despite the fires, *California* and *Duchess of York* lowered most of their boats and these were filled with motley crews of soldiers, airmen, merchant and Royal Navy personnel and civilians. We lowered our whaler and motor boat to pick up swimmers, of whom there were a few. Lying stopped, while boat after boat came alongside silhouetted against the burning ships was not a comfortable situation, and it was made no more comfortable by the wireless room reporting loud nearby transmissions that were by no means of Allied origin.

The boats came alongside our low after deck in a disorganised stream. I looked after the port side and the First Lieutenant the starboard. The boatloads of survivors were suffering from shock and, being fragmented and not from a single unit or crew, *esprit-de-corps* was non-existent and elementary discipline generally absent. Panic was not far away. Strong measures were necessary. When the first boat had arrived there had been a mad scramble for our deck before any painter had been made fast, forward or aft, and the scramblers gave no thought for the wounded or women in the boat. From then on, as each boat approached it was necessary to give short, sharp, clear orders and to back these up with the threat to shoot anyone who disobeyed, illustrating the seriousness of this intent by shining a torch on an automatic pistol held in the right hand.

The rather harsh system worked. There was no repetition of the first boat's panic.

After about a dozen boats had been brought alongside and their crews embarked, someone drew my attention to a small lamp flashing morse a short distance away. I answered with my torch and then read: "Request permission to come alongside", to which I had to reply: "Wait". Then a few minutes later when we had emptied yet another ship's lifeboat of women and wounded, I was able to make: "Come alongside".

Out of the darkness a boat approached, all the oars dipping the water in unison and the voice of a Petty Officer calling the stroke. When a short distance off we heard: "Bows. Two forward 'ands ship your oars and stand by with boat'ook and painter. Smartly now".

To our amazement the boat glided alongside in silence, the painters were passed up and made fast and still no-one moved in the boat. The Petty Officer made sure both painters were made fast and then turned to the only officer in the boat — a Surgeon Lieutenant RNVR — and reported: "Boat secured, sir. May I suggest you ask permission to go on board, sir?"

It was superbly done. It might have been a crew of ordinary seamen returning from an hour's instruction in boat pulling rather than the arrival of a bunch of survivors from a bombed ship. The doctor came on board, saluted and introduced himself before asking if he could be directed to the Sick Bay to give what assistance he could. The remainder embarked quietly and quickly under the detailed direction of the Petty Officer.

By about 2300 the supply of lifeboats dried up. Our own boats were rehoisted and with some relief we heard and felt the engines vibrating at a speed that indicated sixteen knots again. This felt a lot safer.

The word was passed that *Douglas* was about to torpedo the two blazing hulks and several dull explosions were heard, but they were still afloat and burning brightly as we steamed away.

Being on watch at midnight and having a little time to spare, I looked into the Sick Bay to ask if any help was required and the doc explained that deck space was a bit at a premium for the many wounded. Searching for space proved quite a problem since, in addition to our ship's company of one hundred and sixty, we now had over four hundred "passengers", including nine nuns, twenty-six other women and a considerable number of injured.

Going through the ship was like working one's way along a crowded underground, except that everyone was lying down — or trying to — wherever there was room in every compartment and in all the alleyways. In each mess I looked into I called "Any room for any injured here?", which was usually a silly question until in the Petty Officers mess the reply came, "There's a bit of space 'ere, sir, if we get rid of this stiffy".

Cursory examination revealed a swimmer who had not made it and who — in the fashion of the times — had been strapped into a stretcher which was see-sawed violently as the means of artificial respiration. Sadly it failed.

Two passing able-seamen were brought in to carry the stretcher along the crowded alleyways and up on deck to await burial. To reach the upper deck the best route was up an athwartships ladder — a difficult enough operation with the ship rolling in a quartering sea. It was not made any easier by the corpse suddenly sitting up in a most lifelike manner. The three-badge A.B. holding on to the stretcher pushed him roughly on to his back again with the admonition heard so often in peace-time drills, "Lie down, you're dead". A few minutes later we laid him out on the engine room casing and covered him over with a blanket. The irrepressible cockney three-badger arranged the blanket, saying under his breath, "I'll just tuck him up nice and cumfy. Cor blimey, some poor bugger's going to get a shock when he gives him a shake in the morning".

After that there was a middle watch to keep and then the problems of trying to find somewhere to sleep. My cabin (shared with the Gunnery Officer) was now occupied by six nuns which did not really leave space for me, let alone suitable sleeping accommodation.

Daylight brought other little problems like trying to count the survivors on board and endeavouring to feed a ship's company which had suddenly been increased fourfold. There is an old saying "there is nothing the Royal Navy cannot do", so we got on with it. A few extra hands were found to assist the Cook in the galley and a continuous process of cooking and feeding was commenced.

Iroquois had sped on to Casablanca at twenty-eight knots with some six hundred survivors on board, while *Douglas* and ourselves followed on at eighteen knots with over four hundred each. Our expected time of arrival was another twenty-four hours on. *Port*

141

Fairy (the only undamaged ship in the convoy) was now proceeding separately under the escort of *Swale* (a sister ship to *Moyola*) with a further sixty survivors from the other two ships.

As evening approached we wondered if the Focke-Wulfs would return to molest us and signals from the Admiralty warned us that this was likely. Submarine attack was always possible but fairly difficult while zig-zagging at eighteen knots, and an extra danger factor was introduced with the news that two German destroyers were in our area escorting a blockade runner into Bordeaux.

By good luck neither the Focke-Wulfs nor the destroyers found us, but the former found *Port Fairy* and this time they did not miss. She was set on fire and her steering gear became jammed so that *Swale* had to take off all the survivors and a tug had to be brought up to bring her to port.

A further problem beset us the following morning which from innocent beginnings almost proved as fatal as German bombs.

The day was sunny, and with our arrival in African latitudes, the temperature rose rapidly both on deck and (more importantly) in the over-crowded space below decks. Our " passengers " started coming on deck for fresh air, and with a fresh breeze and the sea on the port quarter, the majority chose the starboard side and, as the main deck became crowded, they climbed up onto the Oerlikon platforms, lower bridge and other parts of the superstructure.

Moyola was rolling gently in the quartering sea and making a steady eighteen knots to the accompanying thump of her two four-cylinder steam reciprocating engines. All seemed well. Our destination was only three hours away. The likelihood of air, submarine or destroyer attack — already small — diminished with each mile we steamed.

Walking the deck in the sunlight and endeavouring to answer in a reassuring manner the dozens of questions being asked by our " passengers ", it suddenly became apparent that our roll to starboard was bigger than our roll to port. Furthermore, it was developing a nasty sickening pause at the maximum starboard angle and — seemingly — a disinclination to roll back to port.

Suddenly it struck me. We were light on ammunition, becoming lighter by the minute on fuel and water, and now some four hundred persons, each weighing on average a hundred and fifty pounds, had gradually moved up and to starboard. Sixty thousand pounds — some thirty tons — unexpectedly being moved up and to one side

142

was more than the ship's stability was designed to accommodate.

We were getting into a state of loll. I had experienced the situation before in a smaller vessel in Arctic waters suffering from a build-up of ice on the mast and upper works. The situation was not yet very serious, but it was becoming worse by the moment and the rate of increase was difficult to forecast.

It took only a couple of minutes to reach the bridge and speak to the Captain, who quickly appreciated the situation. Minutes later our "passengers" were being persuaded to go below and, while protesting good-naturedly, they complied on the assurance that our destination was only a few hours away.

It was thus not without some relief, therefore, that we finally berthed alongside in Casablanca at midday and watched our four hundred guests go ashore — a dozen on stretchers, but most happy and smiling and glad to be back on dry land.

The six nuns gathered round me at the gangway and assured me that they would pray for me, while I assured them that I would not tell anyone that they had been in my cabin for not one, but two nights!

※　　※　　※　　※

We later heard that the bombs used so successfully on this occasion were fitted with radio-controlled fins by which means their direction could be controlled during flight. (The were codenamed FX 200). For this to be successful the plane had to maintain a steady course and speed for some minutes before releasing the bombs and for the period that the bombs were in flight. They were normally dropped from twenty thousand feet which — as we had discovered — was above the ceiling of most Naval anti-aircraft fire.

The bomb sight being used was obviously a great improvement over anything used heretofore and the results were spectacular. Quite evidently another of Hitler's much publicised "Secret Weapons". I have never really understood why more use was not made of this weapon by the Germans. It was certainly far more effective than the air-launched glider bomb — the HS 293 — which we encountered a few months afterwards.

Both these weapons would appear to be early examples of what are now called "smart bombs" and I distinctly recall that the feeling that they were less likely to miss than traditional simple shells or bombs gave us a nasty impression that this war business was getting to be unfair, a feeling that was not improved a few months later when the "Gnat" — a torpedo which homed in on a ship's propeller — was introduced.

As soon as all the survivors had been landed at Casablanca, *Moyola* and *Douglas* sailed to Gibraltar to pick up the Lamport & Holt passenger ship *Voltaire* of some fifteen thousand tons and escorted her back to Casablanca to embark the survivors of *California* and *Duchess of York* and take them on to Freetown, their original destination. (Extracts from War Diary are reproduced at Appendix B.)

The Captain, First Lieutenant and myself had all sampled the delights of Freetown before, and we did our best to cheer up the rest of the wardroom with tales of horror, absence of amusement and general disorganisation. In particular, we stressed that as new boys on the scene we would be sent to sea the moment we arrived on some damned-fool errand or other.

We duly arrived at Freetown at 2030 on July 25th and went alongside the oiler to refuel before going to our anchorage. At first I thought that a practical joke was being played by the Captain or First Lieutenant but, in due course, was persuaded that we really had been ordered to go alongside a repair ship and embark salvage gear and pumps and sail as soon as possible to go to the assistance of the Armed Merchant Cruiser *Asturias* which had been torpedoed some five hundred miles away.

Spending less than twelve hours in harbour, we embarked the gear during the night and, sailing at dawn, we reached *Asturias* at dawn the following morning (27th), and after a short exchange of signals went alongside and commenced transferring the salvage gear.

The sea was pretty calm and the conditions by no means dangerous, but even in the very low swell *Moyola* banged uncomfortably against the bigger ship's mountainous topsides. Each bang was greeted with an inward cheer from me (and a few others who had reasons for disliking Freetown) as it became rapidly obvious that more damage was being done to *Moyola* than could be repaired locally and any other port was likely to be an improvement. With a bit of luck, it would be back to the U.K. with the next homeward bound convoy.

In fact by the time we had completed the transfer of equipment the whole of *Moyola*'s bridge structure had been canted over to port about two feet and considerable damage done in way of the motor

144

boats davits and the skiffs davits, all of which were mounted in awkward exterior sponsons that always caused problems when going alongside, even in harbour.

We had to hang about to escort *Asturias* into Freetown but the "buzz" was already round the ship that we would soon be on our way home, and so it turned out. A few days later the news came that we were to be formed into an escort group with the senior officer in *Exe* (an identical twin to *Moyola* from the same shipbuilding yard), the other ships to be two pre-war town class sloops and two corvettes.

A few days later (in fact August 30th), this newly-formed group went to sea together for some training manoeuvres prior to taking a convoy back to the U.K. With amusements ashore for all the services being extremely limited or non-existent, all ships embarked parties of RAF officers and other ranks for a day trip with the Navy, which was to turn out a bit more exciting than they expected.

Around eleven in the morning, after various other exercises, the Escort Group Commander made the signal announcing that the next item on the agenda was to be "Officer of the Watch Manoeuvres", a sort of nautical square dance with the Officer of the Watch in command of each ship rather than the Captain. It was about as popular (and as useful) among experienced officers as parade ground drill is to soldiers nearing their pension. The Captain announced his intention of leaving me to get on with it and he and all the other officers (including our RAF guests) went below to do some drinking. I do not remember why I drew the short straw of being the Officer of the Watch, but there I was — lumbered.

Unfortunately the Escort Group Commander had not had much experience in handling a flotilla — especially a motley bunch consisting of three pairs of ships, each pair with a vastly different turning circle and rate of turn, or certainly he failed to appreciate the results of these facts.

The first few manoeuvres went off reasonably well, but resulted in the three pairs of ships being grossly out of their appointed positions *vis-à-vis* the others. By good fortune the only ship not out of position was ourselves, since at this point — by the rules of the game — we were technically "Guide-of-the-Fleet" and it was therefore incumbent on all other ships to get to the correct bearing and distance from us.

However, before enough time had elapsed for this to happen, the signal was made for all ships to make a ninety degree turn to port at the same time. This produced a situation similar to the famous *Victoria* and *Camperdown* incident of 1893, when the Admiral ordered a manoeuvre which was impossible to complete in safety, but everyone did as they were told and *Victoria* rammed *Camperdown* and sank her, with considerable loss of life.

In these situations, signals are transmitted by flag hoists and all ships, on sighting the signal, hoist an answering pennant "at the dip" (i.e. half way up) to show they have seen the signal. As soon as the signal has been understood in each ship, it hoists the answering pennant all the way up and finally, when the order is to be carried out, the senior officer hauls down his signal hoist and all ships lower their answering pennants and get on with doing whatever is ordered.

Looking around at the other five ships, all of which were a long way from their proper station, it was obvious to me that the ninety degree turn to port would be impossible to do without a collision until all ships were in their right position or nearly so.

Swearing madly at the impending shambles and realising the Catch 22 situation, I told the Yeoman of Signals *not* to hoist the answering pennant "close up" while we checked the order and prayed for time. Inevitably a signal lamp from *Exe* demanded "What is the delay?" and in desperation I ordered the answering pennant "close up", assuming that the senior officer would allow a little time before carrying out this — at present impossible — order. After all, it was hardly the right thing for me — a lowly Sub Lieutenant Royal Naval Reserve — to question the sanity of a Royal Navy Commander of considerable seniority and experience. Anyway, I could be wrong in my estimation of the situation and — just possibly — no collision would occur. There was no-one with whom I could discuss the situation and no time to do so anyway.

Before I had even time to take more bearings of the other ships to see if the situation was perhaps getting better, the flag hoist on *Exe* came fluttering down as our Yeoman bellowed "Executive, sir".

I gave the order "Port fifteen" to the helmsman and quickly took bearings of the ship most likely to hit us and then, mentally forecasting my court martial, countermanded the order and ordered "Hard-a-starboard. Full astern both engines". Next I dashed across the bridge and pressed the bell to call the Captain to the voicepipe, and as soon as his voice answered I said as cheerfully as possible, "Captain, sir, you had better come on the bridge. We are going to

146

have a collision in a couple of minutes. Permission to ring the alarm for all hands on deck and close the water-tight doors?"

"Yes, carry on Sub, I will be right up".

With ships at sea collisions take a lot longer to happen than with motor cars, even when you can see they are going to happen.

When the Captain arrived on the bridge — somewhat breathless about sixty seconds later — I pointed out the corvette, *Petunia*, heading towards us on our port side and said "Both engines are going full speed astern and the helm is hard-a-starboard. I cannot think of anything else to do".

"Nor can I", said the Captain, and we watched spellbound until a minute or so later the corvette's bow cut into the port side of our forecastle with an unpleasant noise of rending metal.

As *Petunia* approached, apparently intent upon cutting us in half, the figure of one of the aircraftmen "guests" was clearly visible standing right at the point of the bow, oblivious to the impending danger and enjoying the view of *Moyola*, which was rapidly getting nearer. Soon everyone on our deck was waving and shouting at him to get the hell out of it, but for an exasperatingly long time he waved back, cheerily thinking what a friendly crowd we must be. With a few seconds to spare he was finally persuaded to retreat from his position of temporary figurehead.

Fortunately, in the last few seconds before the collision, *Petunia*, with her helm hard-a-port, turned rapidly and struck our bow at a fine angle. Previous to that she had been heading for our midship point at right angles, and if she had struck us in that manner, we would inevitably have followed the fate of *Camperdown* with some loss of life.

From the bridge it was not possible to see how much damage had been done to *Moyola*, as the corvette's bows had entered us below the level of our forecastle under the flare of the bow. Maybe we were split open down to the waterline, or below, or maybe the damage was more limited.

Finally the report came back to the bridge that the damage was limited to a hole about three feet across leading into the Petty Officers Mess and some ten feet above the waterline, so that regaining the safety of Freetown Harbour represented no danger.

It transpired that when the alarm bells rang, the Petty Officers were just settling down to a cup of tea with the four RAF sergeants who were their guests. Doubtless a few bottles of "neaters" were also being produced in a generous show of hospitality. At the alarm, all the Petty Officers left abruptly, assuming it to be another exercise, and they omitted to inform their " guests " of the situation. The four sergeants decided that they had better stay where they were, pending further instructions and not wishing to get in the way.

About a minute later *Petunia*'s bow must have come through the ship's side plating and then through the plywood lining panels and was then withdrawn as she went astern, leaving a clear view of sea and sky through the newly-constructed " window " just above the bench where they were sitting.

The noise heard on the bridge was pretty horrendous, and I hate to imagine what it must have been like in the Petty Officers Mess, but the four sergeants were still sitting, drinking their tea and rum, unperturbed when the astonished Damage Control Officer, searching the ship from inboard for the damage, opened the door to the mess.

" Jesus Christ on crutches, what in God's name are you doing here? " he exploded.

" Well, sir, we was just having a cuppa when all the P.O.'s left to do some sort of exercise. They didn't say nothing, so we reckoned we should just stay put. "

Ignorance is sometimes a wonderful thing.

* * * *

On the way back into harbour I was feeling slightly glum. After all, justice is not always done and possibly some clever-dick lawyer would be able to prove at the court martial that I had caused the collision and I was not much cheered by a bespectacled RAF administrative officer saying to me in an excited schoolboy type of voice: " Well you know this sort of thing may happen to you chaps every day, but it was jolly exciting for us fellows ".

* * * *

Actually the two or three weeks we remained in Freetown were not so ghastly as I had expected. Firstly I was entertained ashore at the house of Frances Wright and her family, since she had been one of the survivors of the *Duchess of York*, returning to Freetown after being called to the bar. Her photo had been in the *Illustrated London News* the week before we sailed and from this she had been recognised on board. Secondly our Captain encountered an old ship-

. . . But the four sergeants were still sitting,
drinking their tea and rum. . .

mate of his who was in command of a passenger ship awaiting convoy to the U.K. whose passengers, in the main, consisted of Wrens who were being repatriated to the U.K. on account of becoming pregnant, which resulted in frequent references to " a slice off a cut loaf is never missed ".

Finally we made the homeward convoy with Convoy SL 136, arriving in the Clyde September 25th and went up river to Barclay Curle's shipyard to get our damage straightened out, which also took in a period in dry-dock and some leave for all on board in shifts.

While temporarily in command and lying in dry-dock, some visitors were brought to me in the wardroom one afternoon who enquired after the health and well-being of our storekeeper (actually a Leading Stores Assistant, technically). I advised them that he was in good health and currently at work on board, whereupon they identified themselves as police officers and announced their intention of removing the Leading Stores Assistant, since they held a warrant for his arrest on a charge of bigamy. Frankly this inoffensive little man seemed to be a very unlikely bigamist.

However, after getting over the surprise, I had to tell the visitors that they could not remove the man since they held no jurisdiction on board and it would be necessary to obtain a relief for him before he could be released. As is often the case with policemen, who seem to get exaggerated ideas of their powers, they were somewhat put out by my refusal to part with my Lothario — whom they regarded as theirs — and I even had to threaten them with forcible eviction by a party of seamen with fixed bayonets before they departed in high dudgeon. Fortunately, the local Naval Office in Charge (N.O.I.C. Glasgow) cheerfully supported my actions, saying " Quite right, my boy. Good God, if he has more than one wife to support, he has probably flogged half the stores aboard ".

A relief duly arrived a few days later and our sad little storekeeper was handed over to the police to serve a sentence somewhat more chaste than marriage, and surprisingly the police became good friends and entertained us ashore and were duly entertained on board.

On one occasion, after attending a police dance, we forgathered for a bit of drinking in the sergeant's house and in a short while consumed all the alcohol available. Some consideration was given to calling for a police car to go back to the ship for further supplies when one of the policemen remembered he had some booze nearer at hand. These supplies turned out to be six miniature bottles of John Haig and a full bottle of "white" whisky of a hundred and forty proof, straight from a distillery.

After the six small bottles had been consumed, together with half the larger bottle, it was admitted that all the bottles were evidence in a theft case due to come before the beak the following day. Following some hasty discussion, the six small bottles were filled with tea to which a teaspoonful of the "white" whisky had been added, and the larger bottle was topped up with tap water. All were duly returned to the Police Station, and I heard later that the thief had been sentenced to three months. Such is justice.

*   *   *   *

Our period under repair had provided an opportunity for us to be fitted with a new experimental weapon given the imaginative name of "Unicorn". Supposedly it was the answer to a problem in the anti-submarine war of sinking U-boats while they were on the surface. Contrary to what one sees in films, it is extremely difficult to damage the very strong pressure hull of a U-boat with shell fire, and ordinary shells ricochet off the water when aimed correctly at a portion of the hull below the surface. The only really effective wounding point was the base of the conning tower which was a very small target. Ramming was by now considered a poor method of damaging a U-boat as it usually damaged the escort as much as, or more than, the U-boat.

So some boffin devised the Unicorn, which was a single spigot mortar which fired a projectile similar to the Hedgehog but designed to continue its trajectory under water. In a conventional manner the weapon could be elevated and depressed and swivelled left and right to be aimed at the elusive U-boat provided it was within about three hundred yards.

Moyola was fitted with two of these weapons, one each side of the forward gun, for which two massive rivetted mounting sponsons were constructed by Barclay Curle's. Although ships by this time were part-welded and part-rivetted, the specification called for these sponsons to be entirely rivetted, and it was fascinating to watch the rivetting gangs at work. Believe it or not, the gang was actually paid for each rivet and consequently they worked at a furious rate.

Rivetting has now been entirely replaced by welding, but it was indeed fascinating to watch the work. Some rivetting was done with

151

a pneumatic rivetting hammer, but some for reasons of accessibility had to be hand-rivetted. The gang consisted of two hand-rivetters wielding special two-handed hammers rather smaller than a sledge hammer and with a head that was long and thin; they were assisted by a "holder-upper", who held a large hammer levered against the rivet head, a forgeman who heated the rivets in a portable blacksmith's forge, and one or more boys who wielded an empty baked beans tin nailed to a stick in one hand and a pair of tongs in the other.

When the team was ready to start, the forgeman had to be ready with a steady supply of rivets cooked to a bright red at the moment of despatch. Obviously the rivets varied in size according to the job, but generally were about half to three-quarters of an inch in diameter and about an inch and a half long.

The forgeman would pick up a rivet in his tongs and toss it to the boy, who caught it in his tin, picked it up with his tongs and threw it to the "holder-upper's" boy, who caught it in his tin; the "holder-upper" picked it up in his tongs, inserted it in the hole, clamped his big hammer behind it and tapped the steelwork with his tongs to show that he was ready. The two hand-rivetters then beat at the hot soft end of the rivet, swelling it out and knocking it up tight before it became cold and hard. Within a few seconds of finishing one they expected to see another red hot end poking through the next hole waiting to be beaten down, and they did not like to be kept waiting, for each rivet meant money. It was a really skilled team effort.

To revert to the Unicorn. With the refit completed we slipped down river to Greenock and embarked a motley crew of scientists and boffins for the great day of "Unicorn Trials". They were certainly more optimistic than the ships' officers.

Some form of target was towed by a motor launch in the more open part of the Firth of Clyde and the ship was manoeuvred for the correct approach. The starboard Unicorn fired once. There were then some agitated cries, the sound of banging and then the sound of another discharge. Again there were more cries and more banging. An enquiry from the bridge elicited the information that the Unicorn was being bent back into shape after each shot fired and that each aimer only managed one shot as he received a black eye from the weapon and was sent off to the Sick Bay for treatment.

After a few more attempts we returned to the pier at Greenock, the two Unicorns were unbolted and taken ashore, together with what ammunition remained, and we never saw or heard of them again.

The bespectacled boffins looked rather sheepish as they departed to seek fresh inspiration. Some months later we did receive some projectiles code named "Shark", which were about four feet long and were fired out of our 4-inch guns. They appeared to be practical, but we never had the opportunity to use one in anger and I never heard of anyone who did.

✳   ✳   ✳   ✳

We rejoined *Exe* (frigate), *Milford* (sloop), *Clarkia* and *Petunia* (corvettes) and the Indian sloop *Kistna*, now officially formed into the 40th Escort Group and commenced running convoys out to Gibraltar and back — a pleasanter route than the North Atlantic with warmer smoother waters for the most part in the Southern portion. We all painted XL on our funnels and made play of the pun. Gibraltar was quite a good run ashore, with shops fairly well stocked with "ground bait" and the best Spanish wine available at eighteen shillings a dozen (Federico Paternina Banda Azul, as I remember) and the best sherry at two pounds a case.

It was also possible to cross the border into Spain to visit the town of La Linea during the afternoons, provided one had a suit of civilian clothes — generally known as "dog-robbers" from the lack of elegance usually displayed.

La Linea had the air of a Wild West town, and there only seemed to be two trades, of which one was bar-keeping.

By chance I ran into "Dickie", whom I had last seen in Lagos involved in cutting out the Italian cargo ship. He was acting as Diplomatic Courier between Gibraltar and our Embassy in Madrid and went under the name of Captain Richards. In fact his main activity was arranging the safe transit of escaped prisoners-of-war who had managed to get into Spain and needed help to get to Gibraltar. While Spain was technically still neutral, she was still very much pro-German and provided "volunteers" to work in Germany or serve in the German police and armed forces. They provided the manpower for the "Blue Division" which fought on the Russian front and especially provided cavalry to face the Cossacks and other mounted Russian troops who were found to be more practical on the Steppes than tanks as they would "live off the land". Generally the country was not well "disposed" to British prisoners-of-war transiting their territory.

Dickie used to take me to La Linea regularly and he knew it well

153

and spoke Spanish like a Spaniard. On one occasion he suddenly said, "Let's go to another bar, old boy, those Falangists over there might recognise me and there are twenty thousand pesetas on my head in this country". This fact did not seem to inhibit his drinking forays into La Linea or his visits to the rather primitive bull-ring where one's admission ticket also entitled you to a bottle of red wine and where everyone in the audience appeared to be wildly drunk, resulting in some quite hilarious audience participation.

Dickie also introduced me to a very beautiful girl of aristocratic family who instructed me in many elaborate antics in appreciation of some suitable reward. I was further assured that the chance of catching any brand of Liverpool measles was extremely remote as another regular visitor to her modest household was the Surgeon Captain from the Naval Hospital on the Rock. Fortunately he was also a drinking crony of Dickie's and so it was possible always for me to receive advance notice of a visit by the good Doctor.

Reference was made earlier to the pinpointing of the turn in the Battle of the Atlantic from defensive to offensive, and authoritative historians and writers have placed this moment at various dates. For my four-pennyworth, I would put the date at November 21st, 1943 and the action surrounding Convoy SL 139/MKS 30, and will do my best to describe the affair as I remember it from the somewhat blinkered view of an officer of one ship whose action station was never on the bridge and thus one to whom information was limited. Memory is also blurred by the passage of over forty years.

Those who would like to read the more official contemporary accounts are referred to two Appendices in this book. Appendix C consists of a reproduction of the HOME COMMAND WAR DIARY for the days in question, and Appendix D THE ANTI-U-BOAT DIVISION, NAVAL STAFF ANALYSIS of this particular action which was not, in fact, completed until three months later. Copies of these papers have been made available by the Naval Historical Branch of the Ministry of Defence to which I am indebted.

It is interesting to note that the SL 139 (Sierra Leone homeward-bound convoy) joined up with MKS 30 (Mediterranean to U.K. — slow convoy) at noon on November 14th so that we sailed from Gibraltar on that auspicious date, November 13th.

The combined convoy consisted of sixty-seven ships (subsequently reduced to sixty-five) formed into fourteen columns each of four or five ships and escorted by the five ships of the 40th Escort Group —

in all a fairly normal convoy for 1943 in the Atlantic, being neither especially large or small.

Two days after forming up and while still on a course of due West to get out into the Atlantic, the convoy was found by a Focke-Wulf 200 "Condor" or Junkers 90 aircraft which were the types used by the Germans for convoy-spotting and for meteorological data gathering. This aircraft circled the convoy out of gunfire range for about half an hour and doubtless wirelessed back full details to German headquarters. The same drill was carried out the following day and consequent instructions sent to U-boats (and H.F.D.F. fixes on these U-boats' transmissions) soon showed that SL 139/MKS 30 was going to be in for a hot time.

During the course of the battle a total of twenty-one escort vessels were eventually involved and an estimated twenty-five U-boats, while air sorties amounted to seventy-eight, mainly by Liberators, Fortresses and Sunderlands. The efficiency at this stage of the war of our intelligence services with a combination of agents' reports, ENIGMA and other code and cypher-breaking and H.F.D.F. position-fixing was considerable. The resources in ships and aircraft were now adequate — but not over-plentiful — so that sufficient defence could be mustered for this convoy for it to be renamed "Striking Force 31" and for effort to be made to take the convoy through the greatest concentration of U-boats, rather than trying to avoid them.

A portion of the signal from Headquarters Coastal Command to 247 Group (given in full in Appendix C) is worth quoting here to show the sort of battle that was foreseen by those ashore at midday on November 18th at almost exactly the same time as *Exe* sighted a periscope and counter-attacked the first U-boat to make its presence felt.

"...SL 139 will be attacked tonight and again even more heavily night 19th November. Request you keep at least six Leigh-Light Wellingtons for night 19th Nov. Suggest you use maximum possible effort each night on patrols ahead and astern of convoy as present situation will more than likely develop into biggest U-boat battle we have ever had. Any outcome may have critical results on future Gibraltar convoys. Maximum possible daylight effort also first importance. This will be hard going for both air crews and ground personnel but the battle may well put paid to U-boat morale for some time to come. 19 Group will take on the battle on night 20th November."

Such was the view being taken of this developing convoy battle at Coastal Command Headquarters, and presumably much the same view was held in the office of Commander in Chief Western Approaches and the Admiralty in Whitehall.

NOVEMBER 18th

During the early hours of the morning, a Wellington attacked a U-boat some two hundred and seventy miles ahead of the convoy and shortly after dawn we were joined by a German shadowing aircraft for the third day running. This one (possibly with reliefs) stayed with us for some five hours and presumably was busy transmitting homing signals to bring all available U-boats to join the party.

At 1107 *Exe* obtained a good ASDIC contact and also sighted a periscope. She made an immediate depth charge attack and followed this with three more depth charge attacks and a hedgehog attack before obtaining a sample of oil and losing contact. By this time the convoy was beginning to overrun the area, but it was estimated that the U-boat was at least damaged and unlikely to make any attempt to attack.

At 1300 part of the 7th Escort Group — the first support group to join the convoy — hove in sight. This consisted of three modern Bird Class sloops all mounting six twin 4-inch guns, namely *Pheasant* (7th Escort Group Commander), *Crane* and *Chanticleer*.

The arrival of these additional escorts within two hours of the first U-boat making contact with the convoy certainly improved our morale. We knew we were going to be attacked but at least some reinforcements had arrived in time and we knew that more were on their way.

Chanticleer was ordered to sweep astern of the convoy in the hope of finding and despatching the U-boat already attacked by *Exe* and at 1415 she reporting sighting a U-boat which dived some twenty-five miles astern of the convoy. *Crane* was sent to assist.

The V.H.F. radio (called in those days T.B.S., standing for " Talk Between Ships ") told us that *Chanticleer* had picked up a good ASDIC contact and then sighted a periscope. On the bridge of *Moyola* I was keeping the afternoon watch and watching *Chanticleer* through binoculars with some personal interest, since I knew she was commanded by one Bobby Bristow, who hailed from my village and was one of that inimitable band of inter-war Naval officers felled by the Geddes Axe. Suddenly a great column of water appeared at her stern, followed in due course by the sound of an explosion on the ASDIC loudspeaker. The T.B.S. was soon alive with reports which informed us that *Chanticleer* had had her stern blown off with some considerable loss of life.

Our reinforcements had suddenly been reduced within a very short time of joining us. Two further escorts, *Foley* and *Garlies*, joined the screen during the afternoon and they and all subsequent support groups were placed under the orders of the 7th Escort Group Commander in *Pheasant*, who eventually formed an outer screen, leaving the 40th Escort Group to continue to form an inner screen around the convoy. Initially the extended screen was only three vessels, but this gradually increased with fresh arrivals.

Chanticleer was taken in tow by *Salveda*, the rescue tug with the convoy, and proceeded towards Punta Delgada, in the Azores, where she eventually arrived two days later but was declared a constructive loss.

NOVEMBER 19th

A Wellington F179 sweeping astern of the convoy, which was meanwhile plodding on Northwards at around seven knots, attacked a U-boat some fifty miles on the starboard quarter and was credited, in due course, with a "probable" kill.

Calgary and *Snowberry* steaming to join the convoy from the Northward sighted two U-boats on the surface, but one made off on the surface (at a speed in excess of that attainable by the corvettes) and the other dived and eluded them. They joined the outer screen during the forenoon, as did the 5th Escort Group consisting of *Nene*, *Tweed*, *Lunenburg* and *Edmundston*, with *Essington* of the 7th Escort Group in company. This brought the total of supporting escorts to nine vessels over and above 40th Escort Group's six ships.

A shadowing Focke-Wulf Condor appeared yet again, but this was finally chased off by one of the Flying Fortresses in the air escort.

In the early afternoon this or another Fortress sighted a U-boat some twenty-eight miles ahead on the convoy's starboard bow, but it dived before an attack could be made. The 7th Escort Group was sent to the position but found nothing and returned to the outer screen.

It was obviously not possible to remain at action stations for several days at a stretch, but in view of the circumstances prevailing we in *Moyola* did go to the extent of having two officers on watch in daylight as well as dark hours and increasing the number of exercises carried out by the guns crews and depth charge crews on the cruising watch.

The Germans had introduced the "Gnat" homing torpedo shortly before this convoy, which certainly inhibited attacking escorts and required "anti-Gnat" tactics to avoid being destroyed by them. The "Gnat" was a torpedo fired at random by a U-boat which would direct itself towards the propeller noise of an attacking escort and eventually explode on a proximity fuse. They could be defeated by steaming in excess of twenty-five knots, but this was a speed not attainable by sloops, frigates or corvettes and only by destroyers not yet converted to ocean escorts. Conversely, at speeds in excess of twenty-five knots, the ASDIC was virtually useless, so such speeds could only be used for getting to the U-boat's position. Speed had then to be reduced and reliance placed on the "Gnat" antidote, which had the code name "Foxer". This consisted of a system whereby two paravanes were towed astern of the escort, each working its way out onto the quarter by virtue of its aeroplane-like vanes. Then a device not unlike a small kitchen mangle was streamed down each paravane wire on a roller shackle. The water passage caused the "mangles" to rattle violently, which created two areas of noise some one hundred yards astern of the ship and about sixty yards apart, which caused the "Gnat" to circle them in a figure-of-eight pattern until it ran out of power. That was the system and the theory, and there was never any means of knowing that it was working. Mark you, if it did not work you knew soon enough because the stern would get blown off.

"Foxer" was only streamed when required and largely was the province of the quarter deck officer, which was me. Since *Moyola* did not have a power winch at the stern, the operation of streaming and recovery had to be carried out using the power unit of the anchor windlass on the forecastle with two and a half inch wire messengers running through a series of rollers all the way from the stern to the bow providing the link-up. Until we were able to acquire a portable telephone to communicate between the stern and the bow, signals had to be sent in daylight by hand and in the dark by hand-torch through two intermediaries, one on the after Oerlikon platform on

158

each side and one on each bridge wing, and sometimes the inherent delay could be fairly frightening. Recovering the paravanes, which weighed half a ton, in the dark consisted of passing the order to heave in and then peering over the stern with a torch to catch the first sight of the paravane approaching under water. On more than one occasion, by the time the message had arrived at the bow to cease heaving in, the paravane had clanged home on the stern fairlead and the wire between there and the anchor windlass was quiveringly taut.

As I recall, the " Gnat " was also reckoned to be inoperative at very slow speeds with the result that if there was one thing worse than streaming the " Foxer " at night, it was to stand in the stern at action stations knowing a submarine was in the vicinity and being able to feel by the ship's vibration that she was steaming at a critically dangerous speed.

However, back to the convoy. At 2100 *Milford* on the inner screen obtained an ASDIC contact and made an attack, but failing to regain contact she was ordered to resume her station.

Half an hour later *Nene* picked up a radar contact, which she illuminated with starshell some thirty miles ahead of the convoy, and reported a U-boat on the surface. She was joined by *Calgary*, *Snowberry* and *Watchman*. A number of attacks with depth charge and hedgehog were made and two explosions heard shortly after midnight. They then organised a searching sweep around the area.

Meanwhile, *Edmundston* obtained a radar contact on the port beam of the convoy and she made a number of attacks, finally assisted by *Tweed*. Eventually they had to give up the search shortly after midnight.

NOVEMBER 20th

While *Nene*, *Calgary* and *Snowberry* were carrying out their searching sweeping pattern, known by the code name " Observant ", *Nene* picked up yet another ASDIC contact now some sixteen miles ahead of the convoy. A depth charge pattern blew the U-boat (subsequently identified as U-536) to the surface, whereupon all ships opened fire and the crew started to abandon ship. Finally seventeen survivors, including the Captain, were recovered.

As can be imagined, all the conversations on T.B.S. regarding these incidents made pretty exciting listening to us as we kept watch on *Moyola*'s bridge.

159

For the non-technical it should be explained that the T.B.S. radio telephone was what is now referred to as VHF radio, which has very short range and therefore could be used freely during convoy work without it being possible for transmissions to be picked up by the enemy unless he was already so close for it to be unimportant.

There was still some excitement to come. Just as U-536 was actually sinking, *Pheasant* obtained an ASDIC contact close by which was probably *Nene*'s earlier contact. *Pheasant* attacked continuously for an hour, but finally lost contact. H.F.D.F. bearings obtained by escorts and reports from the Admiralty indicated the number of U-boats still in contact with the convoy astern and concentrating ahead of the convoy's track numbered about thirty, so there was still some fun to come although all was quiet from 0400 to 0940.

At this point a Liberator aircraft sighted a U-boat on the surface some twenty-five miles ahead of the convoy and *Tweed* and *Lunenburg* searched for it without success.

In the afternoon *Nene* and *Snowberry* attacked a contact out to port but had to give up after a couple of hours and regain their station.

As night began to fall, H.F.D.F. activity showed that we still had a number of U-boats gathered astern who would probably endeavour to attack during the night.

At 1925 *Essington* obtained a contact and in attacking with depth charges blew a U-boat to the surface, which subsequently disappeared. An underwater explosion was heard and both she and *Winchelsea* observed a quantity of oil on the surface.

As was expected, a number of U-boats were detected by H.F.D.F. creeping up each side of the convoy. The Germans did not seem to realise the importance of maintaining radio silence.

NOVEMBER 21st

However, all the faults were not on their side. *Nene* reported somewhat bitterly that she had twice been illuminated by Leigh-Light aircraft which considerably diminished her chances of catching a U-boat by surprise. *Pheasant* dropped one depth charge pattern on a contact ahead of the convoy but the rest annoyingly appeared and disappeared like will-o-the-wisps, although everyone knew there were plenty of real U-boats around.

However, between 0400 and 1000 *Foley* and *Crane* made

continuous attacks on an elusive U-boat which released a number of false targets and used every trick in the book to escape. Despite running out of depth charges, *Crane* held on to the contact and directed *Foley* (whose ASDIC set was out of action) on several creeping attacks. Contact was lost and oil was sighted, but this could still have been another trick. *Winchelsea* and *Watchman* joined and also picked up some wreckage and made further attacks. This was assessed at Admiralty as a "probable" destruction, but post-war research into German records has shown how often U-boats managed to survive such attacks.

Eventually only bodies or parts of bodies recovered from the sea were considered the absolute proof of a U-boat's destruction and qualifying for a "certain kill".

While all this stuff was going on, the wireless traffic was pretty stupefying and although, in the lower grade of screening, coded messages were decoded by specialist ratings, cypher messages had to be decyphered by officers. In ordinary times the doctor, who had not much else to do, used to undertake this task, but when a steady stream of cyphered messages were arriving it formed another most unpopular task for watch-keeping officers trying to get some sleep in their off-watch periods.

Some messages were, however, quite amusing and we followed with interest the interchange between the Admiralty and an aircraft carrier lying at Belfast, which went something like this:

"Embark forthwith twelve Seafire fighter aircraft and proceed with all despatch to join convoy SL 139/MKS 30 presently in position noon today 46°12′N 19°38′W, Course 004° speed 7½ knots."

This was greeted with hoots of merriment on board and remarks such as "SNAFU again. Just like my Lords of Admiralty to send us fighters while we are up to our balls in U-boats."

Eventually a reply went out from the aircraft carrier:

"Have embarked twelve Swordfish anti-submarine aircraft and sailed at 1400 to join convoy SL 139/MKS 30."

This was naturally greeted with cheers and comments of approbation, but to our surprise it elicited an exceedingly sharp rebuke, to wit:

To aircraft carrier: "When ordered to embark fighter aircraft kindly embark fighter aircraft. Return to port forthwith."

This was followed by a signal to Commander in Chief Plymouth

161

calling for the sailing of *Prince Robert*, an anti-aircraft ship, from Plymouth to join our convoy.

Our estimate of the situation was obviously lacking some essential information and we had good reason some twenty-four hours later to be glad that somebody somewhere knew more than we did.

The battle continued during November 21st, but the action was all in the outfield. A Liberator sighted a U-boat thirty miles astern, but lost touch without managing an attack. After breakfast another Focke-Wulf circled the convoy for a couple of hours occasionally chased by a Liberator, and after lunch yet another support group joined. This was the 4th Escort Group, consisting of *Bentinck*, *Drury*, *Bazely*, *Byard* and *Calder*, bringing the total escorts up to twenty-two, or one for every three merchant ships — an unprecedented level for regular Atlantic convoys.

We were just beginning to feel relatively safe and confident, having survived the efforts of some thirty U-boats without losing a single merchant ship, when a large group of enemy aircraft were sighted coming in from the East and all escorts were required to close the convoy to give maximum covering anti-aircraft fire. The aircraft in question were Heinkel 177's, a type of plane which has gone down in the history of the World's Worst Aircraft, a claim to fame shared by the Fairey Battle in which I had been introduced to the air back in 1940.

It soon became apparent that these aeroplanes were loosing off flying bombs, of which they carried two apiece. Known technically as HS 293 and more affectionately in our Navy as "Chase-Me-Charlies", these were a smaller and earlier version of the flying bombs later launched against London from launching sites in the Calais area of Northern France. They had a wing-span of about fifteen feet and were jet-propelled to a speed of around six hundred miles an hour and were radio-controlled towards their target from the mother plane which launched them. They carried an explosive charge of one thousand pounds of T.N.T.

The use of these devices had been reported a month or so earlier when Captain Walker's "Hunter Group" was attacked in the Bay of Biscay and fortunately a doctor in one ship had obtained some amateur cine film of them in action. Only two antidotes were available. One was difficult and the other somewhat dubious. The first was to shoot the thing down, which was not easy due to its small size and high speed, coupled with the unsophisticated anti-aircraft weapons carried in all but the Bird class sloops. They carried a very advanced bit of kit for those days, which was a gyro-stabilised twin-barrelled Bofors gun which had its own radar set mounted on top and some complicated gadgetry to make it all work.

The second method of dealing with these mosquito-like menaces was — believe it or not — to tune the ship's H.F. radio telephone transmitter to a certain frequency and operate an electric razor near the mouthpiece.

This sounded a most amateur way of dealing with a sophisticated weapon and, of course, there was no way of knowing whether it was successful or not. Perhaps the steady transmissions from two dozen electric razors was responsible for some of the malfunctioning of the HS 293 missiles that afternoon. On the other hand perhaps not. Sadly we shall never know.

It soon became obvious that despite the frightening nature of these flying bombs — particularly the feeling that they could not be avoided — they were not quite so efficient as the designers no doubt wished.

Some could be seen leaving their parent craft and diving straight into the sea, while others even turned around and tried to return whence they had come.

Once again our morale (and faith in shore staffs) was strengthened by the sight of *Prince Robert* appearing over the horizon with all guns blazing within a few minutes of the attack commencing. One could not help contemplating the route by which information of the impending attack had reached our lords and masters in sufficient time for support to be despatched to our aid and arrive in time to be of value.

Post-war information has shown that these aircraft were from II/KG40 based at Bordeaux/M'rignac, that twenty were sent out and that three failed to return.

The SS *Marsa*, which was straggling some three and a half miles behind the convoy, was hit and was finally abandoned after her crew had been picked up by *Petunia* and *Essington*, and one other ship SS *Delius* received a hit on the bridge which killed all but one of her officers and set her on fire. Some of SS *Marsa*'s officers were later transferred to her and she made port safely with the convoy.

At one point a flying bomb was observed coming towards *Moyola* and every effort was made to divert its seemingly relentless progress. It was approaching from the beam and both 4-inch guns were firing short barrage fused shells as fast as they could reload — which was not very fast as the guns were of a simple hand-operated type. As it got closer the two 20mm Oerlikons prepared to do their best.

The mathematics are worth considering. Beyond three thousand yards range a hit was unlikely. From three thousand yards the bomb travelling at six hundred miles an hour would take nine seconds to reach the ship. The Oerlikon magazine held sixty cartridges and probably took about ten seconds to empty in one continuous burst of firing. Replacing with a new full magazine would take between twenty and thirty seconds, but more if a fumbling butter-fingers situation developed. So reloading was out of the question.

There was obviously considerable temptation to open fire too early from sheer excitement (or fear) and it was obviously somewhat dangerous to open fire too late.

Added to this was the problem that no-one had previous experience of those beasts (it would be easier the second and third time) and no device was available for measuring the rapidly-changing range. The missile's small size compared with conventional aeroplanes tended to make it look further away than it actually was.

The bomb approached from the starboard beam and could be seen altering course towards us like an animal which has picked up the scent of a likely prey. Young Petty Officer Taylor was manning the starboard bridge Oerlikon and he rapidly sighted his weapon on the approaching danger.

Ken Clarke, the navigation officer, came up behind him and spoke in his ear, "Steady now. Hold your fire until I tap you on the shoulder".

The tracer bullets could be seen arcing away towards the approaching bomb and it was difficult to see whether they were passing in front of or behind the target, and in any case any alteration of aim might be incorrect by the time the newly-aimed bullet met the approaching target.

Fear was beginning to mount in the minds of all those who could see what was happening, and the view was further confused by the line of tracers from the after Oerlikon and the short fire bursts from both the forward and after 4-inch guns.

Ken tapped Taylor and he opened fire in one long continuous burst of fire. When it looked as though all efforts were in vain, the mini-jet suddenly banked to the left and dived into the sea less than three hundred yards away from *Moyola*.

Relief exploded like escaping steam from all observers and then officers were reminding everyone to keep a sharp lookout on all sectors in case there were any more to come.

Like all the other escorts, we kept our 4-inch guns banging away at any aircraft that seemed remotely within range — or likely to be — and the sky was full of those blobs of black cotton wool where shells had burst.

Then suddenly there were no enemy aircraft to shoot at.

We remained at action stations for another twenty minutes, replenishing ready use stocks of ammunition and reloading Oerlikon magazines, and then stood down and resumed cruising watches on our previous anti-submarine screening station.

The evening submarine situation report from Admiralty advised us that the number of U-boats thought to be in contact with our convoy had now reduced to less than half a dozen and there was a general feeling abroad that the battle was over but that nevertheless we had to be careful not to be too confident as the Germans might still pull a few surprises out of the bag.

In fact it was a quiet night with little or no H.F.D.F. activity and no U-boat contacts or sightings, and the following day "Striking Force 31" started to be disbanded. *Watchman* and *Winchelsea*, whose fuel was running low, were despatched.

NOVEMBER 22nd

During the forenoon there was an enemy aircraft alarm with one being sighted and *Prince Robert* reporting others on her long-range aircraft radar. For a while it was thought that we were in for another attack but nothing developed.

* * * *

The final score at the close of play was:

> Germany: One U-boat definitely sunk
> One U-boat probably sunk
> Three U-boats damaged
> Some aircraft failed to return (some from shadowing and three from glider bomb attack)

Our side: One escort badly damaged (constructive total loss)
One merchant ship sunk (by glider bomb)
One merchant ship damaged (by glider bomb)
Three aircraft failed to return from sorties

The casualties were fairly distributed, but the moral victory was certainly ours, for despite a concentrated effort by between twenty-five and thirty U-boats against a sizeable convoy of sixty-six ships, no merchant ships were sunk by them and only one U-boat penetrated the inner screen, and that at a time when only the original five escorts were present.

The air attack was only slightly more successful, sinking just one ship and damaging another which duly made port.

Our intelligence services had aided those ashore and enabled adequate anti-submarine support groups and some anti-aircraft protection to be despatched to our aid in time for them to be of value. It was unfortunate that no aircraft carrier was available during the U-boat battle and even more sad that despite proper planning no aircraft carrier with fighters aboard was available to make mincemeat of the glider bomb-carrying Heinkel 177's.

In the evening the 5th Escort Group (*Nene*, etc) left the convoy, taking with them some Landing Ships (Tank) which had been in the convoy and *Prince Robert*, whose assistance was no longer considered necessary.

NOVEMBER 23rd

The remaining Support Group escorts were detached during the day and the convoy was split up into Fast and Slow sections, these being escorted as required by 40th Escort Group who finally saw all their charges to different U.K. ports or handed them over to coastal escorts.

The battle was over.

*   *   *   *

The next convoy (OS 62/KMS 36) down to Gibraltar was uneventful. It seemed a bit of a let-down after SL 139.

Both Christmas and new Year's Eve were spent at sea, and apart from striking the traditional sixteen bells at midnight on the latter occasion, both days passed without any celebration as we had decided to combine the two occasions and enjoy them while alongside in Gibraltar.

On the chosen day — around January 3rd — the wardroom was suitably decorated and a great deal of festive spirit was consumed between 1100 and about 1330 when the obligatory roast turkey was served, washed down with some excellent Federico Paternina, and followed by plum pudding and rum butter — the latter the result of some serious "testing for salt" over the previous few days.

Speeches were required by more or less everyone present, including the coxswain who had been invited to join us. It must have been about half past three in the afternoon when a Royal Navy Lieutenant-Commander was brought into the wardroom by the quartermaster. He was greeted with cheers from the merry party still sitting at the lunch table, given several drinks and required to make a speech before anyone even asked his name or enquired as to the purpose of his visit. In fact I recognised him as Lieutenant-Commander McKendrick who had been a term officer at Dartmouth in 1939.

His speech is clearly remembered, but before reproducing it here, it should be explained that devices based on radar, H.F. radio and other mysteries only understood by boffins were appearing at a greater rate than could be fully understood or explained to those not directly involved.

Some required aerials which bore a resemblance to some common or garden article and duly carried this name in general parlance and sometimes in official documents.

There was, for example, an aerial known as "the egg-timer" which actually produced some effect on the radar to indicate whether one was German or British and decoded the same information from any radar echo — its official name was I.F.F. (Indicate Friend or Foe) but the aerial was always known as "the egg-timer". Although not an aerial, there was also a device to allow the captain to look into the navigating plot from the bridge which was known officially as "the what-the-butler-saw" from its similarity to those naughty slot machines usually found on seaside piers between the wars.

It is necessary to understand that these developments and devices were appearing quite frequently and often the first time one heard of them was upon enquiry after seeing something unusual in another ship. Hence the following speech from McKendrick:

"A few months ago, while driving a Hunt Class destroyer in U.K. waters, the wardroom had 'a quiet run ashore'. On the way back we happened to sight a set of golden pawnbrokers balls hanging from a bracket above a shop. The temptation was too great, and in no time at all a pyramid was formed to lift a Sub-Lieutenant up to the necessary height where he quickly unscrewed the bracket with a clasp knife which appeared from God knows where.

"The trophy was proudly carried back aboard and was to be found lying in a corner of the wardroom the following day.

"It was not long before we decided that it would look well screwed to the mast above the bridge and there during the forenoon the carpenter duly mounted it.

"At sea a few days later the Captain (D) of the flotilla ranged alongside to converse over the loud-hailer during which he apparently observed the trophy, and curiosity got the better of him.

"'What are those spheres on your mast, McKendrick?'

"I hardly liked to say 'pawnbrokers balls' — it sounded a bit rude — so I said airily, 'Oh, that's Type 297, sir.'

"Captain (D) not daring to show ignorance in hearing of both ships' companies, said 'Oh yes, of course' and I forgot about the whole thing.

"Unfortunately Captain (D) did not. He was incensed that a ship in his flotilla had been fitted with a new gadget before his own — so incensed, in fact, that on return to port he hurried to the Base Headquarters, breathing fire and brimstone, and headed for the Base Radar Officer's office.

"'Why has a ship in my flotilla been fitted with Type 297 when my ship has not?' he demanded.

"The poor bemused Base Radar Officer had, of course, never heard of Type 297, but being unwilling to admit to such ignorance he stammered out, 'Er, Type 297, sir — I am afraid that is not in my department. If I recall correctly it's Huff Duff — Lieutenant Smithers, sir, in the next office.'

"Captain (D) stormed next door and was directed in the same manner to the Base Wireless Officer, who suggested — with explosive results — an enquiry to the Base Radar Officer.

"In desperation Captain (D) went to the headman — the Admiral — who personally denied all knowledge of any such device or its fitting to any ship. However, to pacify Captain (D) he sent for all his staff officers who all with one voice admitted that while they had all heard of Type 297 it was not actually the responsibility of any one of them and none of them had actually ever seen one, nor could they give any details as to its precise purpose.

"Crustily the Admiral demanded to know the name of the ship fitted with this tiresome new gadget and duly instructed his Flag Lieutenant to make a signal asking for details of Type 297 fitted.

"Very unfortunately when this signal arrived with me I had forgotten the loud-hailer conversation of ten days previously and replied, 'Type 297 not fitted'.

"Then the fat was really in the fire and eventually I had to don sword and medals and explain the whole story to the Admiral. Fortunately he had more sense of humour than the Captain (D) and gave me a large gin before sending me back to my ship with his final word on the matter:

"'Well, McKendrick, it seems to me there will be just enough time for you fellows to transfer Type 297 to Captain (D)'s ship before you sail this evening. Make sure it's done, my boy'."

* * * *

Visits to La Linea having to end by six p.m. and the dockyard gates closing at eleven p.m. resulted in late-night parties developing in one or other of the ships in the group each evening in harbour.

Some ships developed silly games of the type dreamed up these days by university students and rugby clubs. After all, the age of the younger officers was in the same bracket. Drinking a pint of beer while hanging upside down by your toes from a deckhead pipe was one, I recall, and of course there would be sessions of "Here's to the health of Cardinal Puff", apart from endless rounds of "Liar dice" and a silly game played on the floor called "La-de-da".

How it started I do not remember exactly, but *Moyola*'s especial home-produced game was entitled "Operation Neil Robertson" and the essential item of equipment was a Neil Robertson stretcher which was carried in all ships then and — I am pleased to say — has survived into the ultra-modern technological Navy of the 1980s without any modification.

For those who are not acquainted with this marvel of medical science I should explain that it was a sort of well-intertwined straight-jacket made of canvas webbing and lengths of stout bamboo. A severely injured man could be wrapped up in this like an

Egyptian mummy and then carried around the ship or hoisted without doing him much further damage.

Our game was a trial of strength between the doctor and the rest of those present. If the majority succeeded in getting him securely strapped up in the device it was hoisted to the deckhead and secured there while the party continued below. It was, in fact, very difficult to get a resisting body into this device and more often than not the honours went to the medical profession.

At one Gibraltar late-night party, the officers of the Royal Indian Navy sloop *Kistna* were amongst those drinking in *Moyola's* wardroom when "Operation Neil Robertson" was mounted. By tacit agreement the doctor of *Kistna* became the target and the game began. He soon got the idea and began to wriggle free, but someone produced a hammock lashing and this was brought into service to help secure him with several turns being taken around his upper body with much enthusiasm and cries of "Up behind, take another turn — haul taught".

It seemed that the mob's efforts were nearing success when the senior officers who were watching the mêlée indulgently joined in on the doctor's side, which was resented. Eventually, however, they were able to bring to our attention a relatively unimportant point which was that, in our enthusiasm, we had taken a turn round the doctor's neck interfering fairly seriously with his breathing and completely cutting off his pleas for mercy.

After he was released he seemed to need an awful lot of brandy to recover, assuring us that it was far more efficacious than any other medical treatment.

※　　※　　※　　※

While on one of my trips to La Linea with Dickie, he had mentioned that his stint at Gibraltar was coming to an end and he was trying to arrange a berth back to England in some ship. On raising this with *Moyola's* Captain, he was agreeable, all formalities were duly completed and Dickie duly embarked for the return trip (Convoy SL 144/MKS 35) with his baggage and a large official weighted and padlocked sack decorated with the Royal Cypher and accompanied by documents authenticating it as a "Diplomatic Bag" in the personal charge of Captain Richards.

Dickie was very fond of sherry and knew that it was virtually

170

unobtainable in England at this stage of the war, so he also embarked a dozen cases of the produce of Williams & Humbert and Pedro Domecq.

The idea of paying duty on this quantity of booze was naturally abhorrent, so a little plan was hatched up. Six G.P.O. mailbags were obtained from the coxswain and two cases of sherry were inserted into each case and they were then sealed with lots of sealing wax and given regular O.H.M.S. tie-on labels (we had plenty of these in the ship's office), upon which was written "Bag A", "Bag B", etc, after which a spurious document was typed on board on Naval Signal Message sheets with wording along the following lines:

TO WHOM IT MAY CONCERN

BE ADVISED THAT SIX SEALED MAILBAGS LABELLED
"A" TO "F" INCLUSIVE HAVE BEEN PUT IN THE
CARE OF CAPTAIN RICHARDS FOR TRANSMISSION
TO THE UNITED KINGDOM

When eventually we arrived in Greenock and were boarded by Customs Officers, as usual, they were bemused and mystified by the genuine Diplomatic Bag and took about half an hour to convince themselves that they could not open it up and search it. When they had finally been satisfied, the other six bags and the accompanying document were shown to them and there were passed without a second glance.

A party of sailors carried the six mailbags, the Diplomatic Bag and Dickie's kit across Greenock pier to the railway platform, with Dickie and myself bringing up the rear. At his suggestion I was accompanying him to Glasgow to have dinner there before he caught the night sleeper to London.

"It will be all arranged with a reserved compartment for the Diplomatic Bag," he assured me.

When we got to the platform at Greenock Station, a Lieutenant with green "Intelligence Corps" flashes on his tunic approached Dickie and saluted, saying "Captain Fitzgerald, sir, from Gibraltar?"

"Yes, that's right," said Dickie.

"Please follow me, sir, to your reserved compartment," and he led us to the appropriate First Class carriage.

171

The trip to Glasgow passed without incident and on arrival Dickie mentioned that someone should be there to meet us. Sure enough we had barely alighted on the platform when a Captain (also from Intelligence) approached and saluted Dickie with the greeting "Major Thompson, sir, from Gibraltar? I have some men here to handle the Diplomatic Bag and your gear."

A party of soldiers soon had all the bags on a trolley and Dickie arranged for them all to be kept in safe custody and brought out again to board the sleeper for London which was due to depart at eleven o'clock that evening.

We then repaired to the bar of the Central Hotel adjoining the station to quench our thirst and subsequently our hunger.

It was a very merry occasion since, by chance, a number of old friends happened to be drinking there that evening, including a cousin of mine, an RNVR Lieutenant, who was taking the same train to London.

Shortly before eleven we appeared on the correct platform for the sleeper to London and were met by yet another Intelligence Corps officer with some soldiers hauling our trolley. Time was getting a bit short and I went ahead looking at the lists displayed at the end of each sleeping car trying with a somewhat woosey brain to find one of a bewildering number of names "Captain Richards" or "Captain Fitzgerald" or "Major Thompson", not to mention "Lieutenant Sutherland", my cousin.

Eventually I found the latter and he dived into the carriage. Still I could not find Dickie's berth, but as he was looking at one of the lists I had already scanned he said, "Here it is, I am in this one".

Going back I looked at the list again, but could see none of his names. "Where?" I said. "There it is — number five", he threw over his shoulder as he climbed into the carriage.

I looked at number five on the list and it said — "Major Wilson".

"But Godammit, Dickie. . . ." I started to say, but he just winked at me and said "Didn't you hear the Intelligence Corps Captain when he met us with the baggage on the platform?"

*   *   *   *

When I next saw my cousin a few weeks later I heard that they had a hilarious journey South, teaming up with an American Admiral and consuming more than one bottle of sherry before arriving in London.

There, no doubt, was another band of Intelligence Corps pongos hailing Dickie as "Colonel Smithers".

* * * *

At our first meeting in Middlesborough before *Moyola* commissioned, the Captain and I had naturally discussed previous ships. Principally he was keen to discover how experienced I was and I was curious to know what sort of a chap I was to serve under. After speaking about *Auricula* he mentioned that he had commanded a corvette and gave its name. This rang a bell with me, for I recalled that this corvette had been a wing escort of a convoy about a year earlier in varying visibility and had sighted a German heavy cruiser — *Admiral Hipper*, I think — and very correctly made an immediate sighting report in plain language by wireless. The particular wording of the message got to the popular press, who made quite a thing of it at the time since the message read:

"Have sighted enemy battle cruiser. Am altering course to engage."

The visibility had then closed in again, and nothing more transpired.

It is, of course, probable that the German cruiser heard the transmission and understood it, since all German raiders carried large wireless staffs capable of operating in various languages.

It is just possible that due to some error she believed that the signal came from a powerful British warship or a less powerful one closely supported by capital ships. Whatever the cause, the *Admiral Hipper* apparently made no attempt to close the range and engage and, much to the corvette crew's relief, nothing more was seen of her.

These, then, were the facts of the case.

However, during the next twelve months or so in *Moyola*, we began to realise that whatever "the Old Man" had been celebrating he could, with but little difficulty, be persuaded to give us all yet another first-hand account of the incident and eventually it became a sort of game to see who could be the one to give the final conversational prod that would launch "The Great Story".

What was remarkable and amusing was that every time the story was told it improved a little. Not a lot. Just a little.

From an early beginning of "we only got off one shot from the 4-inch and were probably out of range" to "we managed to fire three shots from the 4-inch and the last one was definitely a hit", we gradually closed the range.

Out of courtesy for our Captain and out of respect for the unwritten rules of the game, no expression of disbelief was ever uttered. Occasionally to lend interest to the occasion someone might ask "What was the range, do you think, sir, when you last saw her?"

It was, in all, a fascinating business because we knew it was actually based on real fact. It was the slow and methodical "improvement" of the story which intrigued us so. Sadly, we never managed to get the story told in a state of absolute sobriety. Looking back it would have been interesting to see how it would have emerged.

To complete this little pastiche I have to put the clock on some four months to a day after *Moyola* had been decommissioned and I was acting C.O. of *Deveron*, a sister ship from the same shipyard. She was preparing to sail for the Far East and I was living in the Captain's cabin.

By some chance I met my old Captain at an alcoholic party in Gladstone Dock and on an impulse invited him back on board for a glass. We sat down at the table in the Captain's cabin — identical to his in *Moyola* — and carried on drinking with that air of "now-that - the - amateurs - have - left - we - can - get - down - to - some - serious - drinking".

Then a naughty thought crept into my mind. Could I, just once more, get him to tell the story of the *Admiral Hipper*?

The temptation was too great to resist.

We were both pretty plastered and I began to fear that I had left it too late and he was going to pass out before he could get to the critical part but, with difficulty, he made it and I can see him now staring intently across the table intense upon projecting the truth and importance of the final sentence of his story:

". . . and do you know, Scott, do you know I honestly believe . . . I honestly believe that we were so close to that battle cruiser that he couldn't depress his guns sufficiently to hit us."

He looked at me for about sixty seconds and then his eyes glazed over and his head fell forward on the table.

It is the matter of greatest regret that I never saw him again after

174

that day, since the imagination boggles at how that apparently final solution could be improved upon but surely in forty years and more something had to be managed.

* * * *

The convoys continued Greenock to Gibraltar, Gibraltar to Greenock. The progress of the build-up of our forces continued so that we found an escort aircraft carrier accompanying us at most times. She had the ubiquitous "Swordfish" to attack submarines and some fighters to deal with shadowing aircraft, and was very effective so that nothing like the battle of SL 139 ever developed again.

Although we now began to have the upper hand in the U-boat battle, there were still mistakes on our side too. On one occasion I had to take away the whaler to pick up wreckage and survivors (if any) after the fighters had shot down an approaching four-engine aircraft observed briefly in cloudy conditions. There was nothing warlike or German about the pieces of debris which we recovered, and these and other information soon pointed to the fact that the target had been an unarmed passenger plane flying from Lisbon to the United Kingdom show down in innocent mistaken identity.

On another occasion when we were without our escort carrier an escorting Liberator had spotted a U-boat on the surface some distance from the convoy, and being at the end of her endurance *Moyola* was despatched at full speed to investigate. We reported being at the last known position of the U-boat by T.B.S. and then heard another Liberator reporting that she was also over the spot and had sighted the U-boat which she was about to attack. We could still see no signs of the U-boat but someone did spot a Liberator diving on us from astern with her bomb doors clearly visible in the open position.

A somewhat hysterical transmission from our radio managed to abort the attack upon us.

* * * *

One evening in the spring of 1944, the Jimmy, the navigator and myself went for a quiet run up to Glasgow from Gourock where we were lying.

Alcohol of all sorts was in fairly short supply ashore, but beer was usually obtainable. Our standard drill was to have a number of large gins on board and then, each carrying a hip flask, we walked the odd fifty yards across Gourock Pier to catch a train for Glasgow, where we planned to consume a quantity of ale in one or two alehouses known to us, before a dinner and more ale. Then — after closing time — we could consume the contents of our hip flasks — usually whisky.

We rather tended to let the evening develop on its own, which it usually had a happy knack of doing.

Although our intake of alcohol was considerable and was sufficient to make a modern breathaliser light up like a neon tube and emit flashes of lightning, it was on the whole a rather uneventful evening, and I began to fear that it might turn out after all to be that really rare occasion — a genuinely quiet run ashore.

Fortunately, however, when we arrived at the station to catch the last train back to Gourock, matters improved.

Presumably it was the idea of what was then referred to as The Second Front (and now called the D-Day landings) which was in everybody's minds that prompted Pilot's feelings as we walked up the dimly-lit platform.

"Let's go and talk to the engine-driver," he said.

"If we must," said Jimmy the One.

"When I've had another snort," said I.

One of my regular contributions to these runs ashore was to bring my Father's silver-plated flask filled to the brim with whisky. It was a heavy load to carry around all evening in the pocket of my burberry, but it was worth it, as it usually managed to create some sort of interesting situation.

By tacit agreement it was only broached after all other hip flasks were empty, and its effect on our little group and any other friends we had gathered to us was then fairly considerable, for this flask had two peculiarities. The first was that it held not just a bottle of whisky but a bottle and a half, and the second was that the cover to the screw top, when detached, made a half-pint drinking mug.

I passed this mug in turn to the other two, and when we were all fortified, we approached the engine, where we found the engine-driver and the fireman leaning out of their cab, relaxing before the trip.

"Good evening engine-driver, good evening fireman," we said

one after the other. "Good evening, sirs," they said politely.

Pilot's brain clicked into the gear that was to set the tone for the night's events.

"We are all naval engineer officers who have been receiving special instruction in driving railway engines so that we can drive engines in France after the Second Front opens up."

"Are ye reely that, sirs. Weel, I never heard tell o' the idea, but it's good to hear that they have conseedered the problem. Can we help ye at all?"

"Well you could actually," said Pilot, warming to his extempore theme, "You see, we have had a lot of instruction but not much practice, and we would like to ride with you to Gourock to increase our experience."

"Weel, o' course it's strictly against the reggylations," replied the engine-driver, looking cautiously up the platform.

"We've got a little whisky to keep the cold out that we would gladly share with you," I volunteered, catching up with Pilot's idea and showing support.

"Aweel, ye see sirs, we couldna do it with the Glaska station master himself watching o'er there. But if ye come back at the first stop, we'll see just what we can do. Ye had better climb in now, sirs, the guard is just after blowing his whistle."

Jimmy the One had not contributed much to the conversation and was definitely looking glassy-eyed and beginning to wobble on his pins, but with Pilot and I on either side, he had no difficulty in reaching the first compartment where we climbed in. Jimmy lay down on one seat and commenced snoring, even before the train had started, while Pilot and I sat opposite and refreshed ourselves from my flask.

"What is all this engineer officer business?" I asked Pilot. "Neither you nor I could tell a piston from a turbine even if it danced a highland fling for our benefit."

"Oh I don't know — it just seemed a good idea at the time. When I was a little sprog, I always wanted to be an engine-driver, and I suppose some Freudian spark of desire still flutters in my heart."

He looked pensive and then, surveying the unconscious Jimmy, he declared: "Well, I doubt if there would have been room for three of us on the footplate, but with Number One here temporarily *hors de combat*, we may be able to have a go — that is — with the aid of that silver-plated bomb of yours."

177

A few minutes later the train ground to a halt, and we nipped out of our compartment and walked forward to the cab.

"How's the steam pressure?" says I, hoping to sound knowledgeable.

"Oh it's alricht the noo," comes the reply.

"How old is this engine?" asks Pilot, not being able to produce a more technical query, despite desperate efforts.

"Och aye! Weel, I ken she's aboot twenty years old. She couldna hae been built much after nineteen twenty fower, on account of the type of stubble-mufflers she had. They went oot o' fashion about that time."

"How about a wee drop to keep the cold out?" says I, offering the flask and feeling decidedly short of further technical queries.

The driver leaned out of his cab and looked intently both ways before reaching out a hand and saying "'Twad be better if you two gennelmen came inside. Ye'll nae see much of the workings frae down there."

Passing the flask to the driver, and to the accompaniment of a deep throated gurgle, I mounted the footplate followed by the Pilot.

After the firemen had quenched his not inconsiderable thirst, we heard the guard's whistle and watched in alcoholic fascination as the machine was got under way. Each movement was explained in detail to the two students of steam locomotive art:

"Opening up the feed check valve"

"Closing the cylinder drain cock"

"Easing off the brake and ever so gently opening the main steam valve"

As we watched and endeavoured to express sober interest, we could feel the giant beast moving and see the dimly-lit platform slipping away.

The fireman opened the fire door and shovelled some coal into the white-hot furnace. "Oh I say, can I have a go at that?" says Pilot.

"I'll jest be showing you how it's done, sir," and suiting the actions to the words, he balanced a pile of coal on his shovel and thrusting it into the furnace, tipped it to the left and shouted in Pilot's ear, above the noise of the engine and the shrieking wind screaming through the cab, "One into the left hand side".

Pilot, listening intently, turned to me and shouted in turn, "D'you see? One into the left hand side."

The fireman tipped his next shovel to the right and shouted "One

178

into the right hand side", and this was duly relayed to me: "One into the right hand side". This was followed by "One right at the back".

The driver, wearing his cap back to front in the traditional style, leaned out of the nearside of the cab staring ahead. I put mine on back to front too, and stared out of the offside. I could not see a thing. My eyes watered with the wind, and smuts and grit bounced on my face. The engine-driver leaned in and pulled a lever twice in quick succession.

"Wooo! Wooo!" went the steam whistle.

Not to be outdone, I leaned in and pulled the same lever in a double motion.

"Wooo! Wooo!" blasted into the night.

Pilot, not to be outdone, put his cap on back to front and indicated to the fireman that he would like to do some stoking. Since he was a navigator and I was only an ignorant torpedo officer, he insisted on repeating the instructions to me yet again with each shovelful:

"One to the left hand side"
"One to the right hand side"
"One right at the back"

On completion he banged the fire door closed with his shovel with the panache of a fifty-year old fireman due for his pension.

It was then time for a little refreshment, and so the flask was passed around from hand to hand. "Ye're verry guid health, sir," said the fireman and driver in turn, as they tried without success to empty the flask.

Although the journey lasted less than an hour, the time passed quickly. Detailed instruction in stopping and starting the train at the various stops along the route followed by the thrill of "going solo" as first Pilot and then I was allowed to apply the brakes to bring the train to a halt and subsequently go through the routine for getting going again.

Between whiles, there was more practice at stoking, a little whistle blowing, some short stints at forward look-out, and from time to time a short pause for refreshment.

"How fast will she go?" bawled Pilot.

"Aboot forrrty-five miles an hour."

"How fast are we going now?"

"Aboot forrrty miles an hour," shouted the driver, with one hand pointing to a grime-encrusted dial barely visible in the murky light from the furnace.

"What about a bit more speed then, eh?" encouraged our valiant navigator, beginning to develop a taste for the sport.

"We'll be needing some more coal, ye ken."

"Oh jolly good show," said Pilot, grasping the shovel with enthusiasm and getting to work.

The steam valve was fully opened; the feed check valve adjusted; the furnace stoked and — as my contribution to our record-breaking attempt — the whistle was blown frequently.

There must have been several little groups of bemused Scotsmen waiting at lonely stations along our route that night for the eleven-forty train from Glasgow who were surprised to see the train thunder through at its brain-shattering record speed of forty-seven miles an hour.

Finally we reached Gourock and the engine-driver wisely took over the controls for our final approach to the terminus buffers.

We offered our profuse thanks for the valuable instruction. We assured both the driver and the fireman that they had made a valuable contribution to the war effort and between us we drained the flask before sauntering off to collect the still unconscious Jimmy the One from his compartment and return on board.

The next morning's awakening was not pleasant, but a cup of tea and three crushed aspirins restored a little life to the body. Donning sunglasses to retain the eyeballs in their sockets and soften the deadly blow of sunlight and, being blessedly dressed by the fairies, I opted for a few circuits of the upper deck, in the belief that the cold fresh air would assist my recovery.

"Morning, sir," said the Chief Bosun's Mate.

"Morning, Buffer," I replied quietly.

"'Ave a quiet run ashore last night, sir?"

"Yes, very pleasant, thank you, Buffer."

"Tell me, sir, did you have anything to do with the fact as wot the last Glasgow train got in five minutes early, sir?"

"Good gracious no, Buffer, whatever gave you that idea?"

"Well, sir, I see'd you, sir, hand the Navigating Officer with your caps on a'back to front, sir, a'carrying the First Lootenant aboard."

"Ah well, yes, I suppose you could say that we had a good quiet run ashore, Buffer."

Later in the morning the staff officers from the shore base, including the Captain (D) and some Wren officers, were being entertained in *Moyola*'s wardroom. For three of us, at least, a "hair-of-the-dog" was very welcome but naturally we were all on our best behaviour, it certainly not being the sort of occasion for a bout of Cardinal Puff or Operation Neil Robertson.

In the midst of this shindig I saw the inimitable Able Seaman Poulter, the quartermaster, at the wardroom door where he was asking for me.

"Yes, Poulter, what's up?"

"There are two gentlemen to see you, sir, wot say you've invited them aboard."

"Oh, very well, bring them along to the wardroom."

"Well, excuse me, sir, but I thought it best to show them to your cabin, sir."

"Good grief, why on earth do that?"

"Well, sir, I understand that they is the fireman and the engine-driver from that train last night wot you and the navigator drove."

They were duly entertained in my cabin with the excuse that confidential matters were being discussed in the wardroom.

*　*　*　*

Carefully organised excursions to music halls occasionally featured amongst our quiet — or not so quiet — runs ashore, usually undertaken by a party from several ships in the group.

To be successful, a small amount of organisation was required and a modicum of pre-planning. In those days, when the Music Hall was an honoured institution, there was frequently a choice of establishments — certainly in cities like Liverpool and Glasgow — and the trick was to select the least high-class of those available.

The Master of Ceremonies was then responsible for booking at least two boxes in this establishment for the second or last house. On some days they would give three shows — a matinée, a "first house" from about 6 p.m. to 8 p.m. and a "last house" starting at about 8.30 p.m. For preference the boxes were those nearest the stage, on opposite sides thereof, and at the height of the Dress Circle.

A suitable number of taxis were ordered to be alongside the host ship at 8 p.m. and a quantity of suitable stores and equipment stockpiled ready for departure. The participants were all bidden to

181

arrive at the host ship at 6 p.m. and each one was required to be armed with a suitably loaded hip flask.

Drinks flowed freely from 6 p.m. and possibly a round of "Liar Dice" played to pass the time and accompany the imbibing.

("Liar Dice", incidentally, was a "Round Robin" version of poker played with five poker dice which involved a good deal of bluffing and giving of false impressions of the value of the dice which were hidden from view. In fact, at one stage some particularly stuffy bunch of Lords of the Admiralty put out an order which stated roughly: "It has come to the notice of their Lordships that it has become common practice for officers to indulge in a game entitled 'Liar Dice'. It is understood that an essential part of the playing of this game is the telling of falsehoods. This practice is to be deprecated and commanding officers are to take all necessary steps to ensure that it ceases forthwith").

At around 8 p.m., on being advised that the taxis were alongside, our Master of Ceremonies would endeavour to persuade all those present to cease drinking and embark in the transport provided, at the same time ensuring that everyone selected a piece of equipment to their taste before leaving the ship. All harmless stuff, but destined to play a part in the evening's entertainment.

Some, therefore, took a boiler gauge glass tube and a bag of dried peas (an extemporary pea-shooter); some a supply of nuts and bolts (these could be dropped on to the cymbals and drums at suitably appropriate moments); some armed themselves with old tennis balls supplied for recreation purposes — and what was this, if not recreation? (They made harmless missiles for projection on to the stage). And always there was an adequate supply of light rope. This latter could be used for a variety of purposes, one of the most popular of which was passing chairs or bottles of beer from box to box across the auditorium in the same way that stores were sometimes passed from ship to ship at sea.

On arrival at the music hall, the party gradually found their way to the reserved boxes via the bar and various interruptions or additions to the programme were carried out without any rehearsal. Generally our activities brightened up a somewhat second-rate show and were enjoyed by the audience. Sometimes even the comics in the cast joined in the game.

Chorus girls could be distracted from their dance steps by packets of Player's cigarettes tossed on to the stage and requiring retrieval.

One girl who jumped like a shot rabbit on being struck on the left tit by a packet of twenty remarked afterwards, "I have been hit in a variety of places by a variety of things, but never there with a packet of Players."

Disaster nearly struck when a comic decided to choose our box from which to deliver a cross-talk act with his on-stage partner. Somehow he offended us, so — gripping him sharply by the ankles — he was hoisted up and lowered face downwards back to the audience over the front of the box from which position his dialogue was somewhat strangled.

There was a bit of a problem getting him back into the box since when hoisted up a foot or so, his knees would not bend the wrong way. Consideration was given to dropping him onto the big drum below, but finally he was recovered in good shape but needed refreshment from practically every flask before returning to the stage.

On one particular evening everything had gone swimmingly. Chairs and bottles had passed to and fro, a tennis ball had struck a female acrobatic dancer dead centre when she was completely inverted — to her surprise — serious songs had been rendered humorous by nuts and bolts falling on the cymbals, and a hearty rendering of "Lloyd George knew my father" to the tune of "Onward Christian Soldiers" had even drawn a round of applause and all this even before the interval.

At this time Ken, the Navigator, had to answer a call of nature and while busily engaged in this found himself standing next to a bespectacled chap in evening dress who enquired whether Ken was "one of those naval gentlemen in the boxes", somewhat disapprovingly.

"Yes," he said, "and who are you?"

"I am the producer."

"Ah," said Ken, "do you know John Black?"

"I know of George Black, naturally," said the producer (George Black being the best-known London impresario at the time, responsible for "Black Velvet" and other shows).

Ken had probably intended to claim some friendship with the great man, but in a hazy alcoholic state he inadvertently got the name wrong, but he recovered quickly and held out his right hand, saying "Well, meet John Black, his son".

That altered everything. The producer was effusive in his

*. . . A tennis ball had struck a female acrobat dancer
dead centre when she was completely inverted.*

eagerness to be of help. The more important members of the cast and the management trooped up to our box to be introduced to " Mr George Black's son and his charming friends ".

We were encouraged to further efforts and at the final curtain the producer even came on stage and called for a round of applause for " Our guests from the Senior Service including the son of the famous London impresario, Mr George Black ".

Some months later I actually met George Black's son in a bar in Sussex and admitted to our innocent impersonation. It transpired that he was also a naval reserve officer and had taken part in similar expeditions but it had never occurred to him to trade on his father's fame.

* * * *

Several more convoys to and from Gibraltar followed in succession but there were few alarms or excursions. The addition of a Woolworth type aircraft carrier to our escort group tended to take the action further away from the convoy perimeter.

The rising cost of general entertainment ashore and the fixed nature of our salaries encouraged a few of us to look into extra ways of earning a few pennies and the relative availability of items in Gibraltar which were in short supply in Britain encouraged us to make some investigations into the import business.

Alcohol and watches seemed interesting at first but really necessitated smuggling into the U.K. to show an " adequate " profit considered to be at least 300%. Finally our little import company settled on olives. We found that we could buy small barrels about eight inches high at eight shillings each in Gib, and these were easily and safely stowed in the magazines and depth charge stores. There was no Customs Duty on them and they did not attract thieves at any stage but with a little bit of enterprise they could be sold to the barmen of the better hotels in London and elsewhere for up to five pounds a barrel, which represented a reasonable return on capital without illegality. The rumour that *Moyola* had inadvertently fired a barrel of olives at an attacking German aircraft can be entirely discounted as false and malicious.

We did look at the idea of bringing back a forty gallon drum of acetone and decanting it into miniature medicine bottles for sale as nail varnish remover — then in very short supply — but the problems of sale and distribution seemed too great.

185

Eventually we were ordered to go to Troon on the Firth of Clyde for a major refit and modernisation and the two hour voyage from Greenock to Troon was planned with meticulous care.

A batch of some thirty Wren officers and Wrens were embarked for the trip and arrangements made for their return by road. They had a great time on board, being looked after by a happy crew anticipating some long leave and they were allowed to do everything possible on board including firing the Oerlikons. On arrival at Troon we entered harbour with the crew fallen in on the forecastle and quarter deck, but as we drew close those gathered on shore were astonished to find that *Moyola* apparently had an entirely female crew. Even the captain on the bridge was wearing a Wren officer's hat. It transpired that our little joke was not appreciated by the Naval-Officer-in-Charge at Troon since he was a confirmed misogynist and did not really approve of Wrens in any capacity.

The summer weather had arrived and the warm weather was enjoyed by all. At rum issue one day the Coxswain remarked,

"I went for a walk in those fields just out of town last evening and by golly there weren't half a lot of fellows giving their arses a bit of sunburn."

It had been originally planned to recommission *Moyola* after the refit with the same ship's company, but this plan went awry and some high authority decided that she should be handed over to the Free French Navy and renamed *Tonkinois*. We had a grand ship's company dance in an old church hall in Troon and then all went our separate ways.

HMS Moyola's Sailing and Arrival Dates
January 1943–April 1944

January 8th 1943 (App)	Commissioning. Sailed to Clyde 19th-20th
January 29th–February 22nd	Tobermory for work-up. February 24th
March 4th–11th	First Atlantic crossing to St Johns to Londonderry. Escort Group 40 (no convoy)
March 14th–26th	Convoy HX229A. St Johns to Londonderry

April 8th–25th	Convoy ONS3. Londonderry to St Johns (April 21st U-boat sunk by *Hastings*)
April 28th–May 12th	Convoy SC128. St Johns to UK (Liverpool) (2 U-boats sighted and driven off. 1830 May 1st). (Drydocked in Birkenhead).
May 25th–26th	Liverpool to Londonderry
May 27th–31st	Londonderry to Hvaljord (Iceland)
May 31st–June 10th	Hvaljord to St Johns, N.F.
5th June 1943	Supporting SC 132
5th June 1943	Supporting ON 187
June 16th–23rd	St Johns to UK. (No convoy mentioned)
July 8th–25th	Londonderry to Casablanca. (Convoy *Faith*)
July 26th–31st	*Asturias* incident
August 13th–17th	Freetown to Patrol and return
August 20th–23rd (1900)	Freetown to escort Convoy LS-10
August 24th–30th	Exercises with E.G. under Commander in *Exe*
August 30th	1107, Collision with *Petunia* (OOW manoeuvres)
September 3rd–24th	Freetown to UK. Convoy SL 136
September 25th–October 22nd	Repairing at Barclay Curle's yard, Elderslie, Clyde
October 23rd–26th	Trials with *Unicorn* projector etc. and at Greenock
October 28th–November 10th	UK to Gibraltar. Convoy OS138/KMS 37. Escort group 40 (XL)
November 13th–26th	Gibraltar to UK. Convoy SL139/MKS30
November 16th	Enemy aircraft commenced shadowing
November 26th–December 16th	Presumably boiler cleaning, etc
December 16th–January 3rd	Convoy UK to Gibraltar OS62/KMS36. Celebrated Christmas and New Year in Gibraltar
January 6th–January 17th	Convoy Gibraltar to UK SL-144/MKS235
January 24th–February 8th	Convoy UK to Gibraltar OS66/KMS-40

187

February 11th–23rd	Convoy Gibraltar to UK SL148/ MKS-39
March 4th–17th	Convoy UK to Gibraltar OS70/ KMS44
March 21st–April 3rd	Convoy Gibraltar to UK SL152/ MKS-43

Chapter Five

LEAVING *Moyola* in Troon and going on leave I was endeavouring to join up with a cloak and dagger outfit with assistance from Dickie, the oddball anti-James Bond who had been our passenger from Gibraltar.

Apparently this "private army" had become dissatisfied with the quality of Coastal Forces personnel who were assigned to landing and picking up agents from enemy-held beaches and wished to recruit their own permanent staff and train them to deal with their particular problems. Various meetings were arranged in London by Dickie but delays occurred and finally the Navy lost patience and appointed me to *Deveron* lying in Gladstone Dock, Liverpool, and fitting out for service with the Eastern Fleet.

By chance she had been the next frigate to be built in Smiths Dock after *Moyola* and, as a ship, was as alike as two peas in a pod, but by that odd freak of fate she had seen absolutely no enemy action since she had commissioned.

The resultant impractical view of the realities of war was further compounded since none of the officers (and very few others) had ever heard a shot fired in anger.

The entire atmosphere on board was curiously unrealistic and any attempt to introduce a serious attitude into warlike exercises fell upon exceedingly stony ground and appeared to be regarded by all as a rather boring intrusion into their somewhat smug peacetime thinking easy-going life.

A few days after I joined the whole ship's company was sent on leave and I was left on board a dead ship with a long defect list to chase and the necessity to beg my meals from other nearby ships. There always seemed to be some ship in the dock aboard which was to be found an erstwhile drinking partner, and I had the use of *Deveron*'s Captain's cabin for sleeping and doing a small amount of entertaining.

(It will be recalled that it was here that I had the opportunity to hear the last version of the "attack" on the battle cruiser *Hipper* by the corvette commanded by *Moyola*'s Captain).

The outlook was bleak, and improved little, but had to be endured. Since my time on board was not a happy one, it is not surprising that, apart from a few incidents, memories are few and dim and recollections of the officers and others of the crew are extremely hazy — in complete contrast to *Moyola*.

One small part of the refit comes to mind and that was finding an item in the defect list to improve the comfort in the officers' bathroom. On inspection it was quite adequate, but in contrast the ship's company's wash place was a revolting nausea. With the time-honoured custom of dispensing alcoholic hospitality in the right direction, the defect list was adjusted so that the lower deck bathing facilities were vastly improved and the officers' bathroom remained unaltered. Neither of these changes seemed to be appreciated by anyone when all returned from leave.

Eventually, suitably equipped with sun helmets and awnings, *Deveron* sailed from Liverpool to meet the deadly slant-eyed foe, and, as I recall dimly, made a largely solitary and uneventful passage to Colombo via Gibraltar, Suez and Aden.

We escorted convoys, carried out sweeps and took part in exercises, but at this time the Japanese were very inactive in the Indian Ocean, and no effort was made to send such a poorly armed vessel into Japanese held waters.

One clear memory comes to mind of an afternoon spent sailing a dinghy from the Colombo Yacht Club in that great harbour and watching with fascination a small full-rigggged ship entering under sail and coming to anchor. She must have been some five hundred tons. All sail was furled by a numerous crew and then, while one hand climbed to the mainmasthead and lashed the "Q" flag, the others swayed out a long boat.

A short while later, when the customs formalities had been completed, the "Q" flag was brought down on deck and the anchor weighed by hand while about twelve of her crew manned the oars in the long boat and towed the ship to her berth.

Altogether a commonplace occurrence a hundred years before, but in 1944 a very unusual sight. She was apparently the main supply boat for the Maldive Islands.

In October news reached us that we were to go to Durban for a refit and my heart rose at the prospect of being reunited with a certain attractive girl there, but sadly it was again a case of "haven't you heard? It's all changed. . ." and we continued our various tasks, making trips to exciting ports like Vizagapatam — a port with about as much charm as Freetown.

By December *Deveron* was sorely in need of docking and some repairs, but much to our disappointment it was not to Durban we were sent, but to Massawa in the Red Sea. Now the main base for the Ethiopian Navy, it had been the Italian Naval Base in their colony Eritrea and the main port for the invasion of Ethiopia (then known as Abyssinia) in 1935.

Like Italian Somaliland and Abyssinia, Eritrea had been overrun by British forces from the Sudan and East Africa and was now officially British Occupied Territory, where we tried to live up to the image of conquering heroes.

The dockyard labour force, while under British control, was partly composed of Italian Navy personnel and partly of Italian and local civilians. The language problem in Eritrea (and presumably other Italian colonies) had been solved by introducing a sort of simplified do-it-yourself Italian, where all verbs were limited to the infinitive and the vocabulary much reduced. The sex of inanimate objects was also forgotten.

The British Army and Navy made one great contribution to this *lingua franca* (or *italia?*) in a phrase which frequently ended any discussion about a job done or being planned. The phrase was used and understood by all — British, Italian, Arab, Eritrean and every other nationality.

The final verdict reached after a lengthy chatter in pidgin Italian could always be heard, regardless of the age, race, colour or creed of the speakers. It was always either "Bono" or alternatively "No fucking bono".

The British Town Major of Massawa recounted the story of the scene in his office on the morning after the first evening during which British troops had been allowed to enjoy the hospitality of the bars, dance halls and other entertainment establishments.

As soon as his office opened, a very distressed Madame of the brothel demanded admission and begged "Le Maggiore" to have prepared without delay a large notice to be posted in the entrance of her emporium to explain to the most welcome British customers that the Italian word "Basta" meant "Enough" or "Stop" or "Finish"

HMS Deveron
(Identical sister ship to HMS Moyola)

and was not to be confused with the English word "Bastard", since this misunderstanding had resulted in all her girls receiving two black eyes.

*   *   *   *

Deveron was in dockyard hands for some weeks and a fair amount of leave was granted. During this time some of us took the opportunity to visit Asmara and stay some days there. It was the capital of Eritrea and a fairly sophisticated Italian town, with a pleasant climate, having an altitude of some eight thousand feet. The Italians had built a beautiful road and a railway, as well as an aerial ropeway to connect Massawa at sea-level with Asmara — only forty miles away horizontally — but having to climb some ten thousand feet and then descend two thousand.

All three routes were marvels of engineering, but only the first two were for passenger traffic. If I remember correctly, a bucket on the ropeway travelled the distance in less than eight hours, which meant that the total cargo of a ship unloading at Massawa would be at Asmara forty miles way and up eight thousand feet only eight hours after unloading was completed.

All had been built for the 1935 invasion of Abyssinia (Ethiopia) when the Italians were persuaded by Mussolini to avenge the defeat they had suffered in 1896 and to increase their African colonies as well as joining up Eritrea with Italian Somaliland.

There was a story around that a lot of cargo was pilfered from the ropeway *en route* as it crossed wild, desolate and deserted territory, and the losses mystified and aggravated the Italians as no culprits could be found and observation of the route was difficult due to the relative absence of roads. Apparently it took a long time to discover that the thieves were monkeys, who delighted in shinning up the pylons and jumping into the passing buckets. Once installed they chucked out anything small enough to handle like a baby tossing stuff out of its pram before jumping from the bucket on to the next pylon.

A visit to Asmara was not complete without a sampling of the Beergarden and a visit to "The Glass House".

The first was a delightful Viennese style drinking establishment plentifully supplied with a locally brewed beer entitled Menotti (and beer was an expensive rarity in those days everywhere else East of Suez), which could be drunk from beautiful glass half-litre or one-litre tankards or — if you were brave and thirsty — from elegant glass wellington boots which came in three sizes: two-and-a-half litres, three-and-a-half litres, and five litres. They all looked deceptively small until you started to drink them, but when the first gigantic swallow from the large boot only dropped the level about half an inch, the size of the task began to show itself.

The Glass House was rather different. It had been set up to cater for the comfort of Italian senior officers, Majors, Lieutenant-Commanders and above, and consisted of a pleasant house with a large garden and a high surrounding wall pierced with a gate having in it a small grilled window through which those desirous of entering could be surveyed and made to show their qualifications before being admitted. If one passed muster all was well.

Once inside the garden it was a short walk to the front door of the house inside which one was greeted by your hostess, a charming large Italian lady with an effervescent personality. In no time at all drinks were produced and the hostess introduced a bevy of extremely attractive — if somewhat scantily clad — girls who were eager to dance and drink and remarkably ready to invite one upstairs to the comfort of the well-furnished bedrooms. The particularly remarkable feature of all those rooms was the large four-poster bed of modern design with chromium-plated bed posts supporting a canopy, the underside of which was a mirror.

This item coupled with the slang name for the Army prisons accounted for the title bestowed upon this house of joy.

The Italians went to some lengths to cater for the love-life of their servicemen, even to the extent of fitting out large Alfa-Romeo buses as mobile brothels for service in the Western Desert. On one occasion when a coastal town was captured by our forces, towards sunset a trio of these "buses of joy" were found in the square and in a sort of Officers-Selection-Board-Initiative-Test a subaltern was instructed to take the occupants to the local convent and have them bedded down for the night. Drills for such emergencies are not published in Army manuals, nor are they the subject for much activity at Sandhurst, and one can just imagine the scene at the nunnery door when our gallant young officer with no knowledge of Italian endeavoured to explain by sign language what was required.

The door was slammed in his face and an official complaint was made in the morning. When the incident was finally explained to the Irish Mother Superior she laughed as loud as anyone.

The essential difference in Italy between "Ladies" and "Gents" as written on certain doors also introduces a deal of confusion. The words are "Signore" and "Signori" and to this day I can never remember which is which. Perhaps I am sub-consciously hoping I will get it wrong again with equally happy results.

New Year's Eve was naturally a great celebration and after much convivial drinking here and there some of us found ourselves in the main hotel in Massawa in the last hour of 1944, where the heat of the night encouraged many to dive into the swimming pool. This seemed a marvelloys idea and so after grabbing a swimming costume, I dashed to the men's changing room. Just before throwing open the door I saw the word "Signori" and decided instantly that this means "Ladies".

Somewhat confused, but topped up with Gordon's and John Dewar, I retreated rapidly and took the alternative door at the run, deducing that, if wrong first time, I must be right the second. I was wrong on both counts, but should not have worried since I was made most welcome.

It was certainly a novel way to see in the New Year.

* * * *

Eventually everything was "Bono" and we set off back to Colombo to continue where we left off.

We embarked as a passenger an Italian submarine captain (they were on our side by this time), whose submarine was used for training escorts at Colombo. During the voyage we had many long interesting discussions (largely in pidgin Italian), during one of which he described to me the monumental Cecil-B-de-Mille type cavalry battles which had been fought on the Russian front and in which his brother — a cavalry officer — had taken part. The German army had entirely given up cavalry in favour of tanks, and when faced with large open spaces in which the cavalry could operate successfully — living off the land — they had to appeal to their allies for help. Italy, Austria, Hungary and even the volunteer Spanish Blue Division provided the necessary units.

Having been recommended for a First Lieutenant's job and there being none immediately available, someone had the brilliant idea of making me "Spare First Lieutenant" for the newly-created "Burma Coast Escort Force", and in due course I left *Deveron* and joined probably the most remarkable ship in the Royal Navy — *HMS Gombroon*.

Where the name came from I have no idea, but the ship herself had a chequered history and her crew was somewhat unusual too.

She was an intermediate passenger/cargo ship of about five thousand tons built around the turn of the century on the Clyde for the Austrian merchant marine. In 1919 she had been handed over to the Italians (on our side in the 1914-18 war) for war reparations, and had been operated by the Italian East Africa Line from then until 1940 between ports in Italy and those in Eritrea and Italian Somaliland. Doubtless she carried supplies for the Abyssinian invasion in 1935 and 1936.

When Italy entered the war in 1940 she was in Massawa and was eventually sunk as a blockship in the entrance to the harbour as British forces closed in. She was later refloated and handed over to the British India Line, who operated her for some time until she was taken over temporarily by the Royal Navy as a repair ship in the Persian Gulf and was actually on her way to be broken up in April

195

1945 when she was pressed into service yet again to be a repair ship in Rangoon (which was to be captured shortly), since the real vessel programmed for this job (*Beachy Head*) was behind schedule at her building yard in Vancouver.

Her crew consisted of British deck and engineer officers, Royal Navy Petty Officer technicians for repair work (mainly C of E, I suppose), and Lascar sailors and engine room staff, who were Muslims. Following P & O practice, the cooks and stewards were Goanese and thus Roman Catholic, while the Chinese carpenter Yeh Chang (of whom more anon) was presumably a Confucian. For the cleaning of the boilers of the escorts we embarked some forty Ceylonese, of whom thirty-nine were Hindu and one was a Buddhist.

Fortunately we never held Sunday Divisions with its attendant church service, which would have been somewhat difficult to organise.

Even joining the ship followed a madcap routine, since she was in Bombay and I in Colombo. A railway journey of several days via Madras got me to Bombay in time to discover that *Gombroon* had sailed for Colombo, and so I had to trek back again by train, since perversely no ships seemed to sail between those ports.

When eventually I mounted the accommodation ladder and arrived on the after well deck, an extraordinary sight met my eyes. The deck was covered in Jerries. No, not Germans, real old fashioned traditional chamber pots.

Part of the preparation for sailing for Rangoon was to clear out a part of Number Three hold which extended forward under the accommodation and had been used as a sort of attic for many years. Anything not required was stored there and now was brought to light to make space.

There were certainly Royal Navy chamber pots of various types, although I did not see any of those with blue foul anchors and gold lines reserved for admirals. There were British India pots, and there were Italian East African pots, and I dare say there were a few Austrian ones and even some dour uncomfortable Clydeside productions. I suppose today they would be worth much money, but at that time they were destined for a flotation test ready in a few hundred years' time to surprise an archaeological researcher who may discover them at the bottom of Colombo harbour.

It transpired that *Gombroon* was not only a repair ship but also a Headquarters for the B.C.E.F. — Burma Coast Escort Force — and this meant that practically all the officers on board had some sort of title, Chief Staff Officer, Staff Navigating Officer, etc., etc., and I felt somewhat left out. However, after spending one day surveying *Gombroon*'s somewhat archaic fire-fighting equipment, I decided to appoint myself "Chief Fire Fighting Officer" and following the local custom, had "C.F.F.O." painted on my cabin door.

The joke backfired a few days later when a large fire-fighting pump arrived on board and I was asked why I had organised this acquisition. The title was graven in letters of stone, as will be seen later.

The next job that was thrust upon me was to be made "Mate of the Upper Deck", which in effect meant taking charge of the Lascar deck crew and supervising painting and cleaning of the deck and upperworks and handling all seamanship activities. I had to get used to the Lascar crew's merchant navy customs and practices — a matter largely of trial and error.

The Lascar heirarchy was that the crew consisted of one chief of chiefs — the Serang — a wizened and wily old codger, who had been at sea since Adam was a boy and *Victory* an oak tree.

Below him were four Sekunnis — quartermasters — who steered the ship at sea and stood gangway watches in harbour. The seaman were divided into Tindals gangs of about twelve men each headed by a Tindal. *Gombroon* had two Tindals gangs. The engine room staff had a similar structure, but I had nothing to do with them and can no longer remember the titles.

In a curious division of his own was Yeh Chang, the Chinese carpenter — an inscrutable character always dressed in a sleeveless white singlet, khaki shorts and a khaki sun helmet.

The Serang and a few others spoke a little bit of pidgin English, but essentially the language was Hindustani, of which I had none to begin with, but gradually acquired a smattering. In fact it took some time for me to realise that some common orders were in fact in English but pronounced so oddly as to be unrecognisable. For example, "Oop salack" actually meant "Up slack". The Lascars could not pronounce an "s" followed by a consonant, so that "slack" became "salack" and "steam" became "issteam". Furthermore, Hindustani had no twentieth century technical terms of its own and just used the English words pronounced as well as possible.

Thus with "Tikh hai" being Hindustani for "It is right", and

"Nay tikh hai" meaning "It is not all right", a fault in a motor car engine might well be described by the phrase "Carburettor nay tikh hai, Sahib".

Although the language difficulty was considerable to begin with, confidence in the ability and long experience of these sailors soon developed a degree of mutual trust. It was necessary for me to discard the Royal Navy tradition of all hands keeping silent so that only the orders of the officer could be heard. The Lascar system called for everyone to give orders simultaneously, but somehow or other the Serang's view prevailed and if I could refrain from interfering the job seemed to get done without any fatal accidents occurring.

The war in Europe seemed very far away, but by listening to the news it was obvious that it was drawing to a close. The end came quite suddenly, and although it was a cause for celebration, we were only too aware of the long haul ahead to defeat Japan. The general opinion was that it would be at least two years of hard slog and possible much more.

Winston Churchill's speech came through to us at about eight p.m. and immediately afterwards all the ships in harbour started blowing their sirens. Determined to join in, I went to the bridge, but soon discovered we had no steam since our boilers were all being cleaned prior to departure.

I looked around for something else to celebrate with, and found some distress rockets. These are pretty superior items compared with the usual titchy things one lets off on Guy Fawkes night, the rocket being about two feet long and the stick about five feet. They are normally discharged by being inserted in a metal tube shaped to contain rocket and stick and having a simple breech mechanism in which one inserted a small igniting cartridge known — for some obscure reason — as a friction tube, and this was fired with a length of cord to keep the firer well clear.

Needless to say I could find no friction tubes, so I put the stick into the rings fitted to receive sun awning stanchions and started lighting matches under the business end of the rocket. Although it nearly blew my eyebrows off, it worked and up it sailed into the sky to burst into a beautiful red star, which floated slowly down.

That really started it. Within a few minutes every ship in the harbour seemed to be competing to produce the greatest effect. Rockets, verey flares, snowflake parachute flares, and even star shell, were soon to be seen floating down in all directions somewhat in

198

contravention of the rather pompous signal which had been sent to all ships a few days previously, worded to the effect ". . . on the occasion of the cessation of hostilities in Europe pyrotechnics are not, repeat not, to be expended".

Going ashore in a motor boat half an hour later was really quite dangerous with rocket sticks (wood and steel) and burning flares raining down from the skies.

Eventually the news came through that Rangoon had been captured and *Gombroon* sailed from Colombo. As was normal wartime practice at sea, we carried out a continuous anti-submarine zig-zag manoeuvre which necessitated making large alterations of course at pre-arranged times, calculated to preserve our intended direction of advance and confuse any observing submarine.

This produced an unexpected problem on the first evening at sea.

Just after six p.m., as the sun was setting over a calm ocean, I was enjoying a welcome gin on the promenade deck when an excited English signalman arrived with the message,

"The Captain's compliments, Sir, and would you come to the bridge immediately. Your Lascars are mutinying."

Swallowing the gin rapidly, I ascended to the bridge, passing through a gathering of excited Indian seamen clustered around the foot of the bridge ladder. Reporting to the Captain, he greeted me with the words,

"Your damned Lascars seem to be in a state of mutiny. Kindly deal with the matter."

Mutinies are not too common in the Royal Navy, and instruction on dealing with them is somewhat limited. Personally I could recall no instruction at all, and I could foresee additionally a language difficulty as I descended into the midst of the highly excited shouting mob whose cries seemed even louder and even somewhat menacing.

Fortunately I caught sight of the Serang, who was emulating the Duke of Plaza Toro — leading his men from behind.

"Hola, Serang. What is all this about?"

The crew fell more or less silent and gathered around to listen.

"Sahib, Sahib, the Sahibs humbug our Mohammad."

("Humbug" is one of those much used words in pidgin English with a variety of meanings to suit the occasion.)

"It not good, Sahib, all men much anger."

"Tell me, Serang, how Sahibs humbug Mohammad?"

"Oh Sahib, it very bad. All men on foredeck praying to Mecca.

All men looking to sun, bowing down very much. Then no more looking to sun, all looking that way."

Suddenly I twigged. By chance a large alteration of some forty degrees had happened to occur right in the middle of their evening praying session and the turning ship had pointed them away from Mecca in mid-prayer.

Desperately I tried to explain to the Serang.

"Oh, I savvy, Serang. But Sahibs not humbugging Mohammad. Sahibs want stop all men going to Seventh Heaven. Savvy nasty chota Nipponese men in Unterseeboten" — pidgin English for submarine failed me — "try to make ship go boom, all men — Sahibs and Lascars all go Seventh Heaven. Sahibs steer ship humbug nasty chota Nipponese. All men live."

The Serang looked at me with the kind of pitying sadness that schoolmasters reserve for small boys who dare to suggest that two plus six might be seven.

"But Sahib, Sahib, if it Allah's will all dis ship men go Seventh Heaven, Sahib not can stop dat, no way."

That foxed me.

"Well, ah, yes, possibly," I mumbled, then with the germ of an idea forming,

"Wait here, Serang, me talk Captain Sahib."

Dashing back to the bridge I endeavoured to explain to the Captain the religious problems of an anti-submarine zig-zag and tentatively suggested that the ship's zig-zag routine might be modified and the ship's course held steady during that time.

Eventually the Captain agreed — much against his principles — and the Lascars returned forward full of smiles. I just hoped that the news did not reach the Japanese Navy and result in instructions to their submarine captains to take advantage of this situation.

* * * *

Like all old ships in the East (and some newer ones), *Gombroon* had a large population of rats who had established regular routes throughout the vessel, mainly behind the wood panelling in the passenger accommodation.

They seemed to like bony material, and would trim one's finger-nails or toenails if given the chance. This practice certainly occasioned a very rude and unpleasant awakening. They also seemed to like the tongues of leather shoes, and trouser fly buttons and shirt buttons when they were made of a material consisting largely of dried milk. This was a sort of predecessor of many of the plastics seen today and was particularly used for the manufacture of handles for table knives, which also tended to be appropriated by the rats.

Various people had different solutions. Mine was to acquire a mosquito net and sleep under that after hanging my shirt, trousers and shoes from a ring more or less in the middle of the cabin deck-head.

During the passage to Rangoon, when I was standing the middle watch, the navigator appeared on the bridge with his face shining whiter and brighter than the moon. His vocal chords were somewhat constricted, and I could get no word out of him until he had been persuaded to drink a cup of coffee while continuously pulling at his shirt and scratching his body frantically.

When at last he could talk, he explained that while lying asleep in the chart room — wearing the normal tropical gear of a shirt and shorts — he had been woken up by a rat which had got down inside his shirt and was running around inside with an uncomfortable scratchy gait. It had taken a few minutes of confused thinking before he was sufficiently awake to stand up and pull his shirt out from inside his trousers to allow the rat to drop free.

In due course we arrived at Rangoon and came to anchor a few miles above the city, where we remained for several months. Every five or six days, four ships would come alongside and do their boiler cleaning and what minor repairs we could manage and as soon as they left four more could take their place while others anchored nearby.

The stream of the river ran strongly, especially with the ebb tide assisting, so that boat traffic presented some problems which were partly alleviated by the appearance of a forty-foot steam boat which had laid immobile throughout the Japanese occupation with essential parts of its engine buried nearby.

Entertainment facilities for the ship's companies of visiting vessels of the Burma Coast Escort Force were non-existent to start with and access to Rangoon city was limited by an absence of motor transport. Since my duties as Mate of the Upper Deck (and C.F.F.O.!) were also almost non-existent, I became official scrounger and E.F.T.O. (Escort Force Transport Officer).

Our pool of motor transport grew steadily from small beginnings, mostly by improper means. Early on I acquired a fifteen cwt. lorry (in exchange for a case of gin) which had been damaged by a Japanese 37mm shell. Its petrol pump being non-existent, a petrol tank was installed on the cab roof and gravity did the rest.

Some jeeps and another truck were acquired from a departing Royal Marine party against some dubious signatures, and after that it was all plain theft. If any of my people saw a damaged or abandoned vehicle anywhere, the news acted like a fire alarm and a raiding party set off with a tow rope and any necessities like a spare wheel. As soon as the acquired vehicle reached our lair (which was the skeleton of a cremation ground coke shed roofed in with *Gombroon*'s spare hatch covers), it was instantly painted R.N. grey and sign written "B.C.E.F.", together with a fictitious registration number.

For myself I acquired a large Dodge saloon, previously a Japanese general's staff car, which soon boasted number plates with the legend E.F.T.O., whilst my uniform was now jungle green battledress with khaki R.N.R. Lieutenant shoulder straps surmounted by a bush hat with an officer's cap badge stitched to the front of the hat band.

Sikh policemen on traffic duty normally stopped all traffic to let me through!

It also goes without saying that, being skilled thieves, we took considerable precautions to stop our own vehicles being stolen. Jeeps and trucks had to have padlocks on the bonnets and a chain and padlock through the steering wheel. The Army and the RAF were too trusting and suffered accordingly.

One obscure religious problem was insoluble, namely the supply of mutton on board *Gombroon*. This had been embarked (unfortunately) in Colombo and not in Bombay. It was shipped from Australia and each carcase was marked with indelible dye on both fore and hind quarters. Every one hundred carcases was accompanied by a certificate in English and Indian stating that the animal had been killed in the correct Muslim manner and thus was fit for consumption by the faithful. Unfortunately the languages spoken in Ceylon (Tamil and Sinhalese) are entirely different from the Hindustani spoken in Bombay and even the writing characters are as different as Russian and European. The further complication being that those on board who spoke Tamil or Sinhalese were all Hindus or Buddhists, so in the unshakable opinion of the Lascars, it was all a con to feed them unholy impure meat. I even went to the extent of getting an Indian Army Sergeant to come aboard and explain, but it was to no avail, although he departed with a carcase and a broad smile, having been living on tinned corned beef for months. The Muslims would not even touch a piece of pork, but, of course, this did not apply to the Goanese, who were all Roman Catholic and were always required to handle any pork.

The Indian attitude to truth is also a little strange — except perhaps to most politicians.

For example, one day some British Military Police escorted on board one of the Sekunnis, named Jaindoo, and informed the Officer of the Watch that he had been found in a brothel. When he was brought before me as a defaulter, the conversation went as follows:

"These policemen say you were in bad house, Jaindoo."

"Oh no, Sahib," he assured me, rocking his head from side to side. "Me just having tea with my brother."

I accepted that "brother" could mean somewhat less than a blood relation and replied,

"Well, that's fine, Jaindoo, you send a message to your brother to come on board and speak for you and everything will be all right."

With more head rocking, Jaindoo said,

"Sahib, perhaps he is not my brother. Perhaps he just very old friend."

"Yes, I understand. You just get your very old friend to come on board and speak for you."

With even more head rocking and a rather guilty expression, Jaindoo said,

"Ah, Sahib, perhaps he is not very, very old friend."

"Well, good God, how long have you known him then?"

"Well, Sahib, I walk along street and he shout from window 'Hello, sailor, come inside.'"

On another occasion the seamen had been loading food stores aboard *Gombroon* and these were duly checked into the store by the British storekeeper. When all was completed, he came to me to advise that a case of jam had gone missing between the upper deck and the store below.

I raised the matter with the Serang, who assured me that none of his men had taken it, but on investigation the evidence was watertight and I later told the Serang,

"No shore leave until we find that case of jam."

Deadlock set in. Nobody went ashore, but the amount of work done by the deck crew sank to a minus quantity. Those uneducated sailors could have given post-graduate courses in "going slow" to the most rabid revolutionary European shop steward.

It was fascinating to watch, and was accompanied by sufficient miserable, doleful hard-done-by expressions to melt the heart of a stone statue.

The battle of wills continued for several weeks with no quarter given on either side. Eventually the Serang chose a moment when I seemed to be in a good mood to say,

"Sahib, Sahib, big feast day next week. Men want to go shore side to buy food."

"Certainly not, Serang," I retorted angrily, "Not until we find that bloody great case of jam."

The Serang adopted a painful and hurt expression, and then gesticulating with his hands he said,

"But Sahib, Sahib, nay burra wallah hai sed chota wallah." (Not a big one, Sahib, only a little one.)

The jam came back, work returned to normal, and I was even invited to the feast held the following week on the forehatch after dark.

Although it took me some time to get used to the different customs and manners of the Lascar seamen, their skills acquired over many years at sea soon became apparent and compared very favourably with the much-diluted professionalism existing by that time in our Navy, where two or three years at sea made an "old hand". Amongst the Lascars it seemed that ten years service was required for Able Seaman status.

V.J. Day (Victory over the Japanese) came very suddenly and quite unexpectedly, when we were all preparing for the invasion of Singapore and Malaya and everyone was entirely used to the idea of the war against the Japanese continuing for several more years.

The manufacture and possible use of the Atom bomb had been a very well-kept secret, and its sudden use a tremendous surprise. Its power was incomprehensible and entirely unappreciated — like the horrors of the German concentration camps — until films and photographs were available some time later.

After very nearly six years — in many cases, like mine, one's total adult life — fighting the war had been the overriding occupation and now suddenly it was over. The surprise was a considerable mental shock. The thought that by some mistake one had actually survived while many that one knew had not was followed by an irrational fear that fate might have some other nasty surprise in store for one before being actually allowed to return home and start enjoying the peace.

There was, of course, a lot of celebrating with yet another splicing of the mainbrace and much speculation as to when one would get home to be demobbed (as the phrase went).

Very rightly an ingenious but simple scheme was devised, whereby your age and length of service were used to calculate a mystic demob number. There may have been other factors, like rank and married status, but mainly it was age and service. As I recall, my "number" was thirty-one, and in fact my relief was appointed on New Year's Eve, but at this moment that was all in the hazy unknown future.

Meanwhile the show had to go on, and a signal was received giving details of a Review of the Burma Coast Escort Force and other naval vessels at Rangoon by the Supreme Allied Commander South-East Asia, none other than Lord Louis Mountbatten. It transpired that the date fixed gave us one day in which to improve the outward appearance of *Gombroon*. Two nights and a day to be exact, since the boiler cleaning escorts would depart one evening, the following day was clear and the Review the day after.

In consultation with the Captain, it was decided to try to paint the starboard side of the ship and, if possible, the starboard side of the large funnel and the four large engine room ventilators.

There had been no opportunity to paint the ship for nearly a year, and with the escorts alongside much of the time quantities of gash had been thrown overboard and much of this had stuck to *Gombroon*'s topside. The funnel and ventilators were streaked with rust.

However, with the tide flooding at the time of Lord Louis' passing our designated anchorage, only the starboard side would be seen by him.

I consulted with the Serang with some trepidation, for by naval standards to paint even one side of the ship was quite an evolution, and *Gombroon*'s high topsides were about twice the area of the same length of naval vessel. Painting the topsides of a naval ship, be she a corvette or a cruiser, normally involved some considerable preparation beforehand and the employment of the whole ship's company for one day. In *Gombroon* we had only twenty-four sailors, four Sekunnis, two Tindals and a Serang — a sum total of thirty-one. Even a corvette could muster fifty-odd, and frigates and sloops around one hundred and fifty.

205

With the Serang being religiously teetotal I could not even think of bribing him with beer and raised the matter somewhat cautiously.

"Serang, next week the King's brother" (the best I could do!) " comes to look at all the ships so we must try to make the ship clean and nice. " (I was almost tempted to say " all same Queen Victoria " in emulation of the traditional dockside pimps' claims.) "Perhaps we could paint all one side of ship. "

I looked hesitantly at the Serang and he seemed unshaken, so I added "and the funnel" and, a few seconds later, "and the ventilators. "

"That will be very all right, Sahib, " said the Serang, and I breathed a sigh of relief and departed in search of a restorative gin.

Just as the escorts were casting off, with thirty-six hours to the Review, the Captain sent for me and I arrived to find him clutching a signal and looking crestfallen.

" My God, Scott, it looks as though we may be bunkered. It now appears that the Review may be at 1100 but that it *may* be delayed until 1600 and confirmation will not be made until tomorrow evening. Whichever side we paint, it is bound by Sod's Law to be the wrong one. "

After discussing the possibilities there seemed to be only one solution, but there was some doubt as to whether it was possible or not, so that with even more trepidation I sent for the Serang and endeavoured to explain the problem, eventually saying,

" Do you think you could paint both sides of the ship in one day . . . and the funnel . . . and the ventilators? "

" Yes indeed, Sahib, we will do this for the King Emperor's brother, but please Sahib, may we start one hour early? "

" Yes, indeed, " I said, mightily relieved.

The next day it seemed to be a matter of pride that the job should be done and in that one day I think they more than made up for the many days of "go slow". As darkness fell all was bright with new paint, except the difficult overhanging counter stern. The Serang came to me and said,

" Almost all finished, Sahib. If Sahib arrange 'lectric lamps under stern all finish tonight. "

The torpedomen in the ship's repair staff quickly conjured up some cargo flood lights and those marvellous Lascars did the rest.

The confirmation of the Review time came later that evening as 1100 with the additional surprise news that "El Supremo" would board certain ships and inspect the ships' companies and, needless to say, *Gombroon* was to be one of the lucky ones!

Although the Lascars were marvellous seamen and although they were officially in the Navy (on the ubiquitous T124 articles) and although they had been issued with naval uniform, they had never received instruction in parade ground drill and had only worn their uniform for going ashore.

There were many last things to do in the morning and eventually I had about fifteen minutes left in which to teach them how to stand at ease, how to stand at attention upon the order, and to persuade them not to spit upon the deck (or over the side) whilst the "King's Brother" was in sight.

Eventually I had them lined up on the forecastle more or less in a straight line with their feet apart and hands behind their backs.

The dreaded moment arrived. "El Supremo" approached, followed by our Captain and a retinue of staff. As he mounted the forecastle ladder I came to attention and shouted,

"*Gombroon*'s Yeh Karo,"

and was gratified to see that almost all managed to bring their feet together and their hands to their sides. Left-right-left-right-halt-salute-and-report.

"*Gombroon* Deck Crew, Sir, present and ready for your inspection."

Mountbatten surveyed them from afar and I could almost hear him quoting Wellington with some remark to the effect of,

". . . by God they frighten me."

In fact he said bravely,

"A fine body of men."

He passed down the front rank, saying,

"Any of these fellas speak English?"

"Oh yes, Sir," I said, "this man speaks some."

Mountbatten paused, eyed the sailor and barked,

"What is your name?"

I realised too late what was coming. Grinning broadly and innocently the seaman said what sounded ominously like,

"Fucker Mohammad, Sahib."

Mountbatten gave me a sideways look which seemed to say "You landed that one on me" and said to F. Mohammad,

"How long have you been at sea?"

"Thirty years, Sahib."

"Fucker Mohammed, Sahib"

Slightly puzzled, Mountbatten said,

"How old are you?"

"Thirty years, Sahib," replied the smiling proud Mohammad.

Mountbatten looked at me in puzzlement in which there may have been a thought that I was putting him on.

"Well, Sir," I said, "You know most of these chaps do not really know how old they are."

With that Mountbatten continued his inspection while refraining from asking any more questions in fear of what further odd replies he might get.

On completion I saluted and watched his retinue disappear down the forecastle ladder before standing at ease in front of my gallant band and once more ordering,

"Yeh Karo."

Obediently they put their legs apart and their hands behind their backs, since even with the small training they had had they could respond to an order of,

"Do This."

        *   *   *   *

By this time the Japanese had been almost completely driven out of Burma by the XIVth Army and to complement their land advance, a seaborne invasion of the Malay Peninsula and eventually Singapore was almost ready to go. Following the final Japanese surrender (the details of which not everyone was confident would be adhered to), the projected invasion was brought forward and put into immediate action and we, in *Gombroon*, were warned to be ready to move down to Singapore as soon as it was properly occupied. With the war officially over, few if any of us aspired to being up at the sharp end and possible getting knocked off by some fanatical Nipponese bent on disobeying the Emperor to save his "honour".

Eventually the order to move came and we set about closing up shop in Rangoon, which for me amounted to a "rabbit distribution party". After some drinks aboard *Gombroon*, attended by various Army friends ashore, I had pleasure in giving away a steamboat and crew, a salved Japanese barge, a number of motor vehicles (including the Dodge saloon), and even a fully-equipped theatre, which had just been completed in anticipation of a long stay in Rangoon.

It only remained to hoist our thirty-two foot cutter which had been our diving boat and disentangle the two anchor cables which had managed to acquire only about ten turns, despite swinging to four tides a day for several months.

We started to prepare the davits for hoisting the cutter, swinging them out and throwing over the heavy lower blocks before overhauling them down to water level. This turned out to be a grievous error, since the sisal rope had become so rotten with sun and rain that it could not even support the weight of the blocks, let alone a boat. They disappeared into the river and I had to improvise some slings and hoist the cutter with derricks on to the after cargo hatches for the voyage.

Disentangling the two twisted anchor cables was another game, since *Gombroon* (unlike proper RN ships) had no mooring swivel to make a proper moor without twists.

It was necessary, therefore, to adopt a very old cure for the problem. After counting the number of twists, a sailor was lowered down on a bosun's chair with a length of four-inch rope to lash the twisted part firmly together in a big sausage.

The starboard cable was then unshackled on deck and a three-and-a-half-inch wire was passed out through the starboard hawsepipe and around the lashed cable several times and brought back up to the hawsepipe and shackled to the outboard end of the starboard cable. This was then released from its slip on deck and allowed to drop outboard. Heaving in on the three-and-a-half-inch wire eventually wound a few turns of cable the opposite way to the original tangle. When an equal number of turns had been achieved the inboard end of the starboard cable was re-shackled to the outboard and all was ready for "*la momente critique*".

How to release the lashing of the two cables which would spring apart rather violently at the last moment?

The Serang approached me with some fear to explain the dangers of cutting or casting off the lashing from a bosun's chair. He was quite right, it would have been pretty close to suicide.

"Aha, Serang," I gloated, "But we are not going to cut the lashing or cast it off."

"How, Sahib, can we get back anchors?"

"Burn it."

"Burn it, Sahib??"

"Yes, fetch some Kerosene and pour it on the lashing and then light it. Bye and bye, rope will burn away and break. That way no man close to chain. Plenty safe."

"Acha, Sahib, that plenty good."

And once more he and all the crew were all smiles.

It was better than a firework display. All the deck crew peered over the rail as a burning piece of rope was lowered down to the lashing soaked in Kerosene, which had become somewhat volatile in the hot sun. The woomph with which the lashing ignited almost blew their moustaches off, but the whole performance delighted them all, and when the chain eventually broke free and clear with horrible noises, they were as puffed up with pride as whores at a christening.

One anchor was then weighed before any more turns could be put in by the forthcoming turn of the tide, and *Gombroon* was "in all respects ready for sea".

By merchant navy custom, Chang — the carpenter — was in charge of the anchor windlass and here again some special pidgin English was required. Clutching up the cable gypsy (connecting the windlass engine to the wheels that pulled in the chain cable) was only done in response to the order,

"Put on the gear,"

and de-clutching was similarly,

"Take away the gear."

No other wording produced any result.

Having duly weighed our second anchor, we departed from Rangoon and once clear of the river mouth set course for Singapore which had been liberated without the expected trouble.

Every morning since I joined *Gombroon*, when I met Chang on deck (resplendent always in his sleeveless white singlet, khaki shorts, khaki sun helmet and sandals), he would smile broadly and say,

"Morning, Sah,"

to which I replied courteously and occasionally added some details of work to be done. It was always done "plopper manner", either "Right away, Sah", or "Bye um bye, Sah".

He was a meticulous craftsman, and somehow the work in *Gombroon* seemed to me to be far below his talents. He lived a curious, lonely life, being in most ways neither part of the Lascar crew nor yet part of the British ship's company in race, religion or philosophy. In our total time in Burma he never went ashore, although there was the usual Chinese community of shopkeepers that were found everywhere in the East and nowadays also all over the world.

211

To my surprise, the first morning after we anchored in Singapore, after his usual morning greeting, he said,

"Chang go shoreside today, Sah?"

This was a turn-up for the book, but knowing there was a large Chinese population there, I said,

"Oh yes, certainly, Chang. I suppose you have friends here."

"Ho yes, Sah, me have bluther here, Sah."

"Good show, Chang. You go shoreside and see your brother," and with that I wandered off on my daily rounds without a further thought. The next morning the same inscrutable smiling Chang tossed out his usual "Morning, Sah" to which I replied, and then remembering the previous day's unusual request, I added,

"How was your brother, Chang?"

Still with a broad smile, he said,

"No findum bluther, Sah. Nip choppum head," and with that he drew his outstretched fingers across his neck in a most demonstrative gesture without reducing his smile a fraction.

Conventional replies to that seemed somewhat inadequate, and I could only do my best with a mumbled,

"Very sorry to hear that, Chang."

I don't think he ever went ashore again.

＊　　＊　　＊　　＊

The habit of "scrounging" motor vehicles and anything else we required seemed to be hard to cast off, but tended to become more personal now that the war was over.

By chance I encountered the officer in charge of the warehouse containing all the Samurai swords which Mountbatten (quite rightly) had required all Japanese officers to surrender. A little bit of barter resulted and I became the possessor of a fine sword which I was assured was a "guaranteed five-header". Sword blades are handed down in the family, with each generation supplying a new hilt but retaining the blade which may be several hundred years old. They are made by forging out a bar of iron to a certain length and then dipping it in powdered charcoal (carbon) and forge welding it to itself and repeating the effect a fixed number of times according to a religious ceremony. If I remember rightly, it is eight folds, which in fact gives two hundred and fifty-six layers of iron and carbon, rather in the same way that the French bakers make croissants with butter

212

and dough. The finished bar is of a very high quality steel which takes an edge like a razor. (One friend rubbed his thumb up the blade while examining it and did not realise he was cutting himself until the cutting edge grated on the bone.)

The final touch, in times gone by, was to apply to the Imperial prison for a batch of convicted prisoners to use as test material. They were lined up in a row, kneeling down, and the official sword tester took a golf stroke and then certified the number of heads which were separated at a single stroke, which was then engraved on the portion of the blade which fits inside the hilt. Any son of Nippon whose family only had a "two-header" would, if he made good, replace his family weapon with a blade of higher rating — hopefully even a five-header, which was apparently top quality.

My other main acquisition was a Japanese Kamikaze motor boat, which again was the result of a bit of barter. My official scrounging activities brought me into contact with the Royal Army Service Corps Motor Boat Company Officer, who had found himself put in charge of a Kamikaze Boat Factory.

Apparently dozens of these factories had been set up all over what the Japanese called "The South East Asia Co-Prosperity Sphere". Each one was scheduled to produce a thousand plywood motor boats about sixteen feet long, designed to carry an explosive charge in the fore part, which was set off by a crude mechanism consisting of a stout bowsprit some two feet long with a pointed after end, which impinged on a detonator. The craft had a crew of one, whose job it was to drive the boat to a point where he could ram an Allied vessel and explode the charge.

The steering gear was, I noticed, fitted with a clamp so that (presumably) the less fanatical sons of Nippon who were not one hundred per cent keen on dying for the Emperor and Fatherland could fix the rudder and dive off the stern at the last minute with some small chance of survival.

While any one of these craft could achieve a speed of over twenty knots, it could probably have been destroyed by 20mm Oerlikon guns before it reached their target, but the situation might have been somewhat fraught if they had appeared in swarms rather than singly and the cloak of night would have assisted them. Their small wooden hulls would have given a very poor radar echo, which would have further increased their chances of reaching the target.

It is interesting to note that the yard where I acquired my boat was kitted up to build a thousand of those craft and I saw stacked up in the yard the one thousand brand new Ford V8 petrol engines still in their packing cases in which they had left the Detroit factory.

Presumably the Export Vice President of Ford had more than earned his Christmas bonus in the last few years before Pearl Harbour.

The arguments in favour of using the Atom Bomb to bring the war to a close generally state that more lives — both Allied and Japanese — would have been lost in the eventual defeat of Japanese forces and this particular weapon was probably only one of many which would have been brought to bear on the Allied invaders.

It is impossible to estimate how many ships might have been sunk by these real "mosquito craft", but one can only imagine with horror the effect of, say, twenty thousand of these little boats even if only operating in "swarms" of a few hundred.

However, to return to my own acquisition, it was to be Yard Number Two, the R.A.S.C. officer having kept Number One for himself. The mass production line had just reached the point where the first boat would be complete, and it seemed a pity not to finish off a number of partly-completed craft, since all the material was at hand and most of the work done.

The crudity of the design was pretty extreme. The engine was connected directly to the propellor shaft with no clutch or astern mechanism. The boat was therefore securely moored while the engine was started with the electric self-starter. As soon as the engine fired, the boat strained at her mooring ropes and continued thus until the engine was fully warmed up. Then the mooring ropes were cast off, hurried good-byes exchanged and at the touch of the self-starter, I shot off like a bolt from a crossbow.

What fun. What glorious exhilaration. Monarch of all I surveyed, I swept across Singapore harbour making a few circuits of frigates containing friends, finally making several circuits of *Gombroon* and shouting for someone to come down to the bottom of the accommodation ladder to take my mooring rope.

As soon as someone was ready, I aimed for the ladder with one hand ready to switch the ignition off, knowing that steering would not be very effective once the propellor stopped turning.

My pride was severely dented when I found that switching off the ignition had no effect whatsoever, and I shot past the accommodation ladder at about twelve knots which seemed to be the craft's minimum speed.

Circling around *Gombroon* I opened the engine hatch ahead of the steering wheel and pulled off all the sparking plug leads, giving myself a violent shock on each one. Still the boat ploughed on. I searched for a petrol tap and eventually switched it off, with the engine stopping once it had drained the carburettor.

I was towed back to *Gombroon*, my millionaire playboy status thoroughly deflated. Slings were rigged and the "prize" hoisted on board.

After some consultations with one of the engineer officers (and some liberal slaking of his thirst for whisky), he diagnosed the fault as inadequate water circulation causing the engine to overheat and run like a diesel without the need for electric power to the sparking plugs.

The next day the repair facilities of *Gombroon*'s engine department were harnessed to cope with the situation, and some brass scoops were fitted to the cooling water inlets on the hull and the boat was lowered into the water for a trial trip. This cure proved entirely successful and the boat (proudly named *Tojo's Pride* and painted in large letters) gave a lot of us a great deal of fun in the weeks ahead.

Thinking about this problem later, I wondered whether it really was a fault in design or whether the devious Japanese designers had carefully built in this factor to prevent the more faint-hearted Kamikase coxswains from aborting their attacks and claiming that the engine had stopped. It seems unlikely that they could be so stupid as to set up all this vast construction programme based on a false design.

Singapore struggled to regain its pre-war elegance and sophistication. The Raffles Hotel had, of course, never closed, and soon it was serving again the type of customer it had known before the unwelcome arrival of the Japanese. Various clubs were taken over by the N.A.A.F.I., the Navy, Army and Air Force Institute and provided canteen facilities for the services, while the enterprising Chinese were soon opening restaurants and bars. The ladies of the town were back in business — if, indeed, they had ever closed — but the Kai-tai had not yet developed into the famous local attraction that they later became.

215

The new repair ship *Beachy Head* arrived from Vancouver and I transferred there, quite sad to leave my Lascars and Chang, and unhappy joining a ship as a spare hand where everyone had already carved out their own niche. Like *Deveron* they had all been so far from the war for so long they lacked any sort of *esprit de corps*, and with the depressing *after-the-ball-is-over* feeling that existed anyway, there was little inclination to improve matters.

Somewhere ashore I encountered another RNR Lieutenant who had been in a Singapore shipping company and who had made contact with some of the Chinese office clerks from those days. They arranged a real Chinese dinner — something far removed from the numbered menus now encountered throughout the land — as I recall it took a week to gather the raw materials. Some came from *Beachy Head*, but most from Chinese country sources. The meal consisted of a modest twenty-four courses — each small and exquisitely tasty — the whole eaten, naturally, with chopsticks and the partaking of it lasted several hours. Quite an education, by and large.

Having met some folks who were with E.N.S.A. while we were in Rangoon, I ran into them again in Singapore and as a result visited them at their accommodation there. This turned out to be a home belonging to a certain Miss Bates (known to one and all as "Batesy"), who had spent the Japanese occupation period in Changhi jail, together with all the other British citizenry. During this time her house had been used as the Japanese senior officers' brothel and as a result had been very well maintained. Now "Batesy" had returned home and found the ladies and gentlemen of E.N.S.A. billeted on her, which caused some confusion among the locals who, at first, tried to bring "clients" to the new establishment.

"Batesy's description of life in Changhi jail was quite astonishing, and I listened to her reminiscences for hours on end. I wish I had had a tape recorder at the time. It is some measure of the impression she made upon me that I still remember certain portions over forty years later.

After the surrender of Singapore, the Japanese rounded up the British civilians and incarcerated them in the newly-built "model" prison at Changhi. The men were separated from the women and all were ordered to sign an oath of allegiance to the Japanese Emperor. When the men refused, the Japanese told them that the women would be punished, and vice versa. So eventually all signed, except

216

"Batesy". She refused and finally after dire threats the Japanese commandant accepted that she would not sign.

In the women's camp the women carried their husbands' ranks with precise protocol and some of their antics must have caused the Japanese commandant to think he was in charge of a lunatic asylum.

Over the years more women were brought in, who — although not European — had some connection with the British administration.

The "Women's Camp Committee" took charge of everything, including any food supplies brought in by the new arrivals. Food of all sorts was desperately short, and children were dying of malnutrition in the camp where medicines and items like vitamin tablets were also virtually non-existent.

Despite the parlous state of affairs, the cat belonging to the chairwomen of the Camp Committee had a saucer of milk every day! (Furthermore it was not even her own cherished cat which she had brought in to the camp, but an alley cat she had found and adopted.)

"Batesy" was a qualified nurse and worked as assistant to the only lady doctor in the camp. With more children's deaths occurring, the doctor eventually made the decision: "That cat must die", and officially ordered "Batesy" to carry out the execution. This was something of an anathema to "Batesy", who was an almost fanatical member of the R.S.P.C.A.

However, an order was an order.

"Batesy" saved a small part of her already meagre rations and enticed the ghastly cat into a temporarily deserted mortuary and killed it. ("Batesy" told me she lived in the mortuary and slept on the slab, which meant that her sleep was disturbed if a body was brought in during the night.)

Getting rid of the cat's body was the next problem. "Batesy" threw it in the large open drainage ditch which ran through the women's camp and then through the men's camp to the open sea. She expected the men who cleaned the ditch just to push the body on. No such luck. One of the men found the body, recognised it as the adopted pet of Lady ———, fished it out of the ditch and — believe it or not — the prisoners petitioned the Japanese camp commandant to investigate the "murder" and attempt to find the culprit. Nothing was proved, but suspicion fell on "Batesy".

The women's camp was polarised. About half would hiss "cat

murderer" as "Batesy" walked by, while the other half would come up to congratulate her.

* * * *

On one occasion I was asked to drive Gracie Fields and her husband some thirty miles to an airfield where she was to give a concert for the troops. I gladly accepted and did all I could to make the trip comfortable, but was sadly disillusioned by enduring the company of this much vaunted "lassie from Lancashire" for a couple of hours. Nothing was right. The jeep was uncomfortable; the road was bumpy; the weather was hot; the insects were unbearable; the stage was too small; the lighting was inadequate; the piano was out of tune; and more and more besides. I was never able to enjoy any performance of hers again after that one.

* * * *

On one evening, "Steve" Donoghue, *Beachy Head*'s navigator, myself and two Army officers took dinner at a restaurant established in what had been the Dutch Club. It was a long, low building like a traditional cricket pavilion with a verandah along the front, entry being up a dozen steps from the drive, which ran parallel to the front of the building. On the other side of this drive, the ground sloped away and part had been levelled off to make tennis courts, resulting in a steep ten foor bank dropping down from drive level to the flat tennis court.

At the end of a convivial evening, I left the party to unlock the jeep and bring it to the front of the Club. After sitting for some minutes with the engine running and no sign of the rest of the party, I became a little impatient and not wanting to lock up the jeep and enter the club on foot (and certainly not stupid enough to leave it unlocked while I entered the restaurant), I decided to drive it in. Slipping into four wheel drive and low ratio, it was easy to turn to the left and drive bumpily up the steps and on to the verandah. Once there it seemed only sensible to carry on into the restaurant. People moved a few tables and chairs obligingly, and amidst ribald comments I drove up to the table where Steve and the others were sitting and suggested it was time to leave.

Once they were aboard, we made three circuits of the dance floor and then out across the verandah and down the steps to the drive.

218

Then, encouraged by the cheering, instead of turning left on to the drive, it suddenly seemed a good idea to go straight ahead, down the near vertical grass bank on to the tennis court. This was all right and even although the front bumper touched down first the four wheel drive soon brought us on to the flat. A couple of circuits of the court to gain speed and we aimed for the bank to get out again. The jeep climbed the bank until the front wheels were scrabbling at the top, but even the four wheel drive would not take her up. We backed down and made three more circuits to gain speed before aiming at another part of the bank which looked easier. Steve by this time was standing up in the back with an Army officer's beret on, brandishing an imaginary whip and yelling various forms of encouragement.

We approached the bank at a good clip, but unfortunately it was more steep rather than less, and instead of climbing the bank the jeep stopped dead. Steve did not. He passed us in the front seat like an aerial torpedo, hit the bank with his head, and passed out lying full length on the bonnet. Fortunately the windscreen was folded flat at the time.

After that, we gave up trying to climb the bank and drove through a thin hedge and across a vegetable garden to return to the ship.

Surprisingly we were always welcome at this restaurant, and made it a regular call on runs ashore for the next few weeks until *Beachy Head* sailed for Colombo just before Christmas.

Touring around Singapore one afternoon I came, by chance, upon the shrine and war memorial built by the Japanese, or rather built for the Japanese by British prisoners of war.

The main memorial was built on a small hill up the front of which was a very long flight of steps. As I recall, it was called the Buketema Memorial, but I have no memory of the spelling — it is just written phonetically from memory.

Surprisingly the Japanese had allowed the prisoners to make and erect a small memorial to the British dead, quite near at hand.

A short distance away a shrine had been built which was — I was told — intended to be the spiritual centre of the South-East Asia Co-Prosperity Sphere, which the Japanese predicted would last (like Hitler's Reich) for a thousand years.

It amused me to note that they did not build with that confidence in the future which was so noticeable amongst engineers in the Victorian era. Even at the time I discovered it the planks of the "willow-pattern" type bridge over the ornamental lake had already

219

rotted to the extent that they would not bear the weight of my jeep.

It caused me even further amusement when I was exploring the altar of the religious shrine nearby to find that underneath the holy edifice was built an effective air raid shelter with a sliding steel door over half an inch thick!!

* * * *

We arrived in Colombo on December 30th, having celebrated Christmas at sea, and I remember being the Officer of the Day on the first night in harbour. However, I made arrangements to meet a Wren officer and take her to the New Year's Eve dance at the Swimming Club the following evening. It already looked like being a humdinger of a party — the first New Year's Eve of peace following a Christmas at sea — but matters hit a new high when, during the forenoon, I received a signal designating my relief and official "Demob orders".

The amusing thing about the signal was that it read:

> Lieutenant A. Bloggs, R.N.R. is appointed to *Beachy Head* to relieve Lieutenant H. Scott, R.N.R. and for duties as C.F.F.O. and E.F.T.O. Lieutenant Scott is to report to . . . . .for passage to UK.

This was official recognition at last.

* * * *

Obtaining a passage to England was not easy, even if one had some sort of priority claim, and I had none. However, I refused the accommodation offered me at the Transit Camp out of town and secured instead a room in the G.O.H. (Grand Oriental Hotel) in the centre of town and set about finding myself some UK-bound transport. A watchkeeping ticket and willingness to stand a watch on the bridge was a help, and eventually I met a bunch of friends in the corvette *Freesia* (our flotilla leader in the attack on Madagascar three and a half years earlier) who were willing to squeeze me in for a passage to the U.K. which had already been ordered.

I slept in the wheelhouse on a camp bed but anything was worth enduring to get home fairly quickly. It turned out to be a grand cruise as we had, eventually, eight watch-keeping officers and so only stood a watch about once a day. With ships burning navigation lights and lighthouses all lit up, it seemed ridiculously easy after the difficult wartime conditions of darkened ships — and, in earlier days — no radar.

We put on as many lights as possible crossing the Indian Ocean and the flying fish came sailing over our bulwarks to knock themselves out against the superstructure. A special "Flying Fish Detail" collected enough to be served up for breakfast for the whole ship's company on several mornings, so that we became blasé and wanted something else rather than this food of princes.

At Aden and Port Said we had silly parties on board and ashore. Commander Martyn Sherwood came aboard, wearing his captain's shoulder boards with one stripe removed with nail scissors — beautifully typical of yet another of that great league of gentlemen who had gone to sea as midshipmen aged fifteen in 1914. (A spell ashore as Naval-Officer-in-Charge at Penang had ended in some disaster, but he was far from disheartened.)

We arrived in Malta in Mediterranean spring weather just before Easter. Admiral Dalrymple-Hamilton, who had been Captain of the Royal Naval College, Dartmouth in 1938 and 1939, was in residence as Commander-in-Chief. I called at Admiralty House and signed the visitors' book. A few days later I had the pleasure of being entertained to lunch. It was a few days before the beginning of Carnival, which being the first peacetime celebration since 1939, was forecast as something extra special. Lady Dalrymple-Hamilton insisted that I should hire an Elizabethan costume without delay, and there was some hilarity when it came to details of how I should keep up the "hose" below the "slashed trunks à la Sir Francis Drake". Some somewhat unmasculine equipment had to be acquired for the purpose.

It was a very strange experience when, a few days later on the first night of Carnival, dressed in my sixteenth century apparel, I hailed a dhaisa (the traditional Valetta boatmen's craft) and was rowed ashore to land at the steps under the mediaeval castle walls built by the Knights of Malta and then climbed into a horse-drawn gharri to go to the opening dance of the 1946 Carnival Season.

It gave me an eerie feeling of having suffered a time-warp and slipped back four centuries. The boat, the castle, my costume and the carriage were all real sixteenth century.

The dance was most enjoyable, and by chance I met two charming sisters and was welcomed into their circle of friends. Everyone was in fancy dress and there were a lot of false beards and moustaches around. It was something of an advantage having the genuine home-grown article.

There were several grand displays of formation dancing by various Carnival Societies and then, with a roll from the drums, an imposing elderly lady announced that she wished to auction a bowl of sweets for the benefit of the Valetta Hospital.

Auctioning for charity is a very specialised art to which I had been introduced during my mother's various fund-raising garden parties and dances, and I had often acted as auctioneer.

While regular auctioneers are reputed to accept bids "from the chandeliers" and elsewhere to liven the bidding, the charity auctioneer often announces bids from notable characters in the crowd who are in no position to deny that they blinked an eyelid.

"Twenty pounds I am bid, thank you, Sir John. Twenty-five pounds from you, Doctor Brown", and so on. The main thing is to get the bidding going in sizeable steps and reach a figure which has no relation at all to the value of the article being auctioned.

Now, while not being the auctioneer, it seemed that I should do all I could to assist the good cause.

A few bids came in for a few shillings, which did not bode well, so I bid a pound. Bids of twenty-one and twenty-two shillings followed, before I bid two pounds, which at last attracted the interest of some of the more obviously wealthy and — presumably — prominent local citizens.

Three pounds was bid, followed by four. I bid five, and several more bids quickly brought the bidding to ten pounds. At this point I hesitated, since it was only my intent to force up the bidding, not to buy the blasted bowl of sweets.

There was a silent pause, and I thought local pride will not allow the prize to go to a stranger.

"Guineas," I called.

There was a ghastly silence. The imposing silence called for some more bids.

"Surely," she cried, "This lovely bowl of sweets is not going to be bought for a mere ten guineas."

The silence continued. I could see I was lumbered.

"Going, going, going, gone," cried the Grande Dame, "Gone to Sir Francis Drake over there."

There was nothing for it but to put on a brave face, and I stepped forward to mild applause and grasped the bowl.

"May I send you a cheque tomorrow?" I said, as I received the bowl.

"Certainly," said the great lady, "Come to tea. We live at Dragonara."

"I would be delighted," and I returned to our party, who were inordinately pleased at my effort.

"What a grand surprise," cried the girls, "she did not expect to get so much for so few sweets."

I handed the bowl round and the top layer of sweets were soon gone, laying bare a bunch of wood wool, which filled the volume of the bowl. I had truly been lumbered, I thought.

"She invited me to tea tomorrow," I admitted.

"Oh good," said the younger of the two girls. "Then we shall meet again tomorrow and I will ask Mama to invite you to join our party tomorrow night."

"Dragonara" I assumed was a village, but I was surprised at the alacrity with which the taxi driver dashed about when I asked to be taken there the next afternoon.

"The Scicluna's house," I said.

"Si, si, Signor. Yessir, certainly, Sir," and the car door was held open for me.

After about fifteen minutes' drive we passed through a large archway set in a high wall and I just had time to glance at the words *Dragonara Palace* engraved across the arch as we drove underneath.

We drove for some enormous distance, it seemed, before drawing up before a beautiful Palladian Palace fronted by an impressive row of pillars.

It appeared that I had arrived at the home of the Marchese and Marchesa Testa-Ferrata di Scicluna, where afternoon tea was served in the drawing room.

I had been regretting my foolhardiness in bidding ten guineas for that bowl of sweets (the cheque in an envelope in my pocket), but soon I was thanking my lucky stars. By that stroke of luck I was accepted into the Scicluna's family party for the rest of Carnival with a marvellous succession of parties every night, and usually a lunch party during the day as well.

It transpired that the family more or less owned Malta. Uncle George owned the bank, Cousin Henry owned the brewery, and so on.

I was questioned about the health of George and Elizabeth (King

George VI and his Queen), and endeavoured to hide my lack of intimate knowledge of their health by pointing out that I had been away from England for some twenty months.

One afternoon the Marchesa gave me a tour of the Palace, which contained some magnificent paintings and superb furniture. I particularly remember being shown a marvellous Boule table and being told that it was one of a pair and that its mate was in the possession of "George and Elizabeth". Some twenty years later, while watching a film on the British royal palaces in a Tunbridge Wells cinema, the camera zoomed in on a well-remembered sight as the commentator seriously announced,

". . . and this magnificent Boule table is one of only two in the world," which brought from me a startled,

"And by Golly I know where the other bugger is," to the somewhat shocked astonishment of those within earshot.

The day after the end of Carnival, *Freesia*'s repairs were completed and I said my farewells to my many new-found friends and we sailed for England with just a brief stop for fuel at Gibraltar, which enabled us to stock up with wine and sherry, still at around one pound a case for the former and two pounds a case for the latter.

Pleasant spring weather and the absence of the need to avoid German submarines and aircraft made for a rapid short passage, much of it in sight of the shore of Portugal, Spain and France by day and the friendly lights at night.

Channel fever broke out with a vengeance as we rounded Ushant. Most aboard had been out East for around two years, and additionally looked forward to leave and demobilisation.

It was a very happy homecoming.

EPILOGUE

ENGLAND, in the summer of 1946, was hardly "a land fit for heroes to live in".

Food rationing was stricter than ever during the war. Petrol rationing was severe. Pubs ran out of beer even, and more often of whisky and gin.

Although not frequenting any Naval establishments, somehow the news reached me that volunteers were being called for to provide crews for a number of sailing yachts being brought to Portsmouth from Germany.

Contrary to that old service adage — "Never volunteer for anything" — I volunteered and duly travelled to Portsmouth to join a destroyer being loaded up with other idiots for a passage to Kiel.

The project was under the command of the redoubtable Commander Martyn Sherwood, whose main claim to fame was having been the cook of the yacht *Tai-Mo-Shan*, which had been sailed from Hong Kong to the U.K. by half a dozen Naval officers shortly before the war.

Enthusiasm was strong, but experience in sailing yachts was pretty thin, to the extent that I found myself designated as skipper of one of the fifty square metre yachts (around forty feet long), faced firstly with finding a crew from amongst the rest of the motley band and secondly of sailing the thing to Portsmouth.

I was allocated *See-Taube* and found a beautifully constructed almost new yacht, which had been built in 1938, laid up throughout the war, and just fitted out by the yard that built her. "Bruno", a German Naval officer and Olympic yachtsman, sorted everything out for us — a task he continued to do for British Services yachtsmen for the following thirty-five years.

Evenings were spent at the bar of the magnificent Imperial Kiel Yacht Club, which had become — for the time being — the British Kiel Yacht Club. Money was no problem, since all British Service personnel could buy cigarettes at sixpence for a packet of twenty and this was easily sold on to the Black Market for a hundred marks, which was equivalent to two pounds ten shillings, or enough to buy a further one hundred packets of cigarettes or drinks at similar duty-free prices in the Yacht Club.

The crew of *See Taube* finally consisted of a Royal Marine Captain, a Shipwright Lieutenant, a Royal Marine Sergeant, and an R.N.V.R. Sub-Lieutenant.

After a wild farewell party in the Yacht Club, during which — at one stage — many of us were using the enormous cut glass chandeliers as trapezes, all the six yachts were towed through the Kiel Canal and then set off under sail down the Elbe River and along the North Coast of Germany and Holland.

I suppose with some hard effort we could have made Portsmouth in less than four days, and there was some talk (soon discarded) of making it a sweepstake race. But, what the hell, it was peacetime; there was no requirement to keep to a timetable; with no engine aboard we could always claim the delay was due to contrary winds or calms.

We took four weeks and were not the slowest.

Choosing to stop at Ijmuiden and Ostende gave us the opportunity to visit Amsterdam and Brussels, and some time was spent in the Dutch inland waters.

Our penultimate stop was Newhaven, from where I nipped home to get a car and then drove to Eastbourne where there was a Naval Establishment entirely manned by the Paymaster branch. Announcing myself as "the Commanding Officer of *See-Taube*, prize of war on passage under sail from Kiel to Portsmouth, delayed by westerly winds", I demanded rations for a mythical crew of much enlarged proportion for the long passage against the wind to Portsmouth. On being asked to estimate the time required, I mentioned two weeks, possibly three if the weather was bad.

The whiff of romantic salt air in the staid "Pusser" organisation worked wonders, and in no time mountains of food were loaded into my car and with a few flourishing signatures, I was off back to Newhaven. It took nearly two days to parcel up all the food and post it off to various closely rationed families before sailing overnight to Portsmouth and handing over our Prize of War to the receiving officer at Whale Island.

A few weeks later I returned to Kiel, and this time even made a short cruise to Denmark before setting off for England on a voyage which took even longer.

After passing the Kiel Canal, we paused in Cuxhaven to await good weather and there met two Dutch yachts and a British yacht, similarly employed.

A good deal of mutual entertainment resulted, and the ridiculosity of the situation was demonstrated when, one evening, I entertained all the crews of the four yachts to dinner at the local officers club.

The twenty of us enjoyed a good meal with wine and liqueurs and then, on calling for the bill, I found that I had left my wallet on board. No problem, I merely called for cigars, and when these had been offered round I took half a dozen myself and went outside the club and sold them to the first available buyer before returning with enough money to pay the bill and last me the rest of the evening.

Martyn Sherwood asked me to go back for a third yacht, but having been actually offered a job I had to decline.

The funny business was finally all over, and prosaic work had to begin.

*   *   *   *

Appendix A

List of Royal Navy ships and FAA Squadrons Involved in
OPERATION IRONCLAD — Capture of Diego Suarez

Battleship (1)	*Ramillies* (Read Admiral E. N. Syfret)	
Aircraft Carriers (2)	*Illustrious* with FAA Squadrons:	Swordfish 810
		Swordfish 829
		Wildcat 881
		Wildcat 882
	Indomitable with FAA Squadrons:	Fulmar 800
		Fulmar 806
		Albacore 827
		Albacore 831
		Hurricane 800

Cruisers (2)	*Devonshire*	
	Hermione	

Destroyers (11)	*Active*	*Lookout*
	Anthony	*Pakenham*
	Duncan	*Paladin*
	Inconstant	*Panther*
	Javelin	
	Laforey	
	Lightning	

Minesweepers (8)	Fleet (4)	Corvettes (4)
	Cromarty	*Freesia* (Commander T. Crick,
		Commanding Minesweepers)
	Cromer	*Auricula*
	Poole	*Nigella*
	Romney	*Cyclamen*

Corvettes (Anti-Submarine) (4)	*Fritillary*
	Genista
	Jasmine
	Thyme

Tank Landing Ship (1)	*Bachaquero*	
Infantry Landing Ships (4)	*Keren*	*Royal Ulsterman*
	Karanja	*Winchester Castle*
Hospital Ship (1)	*Dorsetshire*	
French Ships Sunk (3) (all by aircraft)	*Beveziers*	
	Bougainville	
	Heros (Submarine)	

GROUPS II AND III
(S.O. Captain Oliver,
Devonshire)

● Freesia

Cromer ●   ● Poole

Romney ●   ● Auricula

Cromarty ●   ● Nigella

● Anthony   ● DEVONSHIRE ● Laforey

0 Winchester Castle ⎤   ● Lightning
0 Royal Ulsterman ⎦   Nº 5 Commando; 2nd E. Lancs.
                        (assault Red Beach)

Four Miles or
visibility distance,
whichever least

                                GROUP IV
● Fritillary   (S.O. Capt. Garnons-Williams,
Genista ●   ● Cyclamen   Keren)
Headquarters Ship 0 Keren   1st Royal Scots Fus. (Green Beach)
(S.N.O.(L) and
Brigadier Festing) 0 Karanja   2nd Royal Welsh Fus. (White Beach)

0 Sobieski   Floating Reserve

0 Derwentdale Motor Landing Craft

0 Bachaquero Battery, 8 - 25 pdrs.
              6 - 15 cwt. trucks

Four Miles or
visibility distance,
whichever least

                                GROUP V
● Pakenham   (S.O. Capt. Stevens,
                        Pakenham)
Thyme ●   ● Jasmine
0 Oronsay   ⎤ 17th Infantry Brigade
0 Duchess of Atholl ⎦ (Brigadier Tarleton)

0 Empire Kingsley ⎤
0 Thalatta   ⎪ 17th Infantry Brigade
0 Mahout   ⎬ Stores and M.T.
0 City of Hong-Kong ⎦

0 Easedale   Fleet Oiler

0 Franconia   13th Infantry Brigade
              (Brigadier Russell)

0 Nairnbank   ⎤ 13th Infantry Brigade
0 Martand   ⎦ Stores and M.T.

CBH 1943

British Ship Sunk (1)	*Auricula* (mined 5th May)
Commander of Military Force	Major General R. G. Sturges, Royal Marines

Appendix B

CONVOY "FAITH" details

Ships, *Duchess of York, California* & *Port Fairy.*
Escorts, *Moyola, Douglas, Iroquois* (and *Swale* later).

July 9th	Av. speed 17 knots
10th	Av. speed 14.4 knots
11th	Av. speed 13.75 knots. Attack commenced 2110. *Duchess of York, California* bombed. 438 survivors picked up and proceeded to Casablanca with *Douglas* at 18 knots (see photostat attached).
13th	Arrived Casablanca — landed survivors.
14th	Sailed for Gibraltar to pick up *Voltaire.* Av. 17 knots.
dates unknown	Returned to Casablanca.
19th	Sailed Casablanca for Freetown.
25th	Arrived Freetown. pm. time not noted. Av. 14.5 knots.

Convoy "FAITH"
The loss of *SS California* & *SS Duchess of York*
July, 1943

(Extracts from the War Diary received from Naval Historical Department)

Ref.
No.
1 *NOIC Greenock to Admiralty T.O.O. 06/0956B*
Intend sail *California, Duchess of York* & *Port Fairy* pass Clyde Boom 1200B/8th to R/v *Moyola* & *Douglas* 270° Oversay 6 miles at 2100B/8th thence in accordance with AM 03/1415B. E.T.A. Freetown 2000Z/17th.

2   C *in C Plymouth to Admiralty T.O.O. 06/1807B*
Intend sail *Iroquois* 0800B/9th to R/v with *Moyola* &
Douglas and convoy at 2000B/10th in position (R) 47°11′N
15°23′N.

2.   *Iroquois* to provide additional escort to 40°N and then to
return to Plymouth.

3   *Flag Officer in Charge Greenock to Admiralty. T.O.O.*
08/1304B
My 06/0956 Sailed Codeword "FAITH".

4   *Director of Operations Division (Home) approved assistant*
Chief of Naval Staff to escort Group B1, Allexa for escorts
SL132, C in C Mediterranean repeat F.O.I.C. Gibraltar etc.
12/0106B
In absence of other orders from F.O.I.C. Gibraltar *Hurricane* &
Rockingham proceed at best speed to assistance of *California* &
Duchess of York carrying 500 troops each reported bombed and
on fire at 2145 in estimated position 40°N 15°30W.

5   *F.O.I.C. Gibraltar to Escort Group B1 repeat Admiralty, C in*
C Plymouth, C in C Western Approaches. T.O.O. 12/0137B
Fuel from *Dingledale* forthwith. On completion of fueling
proceed to vicinity of *Duchess of York* on fire in 41°24′N
15°24′W at 11/2210B. U-boat probably in contact.

6   *Deputy Director of Naval Intelligence to F.O.I.C. Gibraltar*
repeat Escorts Convoy Faith etc. T.O.O. 12/0154B
There are indications that the attack on convoy may be re-
newed.

7   *Iroquois to F.O.I.C. Gibraltar 12/0155B*
My 2145 *Swale* escorting *Port Fairy* to Casablanca via normal
route. *Iroquois* proceeding independently at 28 knots. *Moyola*
with *Douglas* proceeding at best speed. Following approximate
survivors:- *Port Fairy* 55, *Iroquois* 660, *Moyola* 500 including
32 women, *Douglas* 600. *Douglas* ordered to torpedo hulks
prior to departure. All ships proceeding Casablanca via normal
route. A great number of survivors require hospital treatment
on arrival.

8   *Deputy Director Naval Intelligence to Swale Iroquois Moyola Douglas Hurricane Rockingham. Repeat F.O.I.C. Gibraltar etc. T.O.O. 12/0758B*
    Inconclusive D/F bearings on 5100 kc/s at 0336Z and 0347Z indicate two U-boats may be in vicinity of 40°30′N 15°30′N.

9   *Moyola to F.O.I.C. Gibraltar T.O.O. 12/0820A*
    My position course and speed at 0800A 39°58′N 13°56′W 141° 17 knots to Casablanca. *Douglas* in company.

10 *F.O.I.C. Gibraltar to C in C Mediterranean, Malta & Algiers repeated Admiralty -CMSF. T.O.O. 12/1931B*
    Duchess of York & *California* were bombed and set on fire in 40°00′N 15°30′W at 11/2145B and subsequently sunk by own forces.

11 *Swale to F.O.I.C. Gibraltar repeat Commorseafron, F.O.I.C. West Africa T.O.O. 12/2221B*
    Your 12/2133B *Port Fairy* seriously on fire. Am taking survivors off and assisting to put out fire by my own hose. Position at 2000B 37°20′N, 14°36′W.

12 *Moyola to Commorseafron repeat F.O.I.C. Gibraltar. T.O.O. 12/2215B*
    Expected time of arrival Casablanca 13/1200Z, 413 survivors 12 cot cases. *Douglas* in company with 435, 18 cot cases.

Appendix C

CONVOY SL 139/MKS 30
Gibraltar to UK
SUMMARY OF INCIDENTS
November 13th — November 26th, 1943

November 13th 1700	Slipped
14th	Av. speed 5.0
15th	Av. speed 7.6
16th	Av. speed 8.2, shadowed by Ju 290.
17th	Av. speed 7.5, shadowed by Ju 290.

18th	Av. speed 7.6, shadowed by Ju 290. *Chanticleer* torpedoed. U-boats in contact. *Exe* carries out attack.
19th	Av. speed 6.3. U-boats in contact, shadowed by Ju 290.
20th	Av. speed 5.5. U-boat sunk by *Snowberry*.
21st	Av. speed 5.5. 1530, attack by 16-25 HE 177 with glider bombs. One straggler hit and abandoned. One M.V. hit but proceeded. Near miss on *Moyola*.
22nd	Av. speed 7.0. Shadowed by FW200 & BV 222.
23rd	Av. speed 6.3.
24th	Av. speed 6.0.
25th	Av. speed 7.2.
26th	1315 Arrived Clyde.

Original escort group was increased by Support Groups to a total of 21 escorts and finally by the addition of an anti-aircraft ship *Prince Robert*.

EXTRACTS FROM ADMIRALTY WAR DIARY HOME COMMANDS

Thursday 18-11-1943

SIGNALS

1   *Exe to Flag Officer Gibraltar as 0901*
I am being shadowed by one enemy aircraft at 5,000 feet. Position 39°27'N 19°42'W Course 000° Speed 7.5 knots.

2   *Exe to Flag Officer Gibraltar and Commander-in-Chief Western Approaches at 1101.*
Periscope sighted, am attacking. Position 30°42'N 19°42'W Course 000° Speed 7.5 knots.

3   *Exe to Commander-in-Chief Western Approaches at 1231*
Reference my 1101 Submarine was two miles ahead of convoy. Have rejoined after five attacks. Junkers 90 aircraft still present.

4   *Commander-in-Chief Western Approaches to Captain (D) Belfast at 1154*
4th Escort Group is to be sailed at noon tomorrow to join & support SL139/MKS30.

5   *Headquarters Coastal Command to 247 Group at 1230*
Appreciate SL139/MKS30 will be attacked tonight and again even more heavily tomorrow night 19th Nov. Request you keep at least six Leigh-Light Wellingtons for night Nov. 19th. Suggest you use maximum effort each night on patrols ahead and astern of convoy as present situation will more than likely develop into biggest U-boat battle we have ever had. Outcome may have critical results in future Gibraltar convoys. Maximum possible day effort also first importance. This will be hard going for both aircrews and ground personnel but the battle may well put paid to U-boat morale for some time to come. 19 Group will take on the battle on night 20th Nov.

6   *Pheasant to Flag Officer Gibraltar at 1535*
Chanticleer torpedoed in 39°47'N 20°12'W. Both engines and steering gear out of action. *Crane* standing by. Salvage tug *Salveda* proceeding to her assistance.

Many signals followed regarding *Chanticleer*'s damage and arrangements for tow to the Azores and the following indicates general attitude of Commander-in-Chief:

7   *Commander-in-Chief Western Approaches to Crane, Chanticleer and Garlies at 2247*
One escort only is to accompany tow and this escort should rejoin convoy as soon as it is considered U-boats have been shaken off. Air cover will be provided.
. For future guidance it is important that striking forces should not be denuded to provide escort for damaged ship which should be sunk when personnel have been transferred.

Friday 19-11-1943

Note: 2 U-boats sighted and 6 believed to be in touch.

SIGNALS

1 *Calgary to Admiralty at 0530*
Position of 2 U-boats on surface and 3 unknown in 43°19'N
19°32'W. One dived and one escaped on surface.

2 *Headquarters Coastal Command to 15 Group and 19 Group at
0930*
Close support is to be provided by one Liberator ahead and one
astern of convoy SL139/MKS20 throughout the hours of daylight 20th Nov. One aircraft in each group to be at immediate
readiness and to be despatched if a sighting is reported. 15 Group
to be prepared to reinforce with stripped Sunderlands during
p.m. 20th Nov. 19 Group to carry out Leigh-Light anti-submarine patrols throughout the hours of darkness on night
20/21st Nov. ahead and astern of SL139 as far as resources
permit, particular attention being paid to pre-dawn period.

3 *Exe to Admiralty at 0931*
One enemy aircraft (Focke-Wulf) shadowing convoy position
42°03'N 19°27'W Course 000° Speed 7.5 knots.

Sunday 20-11-1943

Note: Convoy Attacked by Glider Bombs

46°46'N 18°21'W About 1530 enemy aircraft started attacking the
convoy with Glider bombs and the escorts were ordered to " pack ".
While the attack was at its height the A.A. ship *Prince Robert* joined
and was ordered to zig-zag across the stern of the convoy. *Marsa*
(125), straggling about 3½ miles astern, was repeatedly attacked and
finally hit at 1600 and had to be abandoned. A quarter of an hour
later *Delius* (121) was damaged and set on fire, but eventually
managed to reach harbour. The crew of *Marsa* were picked up by
Petunia and *Essington*, but some of the officers were transferred to
Delius as she had lost all but one of her deck officers. At 1657 the
attack ended and the enemy aircraft withdrew. In all about sixteen
bombs were dropped but only two found their mark. This was
probably due to the heavy A.A. fire put up by the escort which
appeared to deter the enemy aircraft.

Appendix D

ANALYSIS OF OPERATIONS IN THE VICINITY OF CONVOY SL139/MKS30 — 18th to 21st November 1943

Concluding Remarks

1   In anticipation of an attempt by the enemy to concentrate a large pack of U-boats on this Convoy, a strong force was sent out in support. No less than 21 escorts operated in defence of the Convoy and almost continuous air cover was provided by shore-based aircraft during the four days and three nights that the battle lasted. Senior Officer, E.G.40 reports that communication with aircraft was completely successful throughout.

2   On only one occasion did a U-boat succeed in reaching the close screen and this was before any of the Support Forces had arrived. *Exe*, in station ahead, got in three quick counter-attacks in twelve minutes before the Convoy over-ran the target. She succeeded in so damaging the U-boat that it was probably unable to take any further part in the proceedings.

3   Although the cause of the explosion in *Chanticleer* cannot be stated with certainty, it appears probable that she was damaged by an acoustic torpedo. The second explosion may have been due to another "gnat" which either detonated at the end of its run or was counter-mined by the explosion of the first. It is almost certain that there was only one U-boat in the vicinity and that it was hunted by *Crane* shortly afterwards. In view of the fact that the U-boat surfaced after dark and fired a torpedo at *Crane*, it is considered that the attacks could not have been more than slightly damaging.

4   Good co-operation between *Calgary* and *Snowberry* was shown in the destruction of U.536, brought to the surface after only one ten charge pattern by *Nene*.

5   The "creeping" attack by *Crane* and *Foley* on the 21st resulted in the probable destruction of a U-boat. Although the enemy used S.B.T. and violent avoiding tactics *Crane* was able to maintain contact and finally directed *Foley* in an attack which was carried out at the prescribed 5 knots.

6 Once more the enemy must have been disappointed with his efforts. Although he attacked the Convoy with aircraft for about one and a half hours, only two hits were obtained by Glider bombs which resulted in the loss of one merchant ship and damage to another. A destroyer was also "near missed" some distance astern of the Convoy, but reached harbour safely.

7 The enemy was even more unsuccessful with his U-boat attack. At least 25 operated against the Convoy but none succeeded in penetrating the close screen or in torpedoing any merchant ships; in most cases they showed a lack of determination when their presence became known to the defence.

8 The final score against U-boats was one sunk, one probably sunk and three more damaged in varying degrees. As opposed to this only one escort was damaged in the course of a prolonged series of encounters which lasted for four days.

81

2098